In the hands of a free spirit the cinema is a magnificent and dangerous weapon. It is the superlative medium through which to express the world of thought, feeling, and instinct. The creative handling of film images is such that, among all means of human expression, its way of functioning is most reminiscent of the work of the mind during sleep. A film is like an involuntary imitation of a dream. Brunius points out how the darkness that slowly settles over a movie theater is equivalent to the act of closing the eyes. Then, on the screen, as within the human being, the nocturnal voyage into the unconscious begins. The device of fading allows images to appear and disappear as in a dream; time and space become flexible, shrinking and expanding at will; chronological order and the relative values of time duration no longer correspond to reality; cyclical action can last a few minutes or several centuries; shifts from slow motion to accelerated motion heighten the impact of each.

The cinema seems to have been invented to express the life of the subconscious, the roots of which penetrate poetry so deeply.

Luis Buñuel

ELEMENTS

OF FILM

SECOND EDITION

LEE R. BOBKER
New York University and Vision Associates, Inc.

Harcourt Brace Jovanovich, Inc.

New York   Chicago   San Francisco   Atlanta

ELEMENTS OF FILM   Second Edition

ISBN: 0-15-522095-0

Library of Congress Catalog Card Number: 74-2561

Printed in the United States of America

Cover photo from Ingmar Bergman's *Cries and Whispers* courtesy of Jon Davison, New World Pictures.

The author would like to thank the following copyright holders for permission to reprint the selections by Norman Mailer and Michael Wood:

NEW YORK REVIEW OF BOOKS. For the excerpt from "Seeing Bergman" by Michael Wood. Reprinted with permission from *New York Review of Books.* © 1973 by NYREV, Inc.

SCOTT MEREDITH LITERARY AGENCY, INC. For the excerpt from "A Transit to Narcissus" by Norman Mailer. Reprinted by permission of the author and the author's agents, Scott Meredith Literary Agency, Inc., 580 Fifth Avenue, New York, New York 10036.

PREFACE

The art of film requires the successful combination of two distinct groups of elements: (1) the technical elements by which the film is made (camera, lighting, sound, and editing) and (2) the esthetic elements that transform the craft into an art. In *Elements of Film,* Second Edition, I have retained the approach of the first edition by providing technical information about the process of filmmaking while isolating and exploring the esthetic elements that motivate and inspire that process. The emphasis throughout is on the relationship between the techniques of filmmaking (the *how*-to-do-it) and their creative application (the *why*-to-do-it). I have designed the book to appeal to both the serious student of film who wishes to pursue a career in filmmaking and to the general reader who wishes to learn more about this most dynamic of art forms.

The structure of the book reflects the filmmaking process itself. The early chapters follow the order in which a film is made: script, image (camera, lighting, composition), sound, and editing. I have devoted special attention to the roles of script writers, cameramen, film editors, actors, and directors, and to their relationships to one another. A separate chapter—completely revised for this edition—examines the work of eleven major contemporary directors who have contributed to the evolution of film art. This chapter includes biographical information about the directors as well as analysis of their distinctive filmmaking styles. A final chapter defines the function of film criticism and provides sample reviews—several of which are new to this edition—by such prominent critics as Andrew Sarris, Pauline Kael, and Michael Wood.

Film is the most rapidly changing of current art forms. In an effort to keep this new edition up to date, I have used recent works from the modern cinema to illustrate important techniques. I have attempted to include as wide a range of examples as possible. Discussions on a representative group of contemporary filmmakers have been included, and the films selected to illustrate current trends and techniques cover many of the most creative works of the past few years. In this second edition such recent films as *Cries and Whispers,* *State of Siege,* *Deliverance,* and *Last Tango in Paris* have been included for discussion and analysis, and a new selection of color plates features the work of cameramen Sven Nykvist and Vilmos Zsigmond, two of the most innovative of contemporary cinematographers.

Of course, no book on film can be successful unless the reader follows through by viewing the films under discussion. The illustrations in this book will provide strong visual assistance, but in the end only a viewing of the entire motion picture can complete the learning process.

Many people contributed to this book. My deep appreciation is due to Paddy Chayefsky, whose screenplay of *The Hospital* is excerpted for illustrative purposes, and who by dint of many stimulating conversations has been a prime inspiration to me; to two of the best cameramen I have known, Herbert Raditschnig and the late Arthur Fillmore, who in effect *retaught* me the art of the moving image; to the most creative sound man I know, Don Matthews, who helped me to appreciate the art of sound recording; to Michael Rothenberg, who has added so much of his abilities and talents to my own films; to Richard Brown, whose talent and imagination produced much of the visual support for the book; and to Nona Bleetstein, for her warmth, support, and unfailing good humor, and for the major contribution she made to this new edition, which enabled me to continue to make films while the work was in process.

L. R. B.

CONTENTS

VIII

Contents

IX

Contents

ILLUSTRATIONS FROM FILMS

XI

five   THE DIRECTOR

ELEMENTS OF FILM
Second Edition

THE CONJURER'S ART

PROLOGUE

When I was ten years old I received my first, rattling film projector, with its chimney and lamp. I found it both mystifying and fascinating. The first film I had was nine feet long and brown in color. It showed a girl lying asleep in a meadow, who woke up and stretched out her arms, then disappeared to the right. That was all there was to it. The film was a great success and was projected every night until it broke and could not be mended any more.

This little rickety machine was my first conjuring set. And even today I remind myself with childish excitement that I am really a conjurer, since cinematography is based on deception of the human eye. I have worked it out that if I see a film which has a running time of one hour, I sit through twenty-seven minutes of complete darkness—the blankness between frames. When I show a film I am guilty of deceit. I use an apparatus which is constructed to take advantage of a certain human weakness, an apparatus with which I can sway my audience in a highly emotional manner—make them laugh, scream with fright, smile, believe in fairy stories, become indignant, feel shocked, charmed, deeply moved or perhaps yawn with boredom. Thus I am either an imposter or, when the audience is willing to be taken in, a conjurer. I perform conjuring tricks with [an] apparatus so expensive and so wonderful that any entertainer in history would have given anything to have it.

Ingmar Bergman
in *Four Screenplays of Ingmar Bergman*
New York: Simon and Schuster, Inc., 1960, pp. xiv–xv.
Reprinted by permission of the publisher and Janus Films

M
AN HAS ALWAYS BEEN FASCINATED BY THE ILLUSION OF MOTION. WE KNOW that conjurers and magicians in the Middle Ages amused and beguiled their audiences by projecting shadows against a wall, using the flickering firelight as a source of illumination. In subsequent centuries, a number of devices were used to simulate movement. These included wheels spinning in front of a light, revolving discs through which all types of visual phenomena could be observed, and innumerable crude, often homemade devices that created a variety of visual effects (Fig. 1).

These early devices evolved into more sophisticated machines, such as the *praxinoscope* (Fig. 2), invented by the Frenchman Emile Reynaud in 1877. As described in detail by Igor Montagu in *Film World,*[1] the praxinoscope consisted of

> . . . a peculiar circular receptacle on a wooden stand. This receptacle was round and flat with a vertical rim about two inches high and you could tuck inside the rim a strip of equally tall paper that fitted exactly and bore a series of small pictures depicting such images as a rider and horse jumping a fence, or a couple of clothed animals firing off a popgun, printed in colours. In the centre of the receptacle was a polygon of mirror faces; there were grooved wheels on the stand over which you fitted strong rubber loops, and when you turned a handle the circular-receptacle part of the contraption, wobbling in a regular path, revolved rather slowly so that, if you kept your eyes fixed on only one of the faces of the mirror polygon, the riders appeared to jump over the teddy-bears or learned hares or what-not to pursue their altercations.

Reynaud's first praxinoscope was only a partial forerunner of the modern motion picture projector. It created the illusion of motion but made no provision for projecting its images. A design for a projecting device using candlelight and glass lenses had been theorized by Athanasius Kircher in 1648, and by the middle of the nineteenth century a variety of magic lanterns was in use. The lanterns simulated motion by the rapid alteration of two glass slides, each depicting a slight change of an object's position, in front of the light source (Fig. 3). In 1882 Reynaud combined the magic lantern with his praxinoscope to produce the most direct ancestor of the motion picture projector—the *projecting praxinoscope* (Fig. 4), which he continued to modify (Fig. 5).

From this simulation of motion came the next major step toward film as we know it today—the *mutoscope* (Fig. 6). This machine, popular in the early twentieth century, consisted of a series of still photographs mounted on a wheel that could be revolved by a hand crank. Thus, the viewer could create his own movie by rotating the stills one after the other. The speed of the action and the

---

[1] From *Film World* by Igor Montagu (Baltimore: Penguin Books, 1946), p. 18.

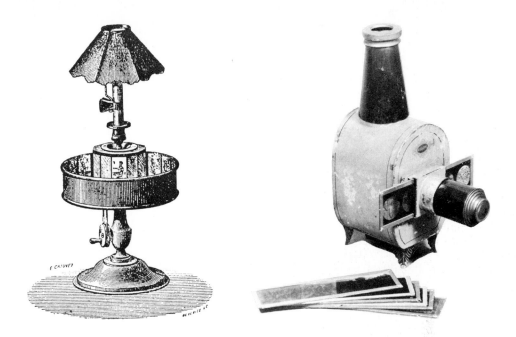

Clockwise, from left: Figures 1, 2, 3, 4.

Figure 5.

smoothness of the motion depended entirely on the viewer. The *kinetoscope*, invented by Thomas Edison, was somewhat similar to the mutoscope but Edison's device employed a rotating strip of film rather than single stills mounted on a wheel.

The single factor that all the antecedents of the motion picture projector had in common was that they attempted to create the illusion of motion. A simple demonstration will illustrate how such an illusion is created. Using a pad of paper, draw a line on the lower right-hand corner of each page. Since it is almost impossible to draw all the lines identically, there will be minute differences in the lines from page to page. Now riffle the pages rapidly with your thumb. You will experience the illusion of a moving line as the pages pass by in succession.

The motion picture camera, equipped with a shutter that opens and closes at high speed, captures a moving image by photographing it as a succession of still frames, each of which records a slightly different phase of the motion. The camera motor advances the film past the shutter at a rapid rate (usually 24 frames per second) and the time lapse between each frame is therefore very brief (one-fiftieth of a second in most modern cameras).

Because of the speed at which the successive frames are photographed, the differences between frames are very slight. The result is a series of still pictures photographed onto a strip of film, like the series of lines drawn onto the corners of the pages. The strip of film is then moved past a light source at the same speed at which the images were photographed (analogous to riffling the pages in the example above). The separate still images projected in this manner create the illusion of motion on screen. Because they are projected at

Figure 6.

a high speed, the images appear to be a continuously moving scene. The appearance of continuity results from the optical phenomenon called *persistence of vision,* first studied by the Belgian Joseph Plateau in 1829. Plateau's investigations showed that the brain retains the sensation of an image for a brief moment after the image is removed from sight. This persistence of vision accounts for the inability of the eye to perceive the separations between single frames of a rapidly projected film. (If, however, the speed of projection is slowed down, a jerkiness begins to appear and the individual frames begin to separate and reveal themselves.)

When the individual frames are projected onto a screen one after the other, and at the same speed at which they were photographed, the perceived motion is the same as the motion that was photographed. However, if the film is projected at a slower speed than the speed of photography, the action will appear to take place in *slow motion.* If the film is projected at a faster speed than the speed of photography, the action will appear faster and jerkier, that is, in *fast motion.* This effect can be seen in the films of the 1920s. Motion in these films (when projected at modern projector speeds) appears mechanical and unreal. Since early motion picture cameras were operated manually, it was difficult to maintain a constant speed in winding the film. Thus, if the cameraman slowed down this movement, the action, when projected later at a fixed rate, would appear to be in "fast motion."

It is the illusion of motion that imparts energy and interest to the people, places, and events depicted in a film. And it is the illusion of motion that gives the art of film its unique ability to move audiences — to excite and arouse their emotions and to transport them beyond their time and place.

STORY AND SCRIPT

ONE

The collaboration between a director and his script writer can take a wide variety of forms. One might almost say that there are as many different methods of work as there are films. Yet the one that seems most frequent in the traditional commercial cinema involves a more or less radical separation of scenario and image, story and style; in short, "content" and "form."

For instance, the author describes a conversation between two characters, providing the words they speak and a few details about the setting; if he is more precise, he specifies their gestures or facial expressions, but it is always the director who subsequently decides how the episode will be photographed, if the characters will be seen from a distance or if their faces will fill the whole screen, what movements the camera will make, how the scene will be cut, etc. Yet the scene as the audience sees it will assume quite different, sometimes even contradictory meanings, depending on whether the characters are looking toward the camera or away from it, or whether the shots cut back and forth between their faces in rapid succession. The camera may also concentrate on something entirely different during their conversation, perhaps merely the setting around them: the walls of the room they are in, the streets where they are walking, the waves that break in front of them. At its extreme, this method produces a scene whose words and gestures are quite ordinary and unmemorable, compared to the forms and movement of the image, which alone has any importance, which alone appears to have a meaning.

This is precisely what makes the cinema an art: it creates a reality with forms. It is in its form that we must look for its true content. The same is true of any work of art, of a novel, for instance:

the choice of a narrative style, of a grammatical tense, of a rhythm of phrasing, of a vocabulary carries more weight than the actual story. What novelist worthy of the name would be satisfied to hand his story over to a "phraseologist" who would write out the final version of the text for the reader? The initial idea for a novel involves both the story and its style; often the latter actually comes first in the author's mind, as a painter may conceive of a canvas entirely in terms of vertical lines before deciding to depict a skyscraper group.

And no doubt the same is true for a film: conceiving of a screen story, it seems to me, would mean already conceiving of it in images, with all the detail this involves, not only with regard to gestures and settings, but to the camera's position and movement, as well as to the sequence of shots in editing. Alain Resnais and I were able to collaborate only because we saw the film in the same way from the start; and not just in the same general way, but exactly, in the construction of the least detail as in its total architecture. What I wrote might have been what was already in his mind; what he added during the shooting was what I might have written.

Alain Robbe-Grillet
Last Year at Marienbad
New York: Grove Press, Inc., 1962, pp. 7–8.
Copyright © 1962 by Grove Press, Inc.
Reprinted by permission of Grove Press, Inc.

THE ART OF THE CINEMA RESTS FIRMLY ON A SQUARE PEDESTAL, MOUNTED, SO TO speak, on a four-sided base: script, direction, camera, and editing. The most artistically successful films are equally strong in these four basic elements. Conversely, a weakness in any one of the four elements can seriously weaken an otherwise fine motion picture.

Most motion pictures begin with the translation of an initial concept into a script or scenario that will serve to guide the film's production. The study of film—the examination of any specific motion picture—is best begun by examining its script.

9

RELATIONSHIP BETWEEN SCRIPT AND FILM

The relationship between script and finished film is unique. In no other art form is the original design (the script) subject to change at so many stages of production. Unlike the novel or the script for a stage play, the film script is not a finished work. It undergoes many reworkings by people other than the script writer—notably by the director, and to a lesser degree by the editor and the cameraman.

Film is primarily a director's medium. The director takes the written word and translates it into film, giving it a breath of life. Occasionally, when director and writer have collaborated quite closely on a film and the director fully understands and concurs with the writer's vision, the film may remain substantively unchanged. The finished work will reflect almost wholly the writer's original conception.

An excellent example of this is the collaboration of the French writer Marguerite Duras with the French director Alain Resnais on the beautiful and important motion picture *Hiroshima, Mon Amour*. In its translation from words to images, the script remained almost unchanged, both in detail and in concept.

Here, exactly as written, is Duras' script for the opening few minutes of the film.[1]

> (*As the film opens, two pair of bare shoulders appear, little by little. All we see are these shoulders—cut off from the body at the height of the head and hips—in an embrace, and as if drenched with ashes, rain, dew, or sweat, whichever is preferred. The main thing is that we get the feeling that this dew, this perspiration, has been deposited by the atomic "mushroom" as it moves away and evaporates. It should produce a violent, conflicting feeling of freshness and desire. The shoulders are of different colors, one dark, one light. Fusco's music accompanies this almost shocking embrace. The difference between the hands is also very marked. The woman's hand lies on the darker shoulder: "lies" is perhaps not the word; "grips" would be closer to it. A man's voice, flat and calm, as if reciting, says:*)

HE: You saw nothing in Hiroshima. Nothing.

> (*To be used as often as desired. A woman's voice, also flat, muffled, monotonous, the voice of someone reciting, replies:*)

SHE: I saw *everything. Everything.*

> (*Fusco's music, which has faded before this initial exchange, resumes just long enough to accompany the woman's hand tightening on the shoulder again, then letting go, then caressing it. The mark of fingernails on the darker flesh. As if this scratch could give the illusion of being a punishment for: "No. You saw nothing in Hiroshima." Then the woman's voice begins again, still calm, colorless, incantatory:*)

[1] From *Hiroshima, Mon Amour*, text by Marguerite Duras for the film by Alain Resnais; trans. by Richard Seaver (New York: Grove Press, Inc., 1961), pp. 15–25. Copyright © 1961 by Grove Press, Inc. Reprinted by permission of Grove Press, Inc.

SHE: The hospital, for instance, I saw it. I'm sure I did. There is a hospital in Hiroshima. How could I help seeing it?

(*The hospital, hallways, stairs, patients, the camera coldly objective. [We never see her seeing.] Then we come back to the hand gripping—and not letting go of—the darker shoulder.*)

HE: You did not see the hospital in Hiroshima. You saw nothing in Hiroshima.

(*Then the woman's voice becomes more . . . more impersonal. Shots of the museum. The same blinding light, the same ugly light here as at the hospital. Explanatory signs, pieces of evidence from the bombardment, scale models, mutilated iron, skin, burned hair, wax models, etc.*)

SHE: Four times at the museum . . .

HE: What museum in Hiroshima?

SHE: Four times at the museum in Hiroshima. I saw the people walking around. The people walk around, lost in thought among the photographs, the reconstructions, for want of something else, among the photographs, the photographs, the reconstructions, for want of something else, the explanations, for want of something else.
Four times at the museum in Hiroshima.
I looked at the people. I myself looked thoughtfully at the iron. The burned iron. The broken iron, the iron made vulnerable as flesh. I saw the bouquet of bottle caps: who would have suspected that? Human skin floating, surviving, still in the bloom of its agony. Stones. Burned stones. Shattered stones. Anonymous heads of hair that the women of Hiroshima, when they awoke in the morning, discovered had fallen out.
I was hot at Peace Square. Ten thousand degrees at Peace Square. I know it. The temperature of the sun at Peace Square. How can you not know it? . . . The grass, it's quite simple . . .

HE: You saw nothing in Hiroshima. Nothing.

(*More shots of the museum. Then a shot of Peace Square taken with a burned skull in the foreground. Glass display cases with burned models inside. Newsreel shots of Hiroshima.*)

SHE: The reconstructions have been made as authentically as possible.
The films have been made as authentically as possible.
The illusion, it's quite simple, the illusion is so perfect that the tourists cry.
One can always scoff, but what else can a tourist do, really, but cry?
I've always wept over the fate of Hiroshima. Always.

(*A panorama of a photograph taken of Hiroshima after the bomb, a "new desert" without reference to the other deserts of the world.*)

HE: No. What would you have cried about?

(*Peace Square, empty under a blinding sun that recalls the blinding light of the bomb. Newsreels taken after August 6, 1945. Ants, worms, emerge from the ground. Interspersed with shots of the shoulders. The woman's voice begins again, gone mad, as the sequence of pictures has also gone mad.*)

SHE: I saw the newsreels.

On the second day, History tells, I'm not making it up, on the second day certain species of animals rose again from the depths of the earth and from the ashes.

Dogs were photographed.
I saw them.
I *saw* the newsreels.
I *saw* them.
On the first day.
On the second day.
On the third day.

HE: (*interrupting her*): You saw nothing. Nothing.

(*A dog with a leg amputated. People, children. Wounds. Burned children screaming.*)

SHE: . . . on the fifteenth day too.

Hiroshima was blanketed with flowers. There were cornflowers and gladiolas everywhere, and morning glories and day lilies that rose again from the ashes with an extraordinary vigor, quite unheard of for flowers till then.

I didn't make anything up.

HE: You made it *all* up.

SHE: *Nothing.*

Just as in love this illusion exists, this illusion of being able never to forget, so I was under the illusion that I would never forget Hiroshima.

Just as in love.

(*Surgical forceps approach an eye to extract it. More newsreel shots.*)

I also saw the survivors and those who were in the wombs of the women of Hiroshima.

(*Shots of various survivors: a beautiful child who, upon turning around, is blind in one eye; a girl looking at her burned face in the mirror; a blind girl with twisted hands playing the zither; a woman praying near her dying children; a man, who has not slept for several years, dying. [Once a week they bring his children to see him.]*)

I saw the patience, the innocence, the apparent meekness with which the temporary survivors of Hiroshima adapted themselves to a fate so unjust that the imagination, normally so fertile, cannot conceive it.

(*And again a return to the perfect embrace of the bodies.*)

Listen . . .
I know . . .
I know *everything.*
It went on.

HE: *Nothing.* You know *nothing.*

The key elements in this script are:

(1) The clipped, repetitive cadence of the dialogue, coupled with its poetic imagery.

SHE: Four times at the museum in Hiroshima. I saw the people walking around. The people walk around, lost in thought, among the photographs, the reconstructions, for want of something else, among the photographs, the photographs, the reconstructions, for want of something else, the explanations, for want of something else.

Four times at the museum in Hiroshima.

I looked at the people. I myself looked thoughtfully at the iron. The burned iron. The broken iron, the iron made vulnerable as flesh. I saw the bouquet of bottle caps: who would have suspected that? Human skin floating, surviving, still in the bloom of its agony. . . .

(2) The very specific instructions for the delivery of key lines.

> A woman's voice, also flat, muffled, monotonous. . . .
> Then the woman's voice begins again, still calm, colorless, incantatory.
> Then the woman's voice becomes more . . . more impersonal.
> The woman's voice begins again, gone mad, as the sequence of pictures has also gone mad.

(3) The brief but almost complete descriptions of the elements that the writer "sees" contained within the visual action.

> As the film opens, two pair of bare shoulders appear, little by little. All we see are these shoulders—cut off from the body at the height of the head

Hiroshima, Mon Amour.

and hips — in an embrace, and as if drenched with ashes, rain, dew, or sweat, whichever is preferred. The main thing is that we get the feeling that this dew, this perspiration, has been deposited by the atomic "mushroom" as it moves away and evaporates. It should produce a violent, conflicting feeling of freshness and desire.

Shots of various survivors: a beautiful child who, upon turning around, is blind in one eye; a girl looking at her burned face in the mirror; a blind girl with twisted hands playing the zither; a woman praying near her dying children; a man, who has not slept for several years, dying. [Once a week they bring his children to see him.]

(4) Clear directives concerning supportive elements (sound, musical effects, and so forth) and a delineation of special relationships.

Fusco's music, which has faded before this initial exchange, resumes just long enough to accompany the woman's hand tightening on the shoulder again, then letting go, then caressing it. The mark of fingernails on the darker flesh. As if this scratch could give the illusion of being a punishment for: "No, You saw nothing in Hiroshima."

(5) Editing instructions on the order and intention of a sequence.

Peace Square, empty under a blinding sun that recalls the blinding light of the bomb. Newsreels taken after August 6, 1945. Ants, worms, emerge from the ground. Interspersed with shots of the shoulders.

The basic concept of the film is contained in its script. The constant shifting back and forth between past and present is established at the very beginning. The *form* of the film, as shown in the elements listed above, was designed to complement its content and theme (i.e., the constant intrusion of memory into present reality, and the final failings of memory itself).

The finished film was executed in precisely the above manner. Here, the director, cameraman, and editor simply took the writer's vision from the inanimate page of the script and brought it to life on the screen.

In most films, however, the script is reworked in varying degrees during its metamorphosis from words on paper to images on screen. The following is the screenplay for the opening minutes of Ingmar Bergman's classic film *The Seventh Seal.*[2] Although this script is replete with rough visual description and dialogue, there is nowhere the specific detail that the director, cameraman, and editor imparted to the scenes as they changed script into film.

The night had brought little relief from the heat, and at dawn a hot gust of wind blows across the colorless sea.

The knight, Antonius Block, lies prostrate on some spruce branches spread over the fine sand. His eyes are wide-open and bloodshot from lack of sleep.

Nearby his squire Jöns is snoring loudly. He has fallen asleep where he collapsed, at the edge of the forest among the wind-gnarled fir trees. His

[2] From *The Seventh Seal,* text and film by Ingmar Bergman, in *Four Screenplays of Ingmar Bergman,* trans. by Lars Malmstrom and David Kushner (New York: Simon and Schuster, Inc., 1960), pp. 99–101. Reprinted by permission of the publisher and Janus Films.

The Seventh Seal.

open mouth gapes toward the dawn, and unearthly sounds come from his
throat.

At the sudden gust of wind the horses stir, stretching their parched
muzzles toward the sea. They are as thin and worn as their masters.

The knight has risen and waded into the shallow water, where he rinses
his sunburned face and blistered lips.

Jöns rolls over to face the forest and the darkness. He moans in his sleep
and vigorously scratches the stubbled hair on his head. A scar stretches
diagonally across his scalp, as white as lightning against the grime.

The knight returns to the beach and falls on his knees. With his eyes
closed and brow furrowed, he says his morning prayers. His hands are
clenched together and his lips form the words silently. His face is sad and
bitter. He opens his eyes and stares directly into the morning sun which
wallows up from the misty sea like some bloated, dying fish. The sky is
gray and immobile, a dome of lead. A cloud hangs mute and dark over
the western horizon. High up, barely visible, a sea gull floats on motionless wings. Its cry is weird and restless.

The knight's large gray horse lifts its head and whinnies. Antonius
Block turns around.

Behind him stands a man in black. His face is very pale and he keeps his
hands hidden in the wide folds of his cloak.

KNIGHT: Who are you?
DEATH: I am Death.
KNIGHT: Have you come for me?
DEATH: I have been walking by your side for a long time.
KNIGHT: That I know.
DEATH: Are you prepared?
KNIGHT: My body is frightened, but I am not.
DEATH: Well, there is no shame in that.

The knight has risen to his feet. He shivers. Death opens his cloak to place it around the knight's shoulders.

KNIGHT: Wait a moment.
DEATH: That's what they all say. I grant no reprieves.
KNIGHT: You play chess, don't you?

A gleam of interest kindles in Death's eyes.

DEATH: How did you know that?
KNIGHT: I have seen it in paintings and heard it sung in ballads.
DEATH: Yes, in fact I'm quite a good chess player.
KNIGHT: But you can't be better than I am.

The knight rummages in the big black bag which he keeps beside him and takes out a small chessboard. He places it carefully on the ground and begins setting up the pieces.

DEATH: Why do you want to play chess with me?
KNIGHT: I have my reasons.
DEATH: That is your privilege.
KNIGHT: The condition is that I may live as long as I hold out against you. If I win, you will release me. Is it agreed?

The knight holds out his two fists to Death, who smiles at him suddenly. Death points to one of the knight's hands; it contains a black pawn.

KNIGHT: You drew black!
DEATH: Very appropriate. Don't you think so?

Among the elements added by the continuing process of creating the film were:

(1) The eerie black-and-white photography emphasizing an almost time-less melancholy.
(2) The sounds of the sea and the birds throughout the entire scene.
(3) The sudden cut that made the appearance of Death almost magical.
(4) The stylized performance of the actors, which immediately identifies the allegorical (passion play) nature of the film.

The script for a motion picture usually exists primarily as a basic design revealing the writer's concept of the film. It is neither a novel nor a play, and it cannot, indeed must not, exist completely as words on paper.

It is this fact that makes the film script unique. The script will undergo a continual process of development as it is handled by other "creators." It must, however, be completely "seen" by the writer—in structure, in what is heard, and most important, in the visual images that will form the finished work.

Over the past decade, filmmakers such as Bergman, Resnais, Bertolucci, Fellini, and Kubrick have produced motion picture scripts that represent an ideal for the form. Paddy Chayefsky's scripts, on the other hand, are examples of a different kind of film script. Highly literate and brilliant in their consideration of human beings and events, they give detailed descriptions of the characters involved, but they do not by and large define a "cinema" style for the finished film.

Although Chayefsky and Duras script their films in very different terms, both conceive of a complete motion picture. Compare the following segment from *The Hospital*[3] with the earlier section of *Hiroshima, Mon Amour*.

60 EXT. NIGHT.

CRASH OF THUNDER. CRACKLE OF LIGHTNING.
THE HOSPITAL — 10:00 P.M.

A horror-film rainstorm slashes across the vast dark complex of buildings.

61 INT. HOLLY PAVILION — EXECUTIVE CORRIDOR

Dark, silent. The doors on both sides are closed except for one on the Director's side which is slightly ajar and leaks a thin stream of light.

62 INT. THE DIRECTOR'S OFFICE

Sundstrom, as impeccable as ever, is at his desk, shadowed by the desk lamp. He is on the phone.

SUNDSTROM

(on phone)

—no, I just got off the phone with Barry, The Relocation Bureau isn't going to help at all. George, we've got to get those people who were evicted into decent apartments. They're living two and three families to a room in welfare hotels. All kinds of fringe groups are exploiting it now. Face it, George. We're in the public housing business. You and/or some other director on the Board has got to dig up four hundred housing units. I want to be able to tell the tenants' committee that tomorrow . . . George, I don't want a riot here like what happened at Lincoln Hospital last month . . . All right, call me back. I'll be here. My wife's going to kill me, but I'll be here. . . .

63 INT. HOLLY PAVILION — THIRD FLOOR — DEPT. OF MEDICINE CORRIDOR

Dark, empty, silent. One lonely light at the lobby end of the long, closed corridor of offices. The door to Bock's office is ajar. A tracing of light issues from there.

64 INT. BOCK'S OFFICE

[3] From *The Hospital*, script by Paddy Chayefsky. Reprinted by permission.

Across the silent, dark, typewriter-covered desks of the two secretaries through the half-open doorway to Bock's private office where we can see Bock at his desk, lit by the desk lamp. He is in his shirtsleeves. He has a bottle of booze on his desk, and he is getting stoned. He gets up from his desk. He has made a decision.

65   INT. HOLLY PAVILION — FOURTH FLOOR

The corridors are silent and sleeping; the night lights are on, subdued, hushed. Head Evening Nurse, MRS. DUNNE, *is back at her desk, hunched over paper work. In b.g., Resident* BRUBAKER *passes by.*

66   INT. FOURTH FLOOR — PHARMACY

Nurse SHERLEE DEVINE, *a black girl in her mid-20's, has a porcelain tray on the shelf into which she puts a small jar of alcohol, some cotton swabs, a bottle of medication, a wrapped hypodermic needle and syringe. She moves out into —*

67   INT. FOURTH FLOOR — NURSES' STATION

where Mrs. Dunne looks up as she passes.

>NURSE DEVINE
>
>(*murmurs*)

Mead.

Mrs. Dunne nods. Nurse Devine pads silently down the sleeping doors to —

68   INT. FOURTH FLOOR — ROOM 406

Silent, dark, sleeping. The bathroom light is on, but the door is nearly closed and only a thin stream of yellow light trickles into the room. THUNDER CRASHES O.S. *William Mead, already sedated with sparine, sleeps fitfully. The other patient has been entirely curtained off. Nurse Devine sets her tray quietly down on Mead's bedtable, turns on the goose-neck lamp, keeping it from glaring into Mead's eyes. She unwraps the hypodermic syringe, sets in the needle, now draws the required dosage from the bottle of medication, reaches over and gently shakes the sleeping Mead by the shoulder.*

>NURSE DEVINE
>(*softly, almost sinisterly*)

Mr. Mead . . . Mr. Mead, I'm going to give you your shot of pheno-barbital now.

Mead sleeps on. Expressionlessly, Nurse Devine extracts Mead's right arm from under the sheets, wets a swab with alcohol and rubs the vein down. CAMERA MOVES DOWN *on the needle of the syringe as it slides silently into Mead's vein.* OVER THIS, *we begin to hear the suggestion of* CURIOUS SOUNDS — *distant sibilant* HISSING, *erratic, indistinct, like the leakage of a bad heart, and an occasional soft* HALF-GRUNT. CAMERA PULLS BACK SLOWLY *to* FULL SHOT *of Nurse Devine withdrawing the hypodermic needle, looking up, frowning, for she too has heard the strange, soft sounds. They seem to emanate from behind the curtains around the other bed in the room.*

Frowning, Nurse Devine returns the syringe to the porcelain tray, gathers the tray up, and, frowning, she pads silently around Mead's bed to Drummond's bed. With her free hand, she opens the curtains a little and stares in.

NURSE DEVINE'S P.O.V. The Indian and the patient's daughter are bent over Drummond performing some kind of pagan ritual. The odd hissing SOUNDS are coming from the girl; this is her contribution to the ceremony. (It sounds like pis-pis; and is in fact an imitation of the nighthawk and is meant to appease the spirit of the thunder.) The old Indian has stripped to the waist and has marked his body with smears of dye and tule pollen. He wears a ceremonial hat which is a sort of beaded beanie. He is putting a buckskin bag of pollen to the four directions—i.e., he is holding the small buckskin bag in the cupped palms of both hands and is facing north, east, south and west, offering the bag in each direction and murmuring prayers under his breath as he does. A beaded amulet lies stretched across the white sheet covering the comatose Drummond. At any rate, when Nurse Devine draws the bed-curtains, the patient's daughter turns to the interruption, frowns at Nurse Devine, holds a cautioning finger to her lips and draws the curtains closed again. Nurse Devine, carrying her porcelain tray, exits.

69   INT. FOURTH FLOOR—NURSES' STATION

as Bock comes out of the elevator, jacketed now, pretty drunk but holding it well. He heads for the nurses' desk as, in b.g., Nurse Devine comes down the west corridor. Bock grunts at Mrs. Dunne and goes into—

70   INT. FOURTH FLOOR—PHARMACY

—where he quickly runs his finger along the second shelf of medicines until he comes to the bottle of potassium which he filches off the shelf and slips into his pocket. He now rummages in the drawers for a hypodermic syringe. Through the open doorway, in b.g., we see Nurse Devine padding swiftly up to Mrs. Dunne at the desk.

71   INT. FOURTH FLOOR—NURSING STATION

NURSE DEVINE

(to Mrs. Dunne)

Well, baby, we got a witch-doctor in Four-oh-six, and you better go in there. You know that Indian that was sitting there in Four-oh-six all night? He's still there, and the girl's there, and they're doing some voodoo in there, and I ain't kidding.

Behind Mrs. Dunne, Bock appears in the doorway to the pharmacy where he stands listening.

MRS. DUNNE

(looking up from her work)

What do you mean?

NURSE DEVINE

I mean, that Indian's in there, half-naked and going pis-pis-pis with a little bag. You just better get in there, Mrs. Dunne.

Mrs. Dunne, annoyed, gets up and heads for the west corridor, followed by

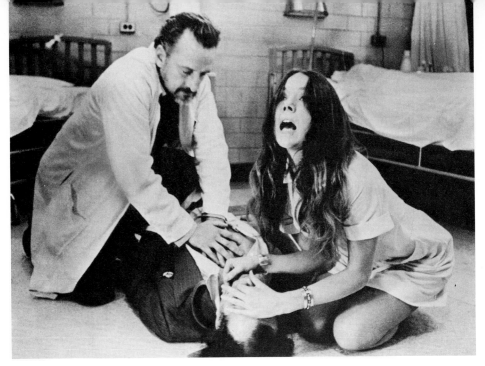

The Hospital.

Nurse Devine, still holding her porcelain tray, and by an intrigued Dr. Bock clumping along a few paces behind.

NURSE DEVINE

(*to Nurse Weitzenbaum, coming out of another room*)

You want to see something, baby? You just come here.

As the small procession bears down on Room 406, Barbara Drummond slips out of that room to intercept them.

BARBARA

(*keeping her voice down*)

Look, it's a perfectly harmless ceremony, nothing to get excited about. It'll be over in a few minutes anyway. But Mr. Blacktree is a shaman who gets his power from the thunder, and it's imperative he conclude his rituals while the storm is still going on.

MRS. DUNNE

(*with asperity*)

Visiting hours were over at nine o'clock, Miss.

Bock reaches for the door to the room.

BARBARA

All that's going on in there, Doctor, is a simple Apache prayer for my father's recovery.

Bock grunts and continues into—

72   INT. ROOM 406

as Bock slides in, a bit of the subdued corridor light coming in with him. The curtains have been left sufficiently open to reveal Mr. Blacktree, still stripped to the waist and marked on both cheeks with crosses of pollen, now extending two twigs to the four directions after which he places the two twigs carefully on the white sheet covering Drummond in a pattern with the embroidered amulet already there. Behind Bock, Mrs. Dunne can be seen peeking in. The Indian is oblivious to both of them. Bock watches it all with interest for a moment and then backs out into—

73   INT. FOURTH FLOOR — CORRIDOR

—closing the door after him.

BARBARA

The markings he's made on my father's arms are from the pollen of the tule plant. The twigs have no significance other than they've been struck by lightning and are consequently appeals to the spirit of lightning. It's all entirely harmless, a religious ceremony, not a medical one.

BOCK

You don't seriously believe that mumbo-jumbo will cure him.

BARBARA

On the other hand, it won't kill him, Doctor.

They regard each other levelly.

BOCK

(grunts)

Okay. Go ahead.

He wheels and clumps off for the stairway exit at the end of the darkish corridor.

BARBARA

(murmurs)

Thank you.

Nurse Weitzenbaum opens the door of the room and peeks in. At the stairway exit door, Bock pauses, looks back to the little clutch of women standing in front of Room 406.

BOCK

Are you still taking your father out, Miss Drummond?

BARBARA

Yes. I still have to arrange an ambulance service. Is there a phone around I could use?

BOCK

You can use my office.

Thank you.

Bock exits. Barbara edges past the fascinated Nurse Weitzenbaum, still peeking into the room.

74   INT. ROOM 406

as Barbara comes in, gathers her coat and purse from one of the chairs and moves to the old, half-naked Indian, now occupied with what seems to be the rolling of a cigarette. The two exchange a brief muttered dialogue in Apache. The old Indian nods. The girl turns and exits, taking Nurse Weitzenbaum out with her and closing the door. The room is dark, silent, hushed again. The old Indian lights his cigarette and "sends the smoke up," a ritual which consists of puffing smoke to each of the four directions, muttering in Apache after each puff: "May all be well." He also goes pis-pis-pis with each puff.

CAMERA SLOWLY PANS *across the room to the other bed where William Mead is sleeping fitfully. The* SOUNDS *of the soft Apache words and the pis-pis-pis penetrate Mead's drugged sleep. He opens one eyelid and stares glazedly at the dark air around him. The* SOUNDS *persist. He turns his groggy head to look at the other bed. Mr. Blacktree chooses this moment to sidle out from behind the curtains and to continue his ritual in the less confined space at the head of Drummond's bed. It's something of a sight for a nervous, sedated man to wake up to — a half-naked Indian with blue, red and white markings on his face and chest and arms, standing in the middle of a dark hospital, puffing a cigarette with curiously formal and ritualistic gestures, and saying pis-pis-pis to the window, outside of which the thunder* RUMBLES *and the rain* SLASHES *and a sudden, savage streak of lightning briefly illuminates it all. Mead figures it's all a bad dream, and, after a moment of dully regarding the odd spectacle, he closes his one eye and goes back to sleep.*

Note that, whereas in *Hiroshima, Mon Amour* Duras gives specific instructions about images, music, and editing, Chayefsky confines himself to the characters and the settings in which they interact. His directions deal with how he wants the characters portrayed and with the mood he wants to create; he is willing to leave other matters in the hands of his director.

The relationship of the script to the film is the springboard from which the art of the motion picture is launched. When clearly "seen" by the writer, the script becomes the starting point for the creation of a film, a work upon which to build.

THEME

The first consideration of any film must be one of *theme.* If audiences do not grasp what a film is about, they can scarcely be expected to criticize, analyze, and study it. If the filmmaker does not know what he wants to say, he can hardly produce a communicative work of art.

This is not to impose an old-fashioned or didactic rule on a modern and open-ended art form. There are many themes and an endless variety of ways to communicate them. It is important, however, to avoid the kind of artistic nihilism that characterizes the "anything goes" approach.

Despite the wide variety of film styles and movements within the past twenty years, the artistically successful films of the period have all shown a common trait: a discernible theme that is both intellectually and philosophically arresting. Bergman's examination of man's relationship to God (*The Seventh Seal, Winter Light*), Antonioni's examination of alienation and the nature of "involvement" (*L'Avventura, Blow-Up*), and Fellini's probing into the institutions of society (*La Dolce Vita, 8½*) are all themes, clearly present in the initial scripts and carefully worked out in the films themselves.

A theme may be a social comment (*The Conformist*), an examination of a philosophical idea (*McCabe & Mrs. Miller*), a statement of a particular reality (*A Clockwork Orange*), an exploration into mystery (*The Seventh Seal, Through a Glass Darkly*), a view of human relationships (*Cries and Whispers, Last Tango in Paris*), or a study of the ills of a particular time and place (*Z, State of Siege*). There is no restriction on the choice of theme, but the script must communicate a theme and must have a consistency in relationship to that theme.

The theme of a film need not be a "message" or even a point of view. It is quite possible for a script to indicate simply a mood; the mood then becomes the theme. Claude LeLouche's *A Man and a Woman* and Bo Widerberg's *Elvira Madigan* state no philosophical theme or intellectual idea but both are content to create a pervasive mood of romance that dictates the handling of all elements, including camera style, acting, editing, and music. Thus theme can be many things; but whether it is a philosophical idea or simply the statement of a mood, it must be clearly presented in the script, for the theme becomes the guiding force in the making of a film.

The most important development in modern cinema was the recognition that film is capable of dealing with the most profound ideas of our time. Thus cinema moved out of the realm of folk entertainment to take its place beside the theater and the novel as a major art form.

In Fellini's film *La Strada*, the theme—the self-imposed isolation of mankind in a world without love—was carefully worked out in the script. The plot deals with an itinerant circus performer, Zampano, who travels over a bleak and barren Italian countryside performing a single tawdry trick. For his act, billed as a feat of prodigious strength, he ties a chain around his chest and breaks it by swelling his chest. Zampano is a crude, bestial, joyless man who performs for the village, eats, sleeps and is otherwise without those qualities that separate man from animals.

In his travels, Zampano meets Gelsomina—a strange, fey creature, half child and half woman. She is a "miracle" child whose retardation has kept her close to nature, free to express love and joy. Zampano buys her from her mother and teaches her to accompany him on the trumpet in his act. She grows in this role, assuming the quality of a circus clown with Chaplinesque

La Strada.

overtones. Most important, she comes to love and care for Zampano and to accept him as he is.

The crisis of the script occurs when a Christ figure, the tightrope walker Matto, enters their lives. As they work together in a small circus, Matto goads Zampano repeatedly, contrasting his own joy and sense of the beauty of the world with Zampano's animalistic behavior. He is kind and loving to Gelsomina and tries to give her a sense of her own worth through love. Finally, with the inevitability of a Greek drama, he goads Zampano until Zampano kills him. This act of violence horrifies Gelsomina and she retreats into a catatonic shell.

Zampano, motivated by his own baser nature, pragmatic and without those qualities that raise man to the angels, leaves her asleep by the side of the road. This desertion of Gelsomina ends Zampano's only opportunity to know love. He lives his life out in squalor and sadness. Strangely, he misses Gelsomina and, after searching, finds out she has died. In the end of the film Zampano lies alone on a beach crying out his own name.

Each major dramatic incident in the film is carefully constructed to reveal the contrasting qualities of the leading characters, and every detail furthers the *theme* of the film. Zampano is placed in situations that demonstrate his inability to respond with any actions above those elemental ones that fill his physical needs. Even his "great" feat of strength is shown for what it really is — a cheap deception. In counterpoint to Zampano is the joyful and loving Gelsomina — her trumpet playing, her dancing walk, her wonder at nature and the universe. Every detail of the film—the narrative, the nature of the visual images, the performances, the sounds—was designed and executed to explore this theme. The harrowing effect of the final scene on the beach where Zampano, realizing how much he has lost by losing the child-woman Gelsomina, cries out to the deaf heavens is a direct result of script structure and script-designed detail that at *all* times relate directly to the theme.

Audiences, sophisticated and unsophisticated, understand the film because Fellini understood what he wanted to say and remained consistent in intent throughout both the scripting and filming.

The following questions should be considered with regard to the theme of a film:

(1) *Is the theme true?* It would be difficult to create a truly great work of art on a theme that is patently false. For example, a film with the theme "Hitler was right in seeking to destroy the Jews" must fail as a work of art, however brilliantly executed.

(2) *Is the theme intellectually or philosophically interesting?* Does it throw new light on the familiar or present a truly new idea or ideas? Does it give us a fresh understanding of old truths or present wholly original ones? For example, a film whose sole idea is "War is bad" must fail as a valid and lasting work of art. On the other hand, *Hiroshima, Mon Amour* tells us something new about *why* war is totally destructive, to both victor and vanquished; it succeeds as art.

A theme that is not intellectually or philosophically interesting may still have artistic merit if it simply evokes a mood. The Swedish film *Elvira Madigan* —which has little to say intellectually but merely seeks to create a mood of romance in a bygone time—achieves its mood primarily through exquisite long-lens color photography and a sensitive and sparing use of Mozart's Piano Concerto #21. Thus, to examine the *theme* of this film is simply to study the mood it evokes (fantasy, romance) and the means by which this is done. No fruitful debate is possible concerning "ideas" in the film, for there are none. It is important to identify those films that contain themes of intellectual and philosophical depth and those that simply seek to evoke a mood.

(3) *Is the theme (or the mood) presented effectively?* What structure and techniques are used to convey the intellectual and philosophical ideas of the film? What cinematic methods are used to create the mood of the film?

FORM AND STRUCTURE

Traditionally, a motion picture script consists of shots, scenes, and sequences.

(1) A *shot* is a single segment of film from the time the camera begins running to the time it stops running. The composition of the image may change if the camera moves, but it is still a shot as long as no other shot is spliced to it.

(2) A *scene* is a unified action occurring at a single time and place. It may consist of a single shot but usually is a group of shots.

EXAMPLE: Close-up: Face of boxer as fist strikes him
Cut to
Long shot: Entire boxing ring as a fighter falls
Cut to
Close-up: Victorious fighter smiling
Cut to
Close-up: Group of faces in crowd cheering
Fade out

(3) A *sequence* is a group of scenes comprising an entire dramatic segment of a film.

EXAMPLE: The "wedding sequence" at the opening of *The Godfather*, beginning with the scenes of Don Corleone (Brando) receiving petitioners in his study and finishing with the end of the wedding itself.

The script, then, is designed from shots, scenes, and sequences. Shots are planned and described as the writer conceives them. They are then assembled to form coherent scenes designed to contribute something to the whole. Finally, scenes are placed in order to form sequences, which in turn make up the entire film. There is no rule as to how long or short each of these units can run and no rule as to order. The writer is free to use the units of the script in any manner he chooses.

A fine example of writing for the screen is found in the work of Luis Buñuel, a filmmaker whose career spans nearly the entire creative history of the art. The following is an excerpt from the script for Buñuel's *Viridiana*,[4] an almost perfect design for a film. In the script each shot is numbered consecutively.

Viridiana, a young girl, is a convent novice. She has come to spend the days before taking her vows with her uncle Don Jaime. Ramona is Don Jaime's servant and Rita is Ramona's little daughter. Don Jaime, erotically stimulated by his niece's innocence and beauty, asks Viridiana to marry him, and when she refuses him he drugs her in the expectation of seducing her. This sequence follows:

> 67 *Exterior, the garden. Night. General shot. Dolly.*
>
> *Rita draws near the door of the room where she sleeps with her mother. She looks toward the interior, which is plunged in darkness, but she does not dare enter. She goes toward the main building and the household dog, wagging his tail, comes up to her. She pats him, sighing with satisfaction; she*

[4] From *Viridiana*, pp. 164–77. Copyright © 1963 by Ado Kyrou. Reprinted by permission of Simon and Schuster, Inc.

seems to have found in him the protection she was looking for. Quieter now, she pushes the animal by its haunches and goes to sit down on a bench by the doorstep. In the dark courtyard, two beams of light clearly shine out from the upper rooms. Rita, leaning forward, looks in the direction of the light.

68   Interior, living room. Evening.

Viridiana, seated in the same chair as in the preceding scene, is listening to the first movement of César Franck's Sonata in F together with Don Jaime, who listens inattentively, leaning against the console of the record player. Ramona is seated on a low chair near the little table on which is the coffee service. She is finishing her coffee in small sips. As she brings the cup to her lips, she looks at the young novice. With fear? Or is she waiting?

Viridiana, her back to the camera, holds the empty cup in her hand.

Don Jaime rouses himself from his false torpor. He raises his eyebrows, looks at his niece, then at Ramona. He walks about, and his steps lead him behind Viridiana whom he is now observing anxiously.

69   Close-up. Panoramic.

Viridiana's right hand, holding the cup and saucer. The pressure of her fingers slacks and what she holds slips to the floor. Don Jaime holds his breath. He is right behind her. He stops to note her reactions. He looks at Ramona. Then he speaks, in a hesitant voice.

DON JAIME: You seem very tired. Perhaps you should go to bed. *There is no answer. Viridiana's head leans toward one shoulder. Don Jaime moves slowly forward until he is facing the young girl.*

DON JAIME (*shaking her gently*): Viridiana! Viridiana!

He receives no answer. Then, walking cautiously, he approaches the record player and stops it.

70   Exterior, garden. Night.

Rita pushes the dog so that he'll go away. She has decided to go up to Don Jaime's rooms to look for her mother.

RITA: Run away, now, Lucero!

Without giving the dog another thought, she goes slowly toward the stairs. She isn't very sure of how welcome she'll be upstairs, but she starts to go up little by little.

71   Interior, corridor. Evening.

The hallway is lit only by the light that comes from the living room. At the far end, Rita's little silhouette appears as she at last reaches the main floor. She enters the hallway cautiously heading for the living room where she hears half-muffled voices.

VOICE OF DON JAIME: Help me! Take her legs . . .

VOICE OF RAMONA: Lift her up a little higher, sir . . .

There is a pause. Sound of a chair falling.

VOICE OF DON JAIME: Don't think ill of me, Ramona. I just want to keep her near me.

The camera has drawn near Rita. Steps are heard approaching the door and the little girl runs to hide behind a piece of furniture. From there she observes the scene, frightened. Don Jaime and the servant arrive from the living room, carrying the body of Viridiana, who seems dead. They go toward Doña Elvira's room, which they enter.

Rita comes out of her hiding place. Spurred by curiosity, she would like to see more, but she is afraid of being caught. She beats a retreat and turning back her head every so often, she starts slowly down the stairs.

72   *Interior, Doña Elvira's room. Foreground shot.*

They have just placed the novice's inert body on the bed. Don Jaime makes a sign to Ramona to leave, and she obeys in silence. Viridiana is still stretched out on her back in the same position. Her hair is in slight disorder, as it was shortly before she took off the bridal veil. Don Jaime puts it in order again, nervously but with minute artistry. Then he replaces the crown of orange blossoms, crosses her hands on her breast, joins her feet together, arranges the folds of her dress. Stretched out thus, Viridiana looks like a beautiful prostrate statue.

73   *Exterior, garden. Night. General shot.*

The great tree under whose branches little Rita usually plays. We see her drawing near the tree, looking every so often toward the dimly lit window of Doña Elvira's room. After a moment's hesitation, the little girl starts to climb the tree, whose topmost branches are a few yards above the roof of the house.

74   *Crane shot.*

We follow Rita as she climbs. She finally finds a good spot and settles down astride a branch which is about on a level with Doña Elvira's room. From there, she watches with curiosity whatever is going on.

75   *Interior, Doña Elvira's room. Evening. General shot. Middle-distance Shot. Close-up on dolly. (From Rita's point of view.)*

Don Jaime, without taking his eyes off the body of the novice, paces back and forth. He stops for an instant, then goes to sit on the bed. He caresses Viridiana's forehead and hair. He is deeply moved. Then he puts an arm under the young girl's shoulders and lifts her lightly to a sitting position. He bends down and touches her lips with his in a sweet, prolonged kiss.

Suddenly his eyes note the uncurtained window and the night. He carefully lowers Viridiana on the bed and goes toward the window. He closes it and draws the curtains. Then he goes to the door and turns the key.

76   *Exterior, garden. Night. General shot.*

Rita clambers down the tree and jumps to the ground. She sees her mother coming from the farmhouse and runs toward her.

RAMONA: What are you doing here?

RITA: Don Jaime was kissing the lady.

Ramona looks at her daughter with a worried expression. Then she realizes how her daughter could have found out. She frowns, annoyed.

RAMONA: If he's kissing her, that's because she's his niece. Don't I kiss you? You ought to be in bed.

RITA: A black bull came in the room.

RAMONA: Shut up, now! I'm going to put you to bed.

She takes the child by the hand and leads her toward the servants' quarter.

77   *Interior, Doña Elvira's room. Evening. Close-up panning to middle-distance shot.*

We see Don Jaime's trembling hands unhooking the false bride's corsage. Her throat and the upper part of her breasts appear, uncovered. This defenseless body, so long desired, is now at his mercy. He is completely overcome. He places his cheek against Viridiana's breast, feels the delicacy and warmth of her skin. He kisses her, once, twice. Suddenly he recoils. He straightens up and looks almost with dread at the inert body. He sees the calm, serene expression on the novice's face. Don Jaime passes rapidly at this point from the blind world of instinct to that of conscience. He understands the baseness of his act. At bottom, he is a good and gentle man.

Yet his hands are still stretched out toward her. Suddenly resolved, as if moved by fear of himself, he hurries toward the door, opens it, and goes down the hallway.

78   *Interior, corridor. Evening. General shot.*

We see Don Jaime pass by on his way to his room. He is walking with a rapid and nervous step. He opens his door, enters, and shuts it violently. Absolute silence reigns in the house.

79   *Exterior, landscape. Day. From close-up to general shot. Panoramic.*

The camera ranges from a few ruins still barely lit by the rising sun to a general view of the uncultivated fields of the property. The murmur of a stream is heard. The mooing of a cow, the cry of birds.

80   *Interior, Doña Elvira's room. Day. Middle-distance shot. Dolly.*

Viridiana is still sleeping an apparently untroubled sleep. She is between the sheets, dressed in a nightgown. We see an exposed portion of her breast. At the foot of the bed, Ramona is dozing on a chair, keeping watch over the young girl.

The cries of birds continue to be heard from outside. Viridiana slowly opens her eyes. Absent expression. She runs her tongue over her lips. A gesture of displeasure. Then her eyes focus on the indistinct silhouette of the servant.

Ramona, aware that Viridiana is awake, draws near. She smiles at her.

VIRIDIANA: I'm thirsty.

Ramona pours her a glass of water from a bottle standing on the little table. Viridiana drinks eagerly.

VIRIDIANA: My head aches.

RAMONA: It will pass. It's nothing.

Viridiana notices her partial nakedness and, embarrassed, covers herself.

VIRIDIANA: What happened to me?

RAMONA: Last evening, you fainted after dinner. The master and I carried you in here.

The novice covers herself up to her chin with the sheet. She is disturbed at having been undressed and put to bed. The servant is aware of this.

RAMONA: I undressed you this morning.

VIRIDIANA: Did I sleep a long time?

Ramona nods her head in assent.

VIRIDIANA: Give me some more water.

The woman pours her another glass of water which she drinks with the same avidity. Steps are heard approaching the room. Viridiana puts down the water glass and withdraws under the sheets.

The door opens and Don Jaime appears. His face and the disarray of his clothes clearly show the sleepless night he has spent. He stands a moment, undecided, motionless in the shadow. On seeing him, Viridiana wishes to protest but she does not dare. He comes into the room.

DON JAIME: Leave us, Ramona.

VIRIDIANA (*emphatically*): Don't go!

Don Jaime nods toward the servant and she obeys. She leaves the room, closing the door behind her. The uncle and niece are face to face.

VIRIDIANA: Uncle, please leave me. I want to get up.

He does not reply. The old man walks, deep in thought, up and down the room, doubtless not knowing how to begin. She insists, irritated.

VIRIDIANA: I must leave.

Don Jaime reacts to this and approaches the bed. He answers firmly.

DON JAIME: No. Now you can no longer leave.

There is a flash of impatience, almost of anger, in the young girl's eyes.

VIRIDIANA: Last evening you promised me never to speak of that again. I beg you, leave me alone now.

Don Jaime, impassive, sits down at the foot of the bed. Viridiana shows signs of beginning to be afraid.

DON JAIME (*very calmly, his eyes fixed now on her, now on the clouds one sees passing beyond the branches of the great tree*): What can be further apart than an old man like me, withdrawn from the world, and a young girl like you, promised to God? And yet . . .

The young girl, annoyed, sits almost upright.

DON JAIME: For you, I've forgotten everything, even the passion that kept me alive for so many years—everything!

Viridiana.

Viridiana would gladly get up and make him leave the room, but her state of undress prevents her.

DON JAIME: I was mad. I thought that you would agree to marry me, but naturally you refused. And now the day has come for you to leave.

She looks at him, wondering how the conversation will end. Don Jaime straightens up and looks at her fixedly.

DON JAIME (*coldly*): I had to force your will. (*A pause*) That was the only way I could hold you in my arms.

Viridiana is overwhelmed. Increasing anxiety. She stammers.

VIRIDIANA: You lie!

DON JAIME: No, it's true. (*Speaking very distinctly*) Last night, while you were sleeping, you were mine.

She stares at him with horrified eyes. She cannot believe what he is saying. She feels a cold sweat break out on her forehead.

Don Jaime starts to walk up and down before her once more, now fixing her with his eyes, now looking obstinately at the ground.

DON JAIME: Now you can no longer return to your convent. You are no longer the girl who left it a few days ago. You must stay with me forever.

He stops. There is a note of supplication in his voice.

DON JAIME: Everything I have will be yours, and if you prefer not to marry me, if you prefer to go on living as we have until now, I will resign myself to it as long as you stay near me . . .

It takes a visible effort for Viridiana to understand her uncle's words. The shock has been so great that she scarcely reacts. Her distress arouses compassion in Don Jaime.

DON JAIME: Think it over. Don't hurry. Think it over.

VIRIDIANA (*as if waking from a nightmare, almost screaming*): Go away! Leave me alone!

81 *Interior, corridor. Day. Middle-distance shot.*

We see Don Jaime, uncertain and torn by doubt, leave the room. The idea that he has committed an unpardonable error in lying to Viridiana is working within him.

82 *Interior, Don Jaime's room. Day. Middle-distance shot.*

Ramona is waiting for him and Don Jaime passes her without even seeing her. He sits down heavily on the edge of his bed. Ramona slowly approaches him. She dares to ask him:

RAMONA: What did you say to her, sir?

He raises his head toward her.

DON JAIME: How she looked at me, Ramona! Now she hates me. I made a grave mistake. She's going away, she's going away for good.

RAMONA (*tonelessly*): Speak to her again. Tell her seriously how things are.

DON JAIME: What would be the good? She would look at me again like that . . . I can't do it. You go. Perhaps she'll listen to you. Try to convince her.

RAMONA: But sir, what am I to tell her?

DON JAIME: Tell her I lied to her, tell her I did her no harm.

Ramona looks at him open-mouthed, incredulous.

DON JAIME (*with deep sincerity*): I intended to, Ramona. But I came to my senses in time. I spent the night thinking, thinking . . . And then I lied to her so that she would not dare go back there.

He gets up and takes Ramona by the arm.

DON JAIME: Go to her. Explain.

He almost pushes her toward the door. She goes hesitantly, reluctantly.

83 *Interior, Doña Elvira's room. Day. Middle-distance shot.*

Viridiana is finishing getting dressed and is closing her valise at the moment the door opens and the servant timidly shows her face. Viridiana's eyes are full of tears. We see Ramona hesitate a moment, then turn and go rapidly toward Don Jaime's room.

84 *Interior, Don Jaime's room. Day. General shot.*

Don Jaime in the foreground, leaning against his bed. Ramona appears in the doorway.

RAMONA: Come right away, sir; she's going.

Don Jaime straightens up at once. He stares at the servant, then moves rapidly toward the door and goes out.

85 *Interior, Doña Elvira's room. Day. General shot.*

Viridiana places her veil on her head, takes up her valise, and is starting to go when her uncle enters the room. He stands in her way. The young girl's eyes are still tearful.

VIRIDIANA: Let me pass!

DON JAIME: Before you go, you must hear me out.

VIRIDIANA (*bitterly*): I have heard you quite enough. Let me leave.

In lieu of an answer, the old man locks the door and puts the key in his pocket.

Viridiana backs away from him and puts down her valise. She is no longer afraid. She can scarcely feel any emotion other than rage mingled with disgust.

Don Jaime drops into a chair.

DON JAIME: Everything I told you before is a lie. I said it so that you would not go away. I harmed you only in my thoughts. I can't bear to have you hating me.

He looks at her in supplication.

DON JAIME: Tell me that you believe me and I will let you go.

VIRIDIANA: You disgust me . . . even if what you say is true.

DON JAIME (*in a quieter voice*): Then . . . can't you forgive me?

The look the young girl gives him completes Don Jaime's destruction. He gets up painfully, more stooped than ever. Perhaps he wishes to inspire at least a ray of pity in his niece. But she remains impassive. He goes toward the door with faltering steps, puts the key in the lock, and opens it. Without looking at him, she hurries out.

86 *Interior, corridor. Day. General shot.*

We see the novice coming from the far end of the corridor toward the camera. Ramona timidly raises her head to watch her pass. Don Jaime's silhouette is shown dimly against the shadows of the room the young girl has just left. Viridiana passes in front of the camera and we hear her hurried steps on the stairs. Ramona runs to meet Don Jaime.

87 *Interior, Doña Elvira's room. Day. General shot.*

Don Jaime, seen from behind, is looking down from the balcony. Ramona enters, overcome by what has been happening. When Don Jaime hears her steps, he turns around. His expression is not what we might have expected. He seems peaceful enough, without the least trace of sorrow. He seems almost to be smiling. Once what he has so dreaded has come to pass, he finds the courage he had simulated before. The servant stops, eyes downcast, a few steps away from him, not daring to look at him. Don Jaime draws near her.

DON JAIME: You believe me, don't you?

RAMONA: Yes, sir.

She says it in a low voice, absolutely lacking in conviction. Don Jaime is immediately aware of this. He smiles and lightly taps her.

DON JAIME: Don't lie. You don't believe me, either.

RAMONA (*looking for an excuse*): It's because—everything is so out of the ordinary, sir.

Don Jaime nods in commiseration.

DON JAIME: It's all right, my girl. It's all right.

He goes toward the hall. Ramona goes to the bed, strips it and examines the sheets, trying to discover the truth.

88   *Exterior, garden. Day. Close-up.*

Moncho, the manservant, has just finished hitching up the carriage.

A few yards away, Viridiana waits, seated on a stone bench, her back to the camera, her valise nearby.

Rita is playing diabolo beside her. The kind of toy Don Jaime has given the child shows what sort of person he is—certainly, "of another age."

RITA: Look how high I can throw it!

Viridiana does not even turn to look. Rita, to attract her attention, picks up the diabolo, which did not fall along the string as it should have. She whirls it about and then puts it back in place with the aid of one of the sticks.

RITA: Look! You can't do that!

As the young girl continues to sit in thought, Rita grows discouraged and tries to interest Moncho.

RITA: See how high I can throw it!

As usual, he answers her irritably.

MONCHO: Leave me in peace!

Rita keeps on playing, disregarding Moncho's rebuff.

MONCHO (*to Viridiana*): Whenever you're ready . . .

The novice straightens up and goes toward the carriage.

89   *General shot.*

Pan in from behind to a middle-distance focus. Don Jaime is watching his niece's departure from the interior of his room, near the balcony. Downstairs, we see Viridiana approaching the carriage. The little girl says something to her. Viridiana gets in the carriage, and Moncho whips up the horse. The little girl waves goodbye. Then she starts to run after the carriage.

90   *Interior, living room. Day. Middle-distance shot.*

Don Jaime sadly watches the carriage drive away. But he soon pulls himself together and his face takes on an expression of calm, almost of indifference.

He goes toward a worktable in the corner of the room and sits down at it. He passes a hand over his forehead. On the table, all his work tools are in disorder. Certainly months have passed since Don Jaime has touched his work. Meticulously, he starts to put things to rights again. He draws a finger over the table top to see whether there is any dust. He looks at his finger. Seeing that it is clean, he smiles, thinking of Ramona's care.

At last, he takes a piece of paper and a pen and starts to write with great concentration. The camera is right over him.

91   *Exterior, town street. Day. General panoramic shot.*

The bus that runs daily to the station is just about to arrive. It turns a corner of the street.

92   *Exterior, town square. Day. Middle-distance shot. Shot in depth. Crane.*

The bus enters the square and pulls up at the bus stop. A group of people wait for it there. A few of them carry packages. The driver clambers onto the roof to tie on the luggage that is handed him. Viridiana passes up her valise.

93   *From general to middle-distance shot.*

At the other end of the street, a man approaches on a mule. He goes toward the town hall which faces on the same square. Near the main entrance to the building, the mayor is talking with two or three people. The man on muleback gets down and approaches the group. He says something. The reaction of the mayor and his interlocutors is strange. They surround the man, as if asking him for explanations, and they all talk for a moment. Then the mayor turns his head toward where the bus has stopped. He rushes toward it.

94   *Dolly traveling forward.*

Two travelers have just gotten into the bus and Viridiana is about to do likewise when the mayor arrives, almost running, and stops her by taking hold of her sleeve.

THE MAYOR: Excuse me, Miss, but you can't leave.

VIRIDIANA (*surprised*): Why not?

THE MAYOR: (*Looking at her fixedly, scratches his neck. It costs him an effort to speak out.*) Something bad has happened. Come.

Viridiana neither protests nor questions.

Dissolve.

95   *Exterior, garden of the house. Day. General shot.*

Two cars stop before the entrance. The mayor, accompanied by Viridiana and the men who were with him in the square, gets out of one of them.

From the other car two police officers and a man in civilian dress emerge. They all enter the property. We cannot distinguish Viridiana's expression amid this little throng.

96   Exterior, garden. Day. Middle-distance.

Ramona is seated under the great tree that little Rita had climbed. She wipes her tears with a handkerchief. Switch to catch Rita farther off, her eyes wide open and fixed on the tree. A little farther away, a group of four or five peasants, men and women, exchange comments in low tones.

97   General shot. Dolly.

The mayor's group comes toward the camera. Among them is Viridiana. A few yards from the tree, they stop and force themselves to look up at something among the branches. Some of them show horror, others, curiosity.

98   The great tree. In the midst of the foliage, we see a hanging body.

99   Middle-distance shot. Viridiana.

The young girl has just glimpsed it, too. She closes her eyes and covers them with her hand, not to see the frightful sight.

100   Close-up.

The branch on which Don Jaime's body hangs. We do not see the body itself which is suspended below, outside the frame. But we see the knot that attaches the rope to the tree. The rope has a wooden handle. It is little Rita's jumping rope.

Dissolve to darkness.

In this script each numbered section is a *shot*. For example, number 69 is a shot. Shots 68 and 69 form a *scene* occurring at one time and place. Shots 67 through 78 consist of several scenes that form a single *sequence*, beginning with Rita in the garden and following through to Don Jaime's return to his room. Notice that the writer has shaped this sequence from several changes of place and viewpoint, but the cinematic form is that of a single action with a clear beginning (the quiet of the garden and the exterior shot of Rita, the outsider), a dramatic middle (the temptation of Don Jaime as seen within the room juxtaposed against the continued exterior shot of Rita), and a quiet resolution (Don Jaime's flight and the return to the silence of the beginning of the sequence). Shots 79 through 100 consist of several scenes that form a final dramatic sequence.

This film script is designed to provide a visual rendering of the film as seen in the mind of Buñuel. There is a clear form — a workable, recognizable dramatic and artistic structure. The units of the script are not simply a jargon or shorthand; they create a rhythm and an order that Buñuel has carefully constructed to communicate his vision. This is *not* a play to be photographed, but a script for a film. It provides a visual rendition of the story's progress and makes excellent use of the elements that separate film from other narrative and dramatic forms. Some of these elements are:

(1) The interposition of single shots to direct the audience's attention to the theme of the film—the nature of innocence and corruption (for example, shot 72, with its religious ceremony).

(2) The ability to present the action as seen through the eyes of different characters. This projects the audience inside the characters and sets in motion vital dramatic contrasts. Buñuel strengthens his basic theme of the corruption of the innocent by varying his camera's point of view. Shot 75 is seen from the point of view of the innocent child Rita, while 77 is viewed from the vantage point of the corrupt Don Jaime.

(3) Most important, the cadence set up by the progression of shots and by the order of shot, scene, and sequence, which provides a blueprint for a fully realized film.

Most current motion pictures of artistic merit are based on scripts that contain a recognizable form and structure. The sequential ideas are clearly present and the shots, scenes, and sequences define the form of the film. Even such apparently formless films as *Faces* (John Cassavetes) and *Woodstock* (Michael Wadleigh) have a structure that can be seen in the script from which the filmmakers work.

THE ELEMENTS OF A SCRIPT

The finished film is a unified whole consisting of many parts. The script for a motion picture should deal with each of these parts.

The visual images

Each shot, scene, and sequence should be completely described in the final version of the script. While the scriptwriter may use professional jargon (*LS, med shot, segue over, diss to*), it is far more important that he give *complete* descriptions of the images as he envisions them on the screen.

The following excerpt is from Alain Robbe-Grillet's fine script for Alain Resnais' film *Last Year at Marienbad*.[5] Note how completely Robbe-Grillet delineates each shot.

> *The series of views of the hotel ends with a stationary shot possessing all the same characteristics, carried to their extreme. A slow scene. The image*

[5] From *Last Year at Marienbad*, text by Alain Robbe-Grillet for the film by Alain Resnais, trans. by Richard Howard (New York: Grove Press, Inc., 1962), pp. 30–32. Copyright © 1962 by Grove Press, Inc. Reprinted by permission of Grove Press, Inc.

includes, at the far left, a blurred close-up of a man's head, but by the edge of the image and not facing the camera. It is X, the hero of the film, but the spectator can hardly tell him from the other characters who have appeared in similar fashion in the preceding images. In the center of the screen in the middle distance is a clearly visible element of the setting: for instance a monumental mantlepiece with candlelabras and a huge elabo- rately framed mirror. Finally, to the right and in the background (preferably in another room, visible through a doorway), a man and a woman standing, talking in low voices. What they are saying is barely audible as a vague whispering.

X's head, in the foreground, then turns in this direction, but not abruptly; the direction of his gaze is not indicated explicitly: it must seem merely possible that X is looking at the couple. Neither the man nor the woman seems to pay any attention to X (who is, moreover, quite far away).

Their words are at first indistinct, virtually incomprehensible; then the volume rises slightly and we begin to understand the dialogue, particularly the man's remarks, for he speaks louder and louder.

MAN: The others? Who are the others? Don't be so worried about what they are thinking.

WOMAN: You know perfectly well . . .

MAN: I know you said you would listen to no one but me.

WOMAN: I am listening to you.

During these remarks, the camera moves so as to center the image a little more on the couple, but without coming any closer, still keeping them almost in the background. During this movement, X's head leaves the field of vision.

From this moment on, the entire text is audible and distinct (though evi- dently situated at the rear of the set).

MAN: Then listen to my complaints. I can't stand this role any longer. I can't stand this silence, these walls, these whispers you're imprisoning me in . . .

WOMAN: Don't talk so loud, please don't.

MAN: These whisperings, worse than silence, that you're imprisoning me in. These days, worse than death, that we're living through side by side, you and I, like coffins laid side by side underground in a frozen garden . . .

During these last words, the woman has looked away from the speaker; she stares anxiously in front of her (toward the camera) and glances to the right and left (but still forward), as if keeping watch on the surroundings.

WOMAN: Be still!

MAN: A garden reassuringly arranged, with clipped bushes, and regular paths where we walk with measured steps, side by side, day after day, within arm's reach but without ever coming an inch closer to each other, without ever . . .

WOMAN: Be still, be still!

With these words, the woman begins walking forward, leaving her com- panion (who has remained stationary, like her, from the beginning of the

Last Year at Marienbad.

scene). The man makes up his mind to follow her a few seconds later. They both advance side by side, about a foot and a half apart, toward the camera.

Silence. Only the sound of their approaching footsteps is heard, especially the woman's heels on the parquet, which is uncarpeted at this point.

When they have reached the foreground, the camera rotates so as to keep them within the frame while they continue walking without a word through the rooms, disappearing in another direction; the sound of their footsteps dies away.

Note how much minute and seemingly irrelevant material is contained in the description of this single scene. This attention to detail, however, helps to communicate all the essential elements of the scene and is the identifying characteristic of a good script for a motion picture.

The sound

The art of the motion picture does not depend solely on the visual image. It was once believed that the quality of a film could be measured in direct proportion to its dependence on the visual elements, that the less sound, the better the film. But in recent years there has been ample evidence of the fallacy of this approach. For example, the mood and impact of the film adaptation of James Dickey's fine novel *Deliverance* were strongly affected by Eric Weissberg's banjo score. The duet in the early sequence between one of the vacationers and the retarded child remains not only one of the most moving moments in the film, but one that gives the audience a revealing sense of the common humanity that links this one man with the natural world to which he seeks to return. One can hardly imagine the film without this particular music score. The script, then, must include all those elements that are to be heard.

Again, using the script of *Last Year at Marienbad*,[6] note Robbe-Grillet's complete and clearly defined instructions concerning the sound track.

> *Opening with a romantic, passionate, violent burst of music, the kind used at the end of films with powerfully emotional climaxes (a large orchestra of strings, woodwinds, brasses, etc.), the credits are initially of a classical type: the names in fairly simple letters, black against a gray background, or white against a gray background; the names or groups of names are framed with simple lines. These frames follow each other at a normal, even rather slow, rhythm.*

*   *   *

> *Parallel to the development of the image during the credits, the music has gradually been transformed into a man's voice—slow, warm, fairly loud but with a certain neutral quality at the same time: a fine theatrical voice, rhythmical but without any particular emotion.*

> *This voice speaks continuously, but although the music has stopped completely, we cannot yet understand the words (or in any case we understand them only with the greatest difficulty) because of a strong reverberation or some effect of the same sort (two identical sound tracks staggered, gradually superimposing until the voice becomes a normal one).*

> X'S VOICE: Once again—I walk on, once again, down these corridors, through these halls, these galleries, in this structure—of another century, this enormous, luxurious, baroque, lugubrious hotel—where corridors succeed endless corridors—silent deserted corridors overloaded with a dim, cold ornamentation of woodwork, stucco, moldings, marble, black mirrors, dark paintings, columns, heavy hangings—sculptured door frames, series of doorways, galleries—transverse corridors that open in turn on empty salons, rooms overloaded with an ornamentation from another century, silent halls . . .

Note how much aural detail is specified by the writer in the above scene. The aural elements of a script, then, include all or some of the following:

(1) *Dialogue*—the words uttered by characters on screen.

(2) *Narrative and voice-over*—the spoken words accompanying images

---

[6] From *Last Year at Marienbad*, pp. 17–18.

that illustrate, support, or exist in counterpoint to what is being said. In the following excerpt from Marguerite Duras' script for *Hiroshima, Mon Amour*,[7] note how closely the words and images are related even though they seem to exist separately.

(*At Hiroshima. The light is already different. Later. After they have made love.*)

HE: Was he French, the man you loved during the war?

(*At Nevers. A German crosses a square at dusk.*)

SHE: No . . . he wasn't French.

(*At Hiroshima. She is lying on the bed, pleasantly tired. Darker now.*)

SHE: Yes. It was at Nevers.

(*Nevers. A shot of love at Nevers. Bicycles racing. The forest, etc.*)

SHE: At first we met in barns. Then among the ruins. And then in rooms. Like anywhere else.

(*Hiroshima. In the room, the light has faded even more. The bodies in a peaceful embrace.*)

SHE: And then he was dead.

(*Nevers. Shots of Nevers. Rivers. Quays. Poplar trees in the wind, etc. The quay deserted. The garden. Then at Hiroshima again.*)

SHE: I was eighteen and he was twenty-three.

(*Nevers. In a "hut" at night. The "marriage" at Nevers. During the shots of Nevers she answers the questions that he is presumed to have asked, but doesn't out loud. The sequence of shots of Nevers continues. Then:*)

SHE (*calmly*): Why talk of him rather than the others?

HE: Why not?

SHE: No. Why?

HE: Because of Nevers. I can only begin to know you, and among the many thousands of things in your life, I'm choosing Nevers.

SHE: Like you'd choose anything else?

HE: Yes.

(*Do we know he's lying? We suspect it. She becomes almost violent—searching for something to say:*)

SHE: No, it's not by chance. (*Pause*) You have to tell me why.

(*He can reply—a very important point for the film—either:*)

HE: It was there, I seem to have understood, that you were so young . . . so young you still don't belong to anyone in particular. I like that.

(*or:*)

SHE: No, that's not it.

[7] From *Hiroshima, Mon Amour*, pp. 47–52.

HE: It was there, I seem to have understood, that I almost . . . lost you . . . and that I risked never knowing you.

(*or else:*)

HE: It was there, I seem to have understood, that you must have begun to be what you are today.

(*Choose from among the three possibilities, or use all three, either one after the other, or separately, at random with the movements of love in the bed. The last is the solution I would prefer,*[8] *if it doesn't make the scene too long. One last time we come back to them.*)

SHE (*shouting*): I want to leave here. (*She clings to him almost savagely.*)

(3) *Sound effects* — sounds in the immediate environment or sounds of events that occur at another time and place off screen.

(4) *Music* — a key supportive element in film, providing an emotional accompaniment or a rhythmic base for the tempo of the film.

(5) *Silence* — occasionally, a key element in the sound track of a film (for example, the corridors of the hotel in Bergman's *The Silence,* where no footfalls are heard, or the silences in *Cries and Whispers*).

Relationships within the script

Within the script there are three key relationships:

(1) The relationship of each image to the images immediately preceding and following it — the relationship of picture to picture.

(2) The relationship of every sound to the sounds heard before, after, and simultaneously — the relationship of sound to sound.

(3) The relationship between the two — the relationship of sound to picture and picture to sound.

From these elements — and from the dynamics of their interrelationships — the motion picture script is formed, and from this script the film itself is created.

SUMMARY

The script is the beginning. It is the blueprint, the design, the plan. An excellent script has a chance to become an excellent film (*A Clockwork Orange, McCabe & Mrs. Miller, The Last Picture Show*). But a poor script, despite all the efforts

---

[8] Instead of using only one, Resnais decided to use all three.

of director, cameraman, and editor, can never become a good film. The finished work of cinematic art will never exceed in quality the initial concept as expressed in script form.

The screenwriter must understand and be able to "see" all the elements of his own script, and his writing must communicate this vision of a finished film to the director and editor.

A fully realized script must contain all the elements that the writer wishes to see executed, and it is very important that the visual and aural descriptions be complete to the smallest detail. The first requirement for a great film is that the vision of the screenwriter expressed in a script project a finished motion picture in all its aspects. Once such a script is achieved, consideration can be given to the film itself, and to those elements that move the art of film from the printed page to the illuminated screen.

FILMS FOR STUDY

Note: Names and addresses of rental libraries are supplied where available.

The Seventh Seal, Ingmar Bergman. Janus Films, 24 West 58 Street, New York, New York 10019.

Hiroshima, Mon Amour, Alain Resnais. Audio Film Center, 34 MacQuesten Parkway South, Mount Vernon, New York 10550.

SUPPLEMENTARY READING

Four Screenplays of Ingmar Bergman, text and films by Ingmar Bergman, trans. by Lars Malmstrom and David Kushner. New York: Simon and Schuster, Inc., 1960.

Hiroshima, Mon Amour, text by Marguerite Duras for the film by Alain Resnais, trans. by Richard Seaver. New York: Grove Press, Inc., 1961.

Last Year at Marienbad, text by Alain Robbe-Grillet for the film by Alain Resnais, trans. by Richard Howard. New York: Grove Press, Inc., 1962.

A Film Trilogy, text and films by Ingmar Bergman, trans. by Paul Britten Austin. New York: The Orion Press, 1967.

IMAGE

TWO

Like most painters, good moviemen try for a composition which will get away as far as possible from the two-dimensional limitations of the screen. But they are not limited entirely to attempts to produce perspective by relationship of mass to mass within their composition. They can also achieve it by the relationship of movement to movement, or of movement to mass, or both.

Basil Wright
in *Footnotes to the Film,*
ed. by Charles Davy
(London: Peter Davies Ltd., 1937),
pp. 52–53.

See what you're looking at. Don't walk into a situation and remanipulate it. Look at it! There are too many people in this business who find a location that is exciting and then proceed to rebuild it photographically. I don't mean that you shouldn't light anything. I simply mean that you should light it so that you still have what you came there to get. It may mean that you won't have to do any lighting at all. But then again, it may take you quite a while to work it all out so that it still looks the same. But see what you're looking at. Retain what's there.

Gregg Steele
"On Location with the Godfather,"
American Cinematographer (June 1971),
pp. 568–69.

I don't care how well written the script is. You can get into a motel room in Texas, and the dialogue can be exquisite, but what you choose to look at and how you look at it is everything.

Arthur Penn
in Eric Sherman and Martin Rubin,
The Director's Event
(New York: Atheneum, 1970),
pp. 120–21.

ENTRAL TO THE ART OF FILM IS THE CREATIVE ACT OF CAPTURING REALITY ON FILM through motion picture photography. Up to that moment all is preparation. The writing of the film script is literary; the preparing for production, administrative. But the instant the camera is turned on, a film is being made. The filmmaker deals with the image captured on film, and, from the moment of photography on, it is this image that will motivate everyone concerned with creating the finished film.

THE CINEMATIC QUALITY OF THE IMAGE

The quality of the image in all its aspects will, in the final analysis, determine the quality of the motion picture. No amount of clever editing, brilliant music, or tricky laboratory effects can save a film if the original image is mediocre. To be sure, the labors of highly creative people can improve a poor job of directing or can salvage something from an uneven job of acting, but a great film cannot be created if the image is without distinction.

There are two basic creative factors present at the time of filming: (1) directing for film and (2) the art of cinematography. The *director*, who is ideally the artist in full charge of creating the motion picture, prepares and designs the total image. Together with the *cameraman*, he creates that image on film.

It is impossible to separate what occurs in front of the camera from what occurs behind it. In the art of film the two are inextricably linked. Unlike the stage director, who moves and motivates his cast within the confines of the proscenium arch, the film director creates a motion picture out of a succession of ever-changing images.

Each frame is in some minute way different from the preceding or following frame. Action and motion take place in front of the camera, and simultaneously the camera itself moves — changing a point of view, providing a new angle from which to view the action.

The motion picture is a unique art form. It is *not* television, and it is *not* theater. The motion picture is as distinct from these art forms as music is from painting, as poetry is from architecture.

The visual requirements of television are dictated by the fact that the finished work is projected onto a very small screen and is usually viewed by the audience at home, in a semidarkened room, subject to a variety of distractions. Thus long shots, medium shots, and compositional subtleties go largely unnoticed, just as the details of a fine painting are lost when rendered on a postage stamp. Only close-ups have visual impact. Lighting details are also minimized, so that what remains is a simple frame that is either bright or dark. Regardless of the creative effort applied to the visual image, the final telecast is a very small picture totally devoid of the subtle detail that comprises the visual image as created for motion picture projection.

When the art of the motion picture is compared with that of the stage, the factors that make film unique are even more striking. The key element in the creation of the image is the filmmaker's ability to *control the eye of the audience at all times.* The stage director can utilize a variety of tricks to command the audience's attention, but in the final analysis the boundaries of the stage remain fixed and the attention of the audience vagrant.

Derek Golby, a talented young English stage director, effectively staged Tom Stoppard's play *Rosencrantz and Guildenstern Are Dead.* In the closing scene, the two leading characters stand on either side of the stage for their final speeches. Because it is essential that the audience give full attention to their words and to the questioning, uncomprehending expressions on their faces, Golby darkens the entire stage and places a strong white spotlight on each of their faces. Rosencrantz completes his speech, and as his life is snuffed out, so is his spotlight. Now the audience is left in darkness, save for the single white light illuminating the face of Guildenstern.

It would be hard to imagine a more effective means (in the theater) of riveting the audience's attention on the face of a protagonist. Yet, unless one is sitting in the center of the first few rows, one still sees the boundaries of the dark stage, with a small head illuminated in the foreground. And if the actor is not superb, the attention of the audience will stray.

The filmmaker, however, deals with an image in which all is motion. The boundaries of the frame change, contracting and expanding at the command of the director. When it is important to focus attention on the face of an actor, the director simply provides a full close-up — and the audience cannot look elsewhere.

It is this factor of multiple motion, the movement of the frame of the scene itself and the action within the scene, that imparts to film a quality not present in the theater. This ceaseless flow of motion coupled with the ability to view significant acts and action from many vantage points makes the art of film unique.

The first requisite of filmmaking, then, is that the image itself be cinematic — that it utilize those special properties separating film from theater, television, still photography, and painting. To achieve and to recognize this quality, it is necessary to understand the creative elements of cinematography.

THE ELEMENTS OF CINEMATOGRAPHY

The elements of cinematography consist of (1) *the film itself* — the properties and characteristics of different types of raw stock; (2) *composition* — the position of every visual element within a frame; and (3) *illumination* — the character and quality of the lighting of each scene.

Film — the raw material of cinema

The raw material of cinema is a strip of celluloid (cellulose acetate) that has been coated with an emulsion sensitive to light and capable of receiving and retaining images. The film (raw stock) is generally designated by its width — 8mm, 16mm, 35mm, or 70mm. The larger the size of the film, the better the quality of the projected image. Most theatrical films are photographed in 35mm or 70mm, and even larger sizes are used in the new wide-screen processes.

Celluloid is ideal for filming because it is both durable and flexible. It bends freely enough to be channeled through camera and projector but is strong enough not to break or tear easily. These assets are simply results of the physical properties of film. More important to the filmmaker is the fact that many different kinds of film are available. The quality of the reproduced image depends in large measure on exactly which type of film is used.

Each type of film has a specific sensitivity to light. A "fast" film is more sensitive to light than a "slow" film — that is, it requires less light to capture an image. For example, 35mm Eastman Color Stock (type 5254) is three times as sensitive to light as 16mm Commercial Ektachrome (type 7252). In practical terms, this means that at the same lens opening, three times as much light is necessary to photograph a scene with 7252 as with 5254.

Generally, the slower the film (the less sensitive to light), the less the grain content; the less the grain content, the smoother the image. A low-grain film stock tends to reproduce an image with sharpness and clarity. In comparison, a high-grain stock will reproduce the same image with a greater degree of fuzziness. As we view a scene photographed with slower film, we are aware of the clarity and the optical perfection of images that are as free of grain as possible (Fig. 1).

Newsreels are usually photographed with a high-speed fast film that is high in grain content. Thus the presence of grain has come to be associated with documentary reality (Fig. 2). The theatrical film, photographed in a studio (with unlimited light available), traditionally uses a slower film that is almost completely free of grain.

Compare the velvet perfection of the black-and-white tones of Gunnar Fischer's photography in *The Seventh Seal,* or the exquisite color in Bo Widerberg's *Elvira Madigan,* with the harsh, grainy reality of Gillo Pontecorvo's *The Battle of Algiers.*

In *The Seventh Seal,* black, gray, and white flow harmoniously into one another (Fig. 3). In *Elvira Madigan,* the muted tones of color create a lyric visual structure perfectly suited to the romantic subject material. But in *The Battle of Algiers,* a harsh, more naturalistic contrast of light and dark creates a sense of immediate reality that enhances this drama of the Algerian rebellion against the French (Fig. 4). The white houses of Casablanca under the glaring North African sun gleam — almost halate — within a single frame that must also accommodate the dark shadows of the streets, shadows created by that same sun. In *The Battle of Algiers,* Pontecorvo wished to convince the audience that the action was photographed as it happened. Thus, he chose a fast film, a high-grain raw stock, and achieved a sense of reality rarely attained in a directed theatrical film. The sequence of bombings between the French para-

Fig. 1. *In Cold Blood.*

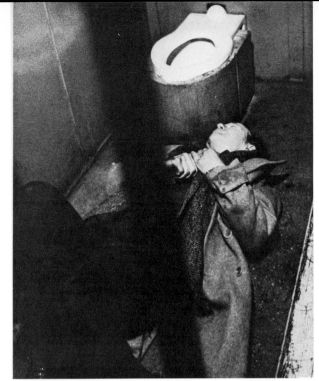

Fig. 2. *The Revolving Door* (Lee R. Bobker).

Fig. 3. *The Seventh Seal.*

Fig. 4. *The Battle of Algiers.*

troopers and the Algerian rebels has an immediacy that can be ascribed not merely to acting, sound, and directing, but in large part to the grainy newsreel effect. Costa-Gavras, working with color stock, achieves the same kind of result in his film about Uruguayan revolutionaries, *State of Siege*.

In addition to its higher grain content, fast film shows greater contrast between light and dark than does slow film. (In all film, the contrast range is between the lightest and the darkest points within the same frame.) This means that a fast film stock is *less* able to accommodate a wide range of brightness and darkness within a single frame. Thus, when a scene in a darkened room is photographed with fast film, a window five or ten times brighter than the interior may glare and halate. The fast film is unable to handle the range of contrast without producing this effect. But often in a "realistic" film this halation can be used to heighten the sense of reality.

In studio photography the contrast range is carefully controlled; in on-location photography, windows are often covered with darkened gelatin (neutral density gel) to reduce the brightness of incoming daylight and to bring the light intensity of the window closer to that of the interior. The contrast ratio can also be reduced by artificially illuminating the interior at an intensity closer to that of the window light. This equalizing of contrast gives us the subtle beauties of studio photography.

Fig. 5. *Wild Strawberries.*

Examine the photography of Gunnar Fischer in Ingmar Bergman's *Wild Strawberries*. The dramatic action of the film revolves around an automobile journey made by an old doctor, Isak Borg, to receive an honorary award at the University of Lund. Because the central concern of the film is Isak's mental traveling between memory, fantasy, and present reality, it is essential at the very beginning to establish a clear visual difference between his various mental states. The main body of the film covers a brief period of time in Isak's life, the last few days before his death. These scenes were photographed on a black-and-white film stock free of grain and capable of absorbing a broad range of black-to-white contrast without distortion. This film stock enabled Fischer to create effective tones and shadows, as well as subtle contrasts (Fig. 5). The opening scenes—Isak writing and sleeping—are fine examples of black-and-white photography that create a view of the old doctor's life with which we can easily become involved.

The entire structure of *Wild Strawberries* depends on the easy flow between past and present *without* traditional optical cues and narrative introductions (for example, the slow dissolve as someone says, "It was many years ago . . ."). Isak's dream contains frightening images of death and symbols of a wasted life. To evoke this nightmare world, which conveys at the very outset the nature of Isak's fears, Bergman used a high-grain, high-contrast film stock. The extreme sensitivity of the film stock produced an immediately discernible difference between reality and dream. The following is the original script description of this sequence.[1]

In the early morning of Saturday, the first of June, I had a strange and very unpleasant dream. I dreamed that I was taking my usual morning stroll through the streets. It was quite early and no human being was in sight. This was a bit surprising to me. I also noted that there were no vehicles parked along the curbs. The city seemed strangely deserted, as if it were a holiday morning in the middle of summer.

The sun was shining brightly and made sharp black shadows, but it gave off no warmth. Even though I walked on the sunny side, I felt chilly.

The stillness was also remarkable. I usually stroll along a broad, tree-lined boulevard, and even before sunrise the sparrows and crows are as a rule extremely noisy. Besides, there is always the perpetual roar from the center of the city. But this morning nothing was heard, the silence was absolute, and my footsteps echoed almost anxiously against the walls of the buildings. I began to wonder what had happened.

Just at that moment I passed the shop of a watchmaker-optometrist, whose sign had always been a large clock that gave the exact time. Under this clock hung a picture of a pair of giant eyeglasses with staring eyes. On my morning walks I had always smiled to myself at this slightly grotesque detail in the street scene.

To my amazement, the hands of the clock had disappeared. The dial was blank, and below it someone had smashed both of the eyes so that they looked like watery, infected sores.

Instinctively I pulled out my own watch to check the time, but I found that my old reliable gold timepiece had also lost its hands. I held it to my ear to find out if it was still ticking. Then I heard my heart beat. It was pounding very fast and irregularly. I was overwhelmed by an inexplicable feeling of frenzy.

I put my watch away and leaned for a few moments against the wall of a building until the feeling had passed. My heart calmed down and I decided to return home.

To my joy, I saw that someone was standing on the street corner. His back was toward me. I rushed up to him and touched his arm. He turned quickly and to my horror I found that the man had no face under his soft felt hat.

I pulled my hand back and in the same moment the entire figure collapsed as if it were made of dust or frail splinters. On the sidewalk lay a pile of clothes. The person himself had disappeared without a trace.

I looked around in bewilderment and realized that I must have lost my way. I was in a part of the city where I had never been before.

I stood on an open square surrounded by high, ugly apartment buildings. From this narrow square, streets spread out in all directions. Everyone was dead; there was not a sign of a living soul.

High above me the sun shone completely white, and light forced its way down between the houses as if it were the blade of a razor-sharp knife. I was so cold that my entire body shivered.

[1] From *Wild Strawberries*, text and film by Ingmar Bergman, in *Four Screenplays of Ingmar Bergman*, trans. by Lars Malmstrom and David Kushner (New York: Simon and Schuster, Inc., 1960), pp. 170–73. Reprinted by permission of the publisher and Janus Films.

The art of color cinematography:
Plates I–VII feature the work of two of the foremost contemporary cinematographers, Vilmos Zsigmond and Sven Nykvist, whose artistry combines a strong sense of cinematic composition with subtle illumination.

Plates I and II. *Images,* directed by Robert Altman. Cinematography by Vilmos Zsigmond.

Plates III–V. *Cries and Whispers,* directed by Ingmar Bergman. Cinematography by Sven Nykvist.

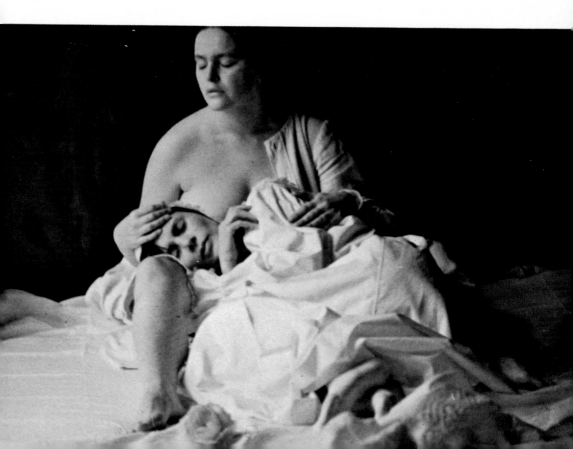

Plates VI and VII. *Deliverance*, directed by John Boorman. Cinematography by Vilmos Zsigmond.

Finally I found the strength to move again and chose one of the narrow streets at random. I walked as quickly as my pounding heart allowed, yet the street seemed to be endless.

Then I heard the tolling of bells and suddenly I was standing on another open square near an unattractive little church of red brick. There was no graveyard next to it and the church was surrounded on all sides by gray-walled buildings.

Not far from the church a funeral procession was wending its way slowly through the streets, led by an ancient hearse and followed by some old-fashioned hired carriages. These were pulled by pairs of meager-looking horses, weighed down under enormous black shabracks.

I stopped and uncovered my head. It was an intense relief to see living creatures, hear the sound of horses trotting and church bells ringing.

Then everything happened very quickly and so frighteningly that even as I write this I still feel a definite uneasiness.

The hearse was just about to turn in front of the church gate when suddenly it began to sway and rock like a ship in a storm. I saw that one of the wheels had come loose and was rolling toward me with a loud clatter. I had to throw myself to one side to avoid being hit. It struck the church wall right behind me and splintered into pieces.

The other carriages stopped at a distance but no one got out or came to help. The huge hearse swayed and teetered on its three wheels. Suddenly the coffin was thrown out and fell into the street. As if relieved, the hearse straightened and rolled on toward a side street, followed by the other carriages.

The tolling of the church bells had stopped and I stood alone with the overturned, partly smashed coffin. Gripped by a fearful curiosity, I approached. A hand stuck out from the pile of splintered boards. When I leaned forward, the dead hand clutched my arm and pulled me down toward the casket with enormous force. I struggled helplessly against it as the corpse slowly rose from the coffin. It was a man dressed in a frock coat.

To my horror, I saw that the corpse was myself. I tried to free my arm, but he held it in a powerful grip. All this time he stared at me without emotion and seemed to be smiling scornfully.

In this moment of senseless horror, I awakened and sat up in my bed. It was three in the morning and the sun was already reflecting from the rooftops opposite my window. I closed my eyes and I muttered words of reality against my dream—against all the evil and frightening dreams which have haunted me these last few years.

The extreme sensitivity to light of the film stock, the high grain content, and the high contrast between black and white create a terrifying nightmare with which we can all identify. The walls of the street gleam in almost unbearable white; the black shadows are Stygian in their gloom. Most important, the range between the two within a single image creates an unreality as effective as the reality produced by the same elements in *The Battle of Algiers*.

The techniques of creating realistic effects with color film are even more critical. Until recently, an interesting paradox was felt to exist in the art of film: we *see* in color and yet we *believe* in black and white. Before the last decade (with films such as *Blow-Up*, *Z*, *The Passion of Anna*, *The French Con-*

nection, *State of Siege*, and others), filmmakers had not successfully used color to deal with real people in real situations *on a contemporary basis*. Color had been used for musicals (*My Fair Lady*), fantasies (*The Red Balloon*), historical films (*A Man for All Seasons*), and pageants (*Henry V*). No one seriously considered doing films like *Grapes of Wrath* or *La Guerre Est Finie* in color.

Because directors and cameramen accepted this apparent limitation, they used color in a very simple way. They employed high-intensity lighting, made little or no attempt at subtle gradations, and emphasized and overlit basic colors to achieve a rich and flamboyant effect.

Sir Laurence Olivier explained why, after the tremendous success of *Henry V*, filmed in color, he chose to produce *Hamlet* in black and white. He felt that *Henry V* was a true pageant play re-creating a bygone time in terms that were not real but larger than life. The bright flags, the richly dressed kings and nobles, the stylized glory of the time — all required the use of color. But *Hamlet*, Olivier felt, dealt with a harsher reality. He saw Hamlet as a contemporary figure and so chose the reality of black and white.

Color, however, has proved to be a far more creative and contemporary instrument than Olivier realized. Indeed, it has opened a new era for film. Today there is no limitation on the ability to create realism in color. Color film is quite sensitive to delicate and subtle shades, and high-speed color raw stock with less and less grain is now available.

Claude LeLouche, in his beautiful film *A Man and a Woman*, employed a number of film stocks — color, black and white, black and white printed on color stock giving blue-gray and sepia tones — as well as flashed and fogged film that rendered a wide variety of effects.

Michelangelo Antonioni helped to change the approach to color film when he made *Blow-Up*. In that film, shot entirely in color, the fantasy world of a photographer's studio — with its bright lights, garish walls, and bizarre images of models in weird costumes — becomes as real as the same studio without lights, the rather mundane place in which the photographer lives.

We see, then, that the film stock itself plays an important role in the ultimate quality of the image. The key factors the filmmaker looks for in choosing a film stock are *the clarity and verity of reproduction, the quality of each color in the full range of color reproduction,* and, of course, *the amount of grain present in the overall frame.*

Each type of raw stock has particular properties, a specific sensitivity to light, and each produces a particular kind of image. The manufacturer describes in detail the properties of the raw stock, rating its degree of light sensitivity according to the ASA (American Standards Association) system. The lower the ASA number, the slower the film. For example, a film with an ASA rating of 50 is twice as slow (or half as fast) as one with a rating of 100, and it requires exactly twice as much light on the scene if the lens opening remains constant.

The film itself, then, is an important factor in the technical and esthetic problem of creating the exact image desired.

Composition in film is unlike composition in any other visual art. The key is *motion*. Because no frame is exactly like any other frame, the image changes constantly, and the director and cameraman must exercise control over it at all times.

The primary goal of all film composition is to project a sense of depth, to create out of a flat two-dimensional strip of celluloid a sense that a third dimension exists. More subtly, the audience must be projected beyond the front layer to a position *within* the frame.

The old taboos of still photography (for example, "Never bisect the frame with the horizon") are totally passé in film composition. Note the power of the scene in Bergman's *The Virgin Spring* in which Töre, the father of the raped and murdered virgin, breaks the birch tree — essentially a bisection of the frame by the horizon (Fig. 6).

There are few, if any, workable rules of film composition. A popular device in modern cinema is the *obscured frame*, a scene in which a foreground object, often in soft focus, blocks a large part of the frame and a significant object in sharp focus is seen far away in the remaining portion. Orson Welles influenced cinematic composition with his use of large foreground figures and small back-

Fig. 6. *The Virgin Spring.*

Fig. 7A. *Doctor Zhivago.* **Fig. 7B.** *Doctor Zhivago.*

ground figures to draw the eye deep into the frame. For example, in a key scene in *Journey into Fear,* the back of a man with a knife sticking out is projected so large in the foreground that it is unrecognizable. Only when the door to his stateroom opens is perspective provided.

The filmmaker's primary purpose in composing each frame is to draw the audience's attention into the scene and to direct it exactly where he desires. No director can be careless or desultory in his visual composition. The success of an entire film often depends on the filmmaker's "eye" for composition.

In the art of the motion picture there are three key factors involved in composition.

(1) Placement of people and objects within the frame   The important factor here is "relationship." Large foreground elements can attract or divert attention depending on how they are used. A full-face close-up in sharp focus in the foreground will divert attention from a soft-focus full figure in the background. In the classic death scene in Welles' *Citizen Kane,* for example, the full head of Kane appears in sharp focus in the foreground, drawing attention from the full figure of the nurse as she enters. On the other hand, a figure in *soft* focus in the foreground can occupy a large part of the frame and yet attract less attention than a smaller figure in the background. Figures 7A–7C illustrate varieties of foreground-background relationships.

"In-depth" composition is usually more cinematic than flat "cross-screen" composition, and the placement of people and objects should be conceived with a full recognition of the third dimension of film (Fig. 8).

The *extended image,* the overlapping of persons and objects with the periphery of the frame, can also be used to enlarge the audience's perception.

Fig. 7C. *Alice's Restaurant.*

Fig. 8. *Fat City.*

Fig. 9. *Lawrence of Arabia.*

For example, the hand of a woman extending into a frame suggests the entire figure seated just beyond the range of what the audience sees. Similarly, a periscope rising up from the bottom of a frame suggests the entire submarine located just below the sight line.

When the frame is totally enclosed, the audience is limited to a "stage" view of the action. By reaching beyond the physical enclosure, the filmmaker enlarges the audience's perception and strengthens the concept of cinematic composition. David Lean and Freddy Young, masters of the art of composition, use the extended image to transmit a sense of size and mass, giving films like *Lawrence of Arabia* (Figs. 9 and 10) and *Doctor Zhivago* their undeniable sweep and power.

Much of what is suggested off screen by an extended image can be supported and enlarged by offscreen sound. Often, the audience is subtly prepared for a cut to the offscreen image by just such a method.

It is through the arrangement and control of all visual elements within the frame that the filmmaker controls the thoughts and emotions of the audience. A scene comprised of elements that are "just there" permits the audience's attention to wander and lapse. Well-composed scenes contain a succession of images in which each element within the frame adds to the total impact.

(2) Movement of people and objects within a fixed frame   Unlike still photography, film is never static. Whenever there is movement within a frame, the composition changes—and the effect of the image upon the audience changes. The motion picture is a constant flow of ever-changing images. Every movement within the frame must be under the filmmaker's control.

Fig. 10. *Lawrence of Arabia.*

In-depth movement is one technique used to overcome the two-dimensional limitation of celluloid. A figure moving from the foreground of the frame directly away from camera draws the eye of the audience deep into the frame. The audience believes in the depth of the image, and thus the illusion of a third dimension is achieved. This is a key concept, and one that is seldom understood. The frame has very real boundaries on either side and above and below, but it has no limit in depth except the limit created by the filmmaker. If a wall is the farthest thing seen within the frame, that is where the frame ends. But the audience can look endlessly beyond the horizon if the frame is given no physical boundary in depth.

Thus, as the filmmaker charts his movement he must bear in mind that horizontal and vertical movements limit film because they remind the viewer of its limitations in dimension—but *within* the frame, movement toward and away from the eye of the camera expands and extends the horizon of film. Again, all movement within the frame must have purpose; it must not simply exist as dramatic "business." Figures moving suddenly toward camera heighten drama; figures moving languidly away from camera increase a sense of sadness or romance. Objects and people moving across screen seem to move more rapidly than those moving in depth.

A brilliant and effective use of motion within a fixed frame appears in *The Seventh Seal.* When Death comes to claim victory, he moves slowly toward the camera, beginning as a full figure and ending with his black cape completely closing the lens. Anxiety grows moment by moment, until we totally identify with the Knight's fear and agony. We *are* the Knight at that moment, and it is our eyes that are closed.

In the final scene of François Truffaut's *The 400 Blows,* the boundaries of the frame remain fixed as Antoine, the unhappy young protagonist, moves away from us toward the sea. Because the frame is totally fixed, the eye of the camera becomes our eyes, and we are drawn *into* the frame after the boy — until finally he turns and returns our view eye to eye, arrested in a haunting visual image. Although the boundaries of the frame remain fixed, the composition changes with each step of the boy as he moves away from camera, turns, and comes back a little.

Movement within a static frame is thus a critical element of composition, for through such movement the film builds its creative impact. Again, there are no absolute rules to guide the filmmaker; there is only the need to comprehend the importance of creating the illusion of depth and of using movement to maintain control over the audience.

(3) Movement of the frame itself Perhaps the most important basic element of cinema composition is the ability of the frame itself to move. This fact alone separates the visual image in film from all other art forms, and it is this element that must be fully exploited.

The mobility of the camera enables the filmmaker to change his vantage point in an instant. It allows action. Even more important, it enables the filmmaker to change the character of the image as the action evolves. For example, the camera moves in on an action and a long shot becomes an extreme close-up. Or the camera pulls away and the scene opens from a microscopic view of a figure to a long shot of the person standing alone in an empty city. Or else, during a psychiatric interview, the camera circles slowly around patient and psychiatrist. With each movement of the camera the composition changes, yet the subjects within the frame have not moved. The frame contracts, expands, and contracts again. Thus, in a single scene uninterrupted by cuts, the character of the image can be changed by simply moving the camera in, out, and around the players.

In the "tango" sequence of Bernardo Bertolucci's *Last Tango in Paris,* the action takes place in various parts of the dance hall. The camera is in almost constant movement. At first it follows the entrance of Paul and Jeanne. They move across the hall to a table and watch the dancers. The movement of the camera is paced to the dance music. After a brief exchange of dialogue at the table, the camera observes the dancers from both moving and stationary vantage points. Finally the lovers leave the table and walk across the dance floor again, accompanied by the camera. Throughout the sequence, the camera continues its slow, seductive motion that subjects the frame and point of view of the audience to constant change. The moving camera gives the sequence vitality and dramatic interest that greatly contribute to its success.

The opening sequence of Orson Welles' *Touch of Evil* is an excellent study in cinematography, for it combines all three basic elements of film composition. The sequence begins on a close-up — a hand places something in the trunk of a car. The camera pulls back. Someone enters the car. We move alongside the car, past a border checkpoint. Finally, the car explodes in our faces. All during this single cinematic sequence, the composition changes. Close-ups open to wide shots, people and objects change position within the frame, and our attention and interest never lapse.

Few filmmakers use composition to its full potential. The concept of the *ever-changing image* seems difficult to execute because it demands the simultaneous control of the three basic elements of composition. The still photographer "composes" his *mise en scène* and freezes it, seeking only to capture a single significant moment. The stage director "moves" his actors within the rigid confines of the stage; regardless of the composition he designs, the boundaries of his arena remain fixed. This is essentially true even in theater-in-the-round. The filmmaker, however, creates his visual compositions in a flexible, ever-changing arena. He can, in effect, propel the audience about, enabling it to view a scene from a thousand positions—each single frame is a different position.

Thus composition in the art of film is never static; it is a process of continuous change created by the control of its three basic elements and by the understanding that the audience must be projected into the frame.

Illumination

Every image in a finished film has in one manner or another been illuminated. Light enables us to see the image, and what we see and how we see it is often determined by the *character* and *quality* of the light. The flat, colorless haze of a noonday sun illuminates an object in quite a different manner than the reddish warmth of a low evening sun that creates long shadows and edge-lights objects and characters with a gentle glow.

Just as composition gives form and substance to an image, light gives the image its distinctive character. A clear understanding of the use of light is essential to the study of the art of film. The two basic types of light are *artificial* (electric light) and *natural* (sunlight). As the filmmaker seeks to achieve images that have an artistic validity related to the entire film, he relies more and more on the creative use of light, both artificial and natural.

In the cinematography of any scene a certain amount of light is necessary to insure an image. The intensity needed will vary depending on the film stock. The technical procedure for computing the intensity is simple. Using the ASA rating of the film stock, the size of the lens opening, and the shutter speed, the cameraman can determine by simple mathematical formula (or light-meter reading) the intensity of light necessary for filming.

With a light meter, the cameraman measures the intensity of light illuminating the object or scene being photographed. The measurement is given in *foot-candles*. This light intensity is then translated (by means of a scale on the meter) into the lens opening required to effect a perfectly exposed image. If the lens is opened too wide, too much light will reach the film and the image will be *overexposed* (too light); if the lens is not opened enough, the image will be *underexposed* (too dark).

But beyond these fairly simple technical procedures are more important questions that relate to the nature and character of light. Everything seen within the frame must be considered in relation to light. The entire scene must be illuminated *in depth*. Therefore, lighting for film is essentially an exercise in creating an endless series of *planes of light*—from the very first layer, as one enters the frame, to the farthest horizontal plane visible in the frame.

In lighting, as in composition, there are three key elements to be considered: (1) the relative intensity of light, (2) the direction of light, and (3) the character of light. Each of these elements plays an equally important role in producing the mood of the image.

Relative intensity of light   Ultimately, it is the artistry with which light is manipulated that imparts much of the visual impact to a scene. All light diminishes in intensity as it travels away from its source. To illuminate a frame in depth, the filmmaker must view it as a three-dimensional box. The gradations of intensity of the light illuminating everything within that box give shape and substance to the whole (Fig. 11).

High-contrast scenes, scenes containing a wide range of lights and darks, tend to create more dramatic and interesting images than scenes that are more

Fig. 11. *Five Easy Pieces.*

Fig. 12. *The Magician.*

even in range. Mystery and suspense films are usually lit in what is called "low-key" lighting, replete with dark shadows. Bright bulbs and shadowed faces are characteristic of mystery scenes. Musicals and comedies, on the other hand, are usually lit with far less contrast.

Gunnar Fischer, the cameraman for many of Bergman's early films, is particularly effective with intense blacks and whites. The opening scenes of *The Magician* are a study in the art of *mood* cinematography, for they establish at once the hypnotic and mystical character of the entire film (Fig. 12).

Light must never be allowed to just fall; as the cameraman plots all movement, he must bear in mind the variations in light intensity within the frame. Actors emerge from or disappear into shadows, giving the entire action a particular emotional character.

Because new film stocks are much more sensitive to subtle gradations between light and dark, and because they can also transmit subtle shades of color, the filmmaker can create relative intensities much in the manner of a painter. The filmmaker, however, must also accommodate the compositional factor of motion, the continually changing scene. The intensity and quality of light within a scene vary with the slightest change in camera angle, and this must be considered when "brush strokes" of light are applied to the image.

The relative intensities of light, then, give the filmmaker a palette, and the range between the brightest and the darkest object in the frame gives him artistic control (Fig. 13).

Fig. 13. *American Graffiti*

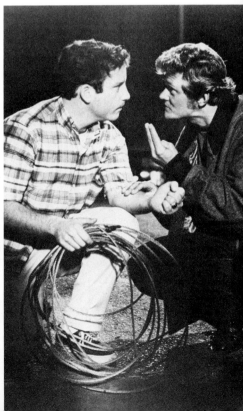

Direction of light   Whether a scene is illuminated artificially or naturally, the direction of the light is of primary importance. Figures 14A and 14B readily demonstrate the emotional effect created by the direction of the primary source of light. Flat overhead lighting imparts a dull, monochromatic quality to a scene (Fig. 14A), whereas light coming from a lower angle creates a more dramatic effect (Fig. 14B).

Scenes can be lit entirely from the front or entirely from the back, but the mood created in each case is quite different. In most dramatic scenes a combination of front and back lighting is used, with varying intensities imparting to the scene its final character.

Gunnar Fischer uses a variety of techniques to create different moods. For example, in the opening scene from *The Magician,* detail is obscured in favor of high silhouette, giving a stark, melancholy feeling to the scene. Blacks are sharply etched and the brooding sky (the source of the back light) seems to overpower and control the entire scene (see Fig. 12). In the "pastoral reverie" scene from *The Seventh Seal,* Fischer uses a front light that softly fills every shadow and gives a feeling of beauty, kindness, peace, and gentleness (Fig. 15).

A simple experiment will demonstrate the effect of direction on the art of cinematic illumination. Stand in front of a mirror and shine a flashlight directly into your face. Note the flatness and lack of character lines in your features. There are no shadows. Now place the flashlight directly under your chin and observe the eerie dramatic quality imparted to your face.

The essential principle demonstrated here is that *the placement of the primary source of light critically affects in mood and character the dramatic quality of the image.*

Character of light   Every source of illumination employed in a scene has a character of its own. The quality of natural light has endless variations, from the harsh, bright light of a clear fall day to the soft, hazy light that fills the corners and the shadows of a foggy summer noon. Sunlight also has special color characteristics that affect the mood and character of the image. Morning sunlight is blue in character and imparts a cool quality to the entire scene, whereas late afternoon sunlight is reddish and warm.

Fig. 14A.   **Fig. 14B.**

Fig. 15. *The Seventh Seal.*

The artistic filmmaker is intimately familiar with the subtlest qualities of natural light. Using filters and devices such as reflectors, he is able to control both the black-and-white and color character of all light that falls within the frame.

The chief sources of artificial light are the carbon arc, the incandescent bulb, the quartz bulb, and the xenon arc lamp. These bulbs are used in a variety of housings and each imparts a special character to light. The *spotlight*, with its harsh, focused beam, and the *floodlight*, with its soft, diffuse quality, are the two basic lights in general use for cinematic lighting.

A scene steeped in sorrow, mystery, or gloom is difficult to illuminate properly with a bright full light. The exclusive use of harshly focused spotlights creates deep shadows and high contrasts that would probably be inappropriate to a lively comedy. Here again, however, there are few fixed rules. Filmmaking remains in large measure a visceral art, dependent on the taste and instincts of the filmmaker. The eye is the judge, but it is essential to understand how the character of light itself can control the impact (emotional and intellectual) of the entire image.

Fig. 16. *The Seventh Seal.*

Generally, we are unaware of the effect of light on our emotions. But the vague feeling of being "down" on an overcast, raw fall day or the lift felt at the first brightness of a spring sun are familiar examples of the emotional impact of light.

Consider, for example, the effect of the daylight exteriors in the opening sequence of *The Seventh Seal*. Throughout the sequence, a generally flat, overall light is used for all exteriors. The effect is much like that experienced on a cloudy, sullen day: a mood of despair and unrelieved sorrow is created. The character of the light subtly affects the audience's emotions at the outset of the film. The waves, the long shot of the sea and the land, the relative absence of shadows, and the oppressive grayness set the mood. Then narration provides the first facts: a land gripped by plague; the sorrowful, hopeless journey homeward.

The grim foreboding of the exterior scene in which Death and the Knight play chess is an almost perfect example of the effect of light on mood. The sky is dotted with black clouds, while far off a cold sun provides gloomy illumination. The figures are edge-lit, and there is a broad contrast between darks and lights within the frame (Fig. 16).

Compare these scenes with the daylight exteriors that include Jof and Mia —the symbols of the Holy Family, the single presence of light and hope. Here the lighting is sharply etched, luminous. It has the character of a bright spring

Fig. 17. *The Seventh Seal.*

day and relieves the oppressive gloom of the land. During the beautiful "sacrament" scene, as Jof and Mia share their strawberries and cream with the Knight, the audience almost forgets the plague and all that has gone before it (Fig. 17). The presence of Death, so ominous in the film, is almost washed away in the sunlit character of this idyllic scene.

Throughout *The Seventh Seal,* Fischer displays his versatility in employing the character of light to support and indeed *create* the desired mood. Death is always lit in sharp, high contrast. His face, overexposed and stark in its whiteness, contrasts with the deep blacks of his robe. The majority of the interiors are lit by a sharp, contrasting light that emphasizes shadows and firelight and evokes a mood of mystery and gloom.

Another example of the control of the character of light is seen in Sven Nykvist's camera work in *Through a Glass Darkly.* This film, the first of Bergman's trilogy that includes *Winter Light* and *The Silence,* deals with the destructive effects of a loveless atmosphere on a schizophrenic young wife, Karin. The barren, cold light of the Baltic island, with an unseen sun that lies low on the horizon and casts no warmth and no shadow, reflects the inner life of the characters (Fig. 18). Here is the most subtle use of light possible: the exteriors not only create mood but project an *external* expression of *internal* conflicts. Nykvist tells of making a careful study of the island light before shooting the film:

Fig. 18. *Through a Glass Darkly.*

> I remember when we filmed *Through a Glass Darkly* on the island of Gotland in the Baltic Sea. We would go out in the early, gray light, noting the values that were to be had and how these values changed and new light patterns and effects were created whenever the sun broke through. We wanted a graphite tone, one without extreme contrasts, and we determined the exact hours when this mood could be obtained naturally.[2]

As Karin's father and husband sit in a rowboat discussing her madness and the apparent hopelessness of her schizophrenia, we sense their total self-involvement, their inability to love. The power and communicative quality of this scene gain immeasurably by the character of the sunlight, which is devoid of warmth or comfort. The character of the light remains flat — gray and cold.

Color

It has already been noted that all light has its own color and that the potential in color mood lighting has only recently been realized as equal to, if not greater than, that of black and white. In color mood lighting there must be exact control because colors in themselves produce emotional responses. Thus the *intensity of the light* can vary the strength of hues, the *direction of the light* can vary the "shape" of objects and people, and the *character of the light* can impart within a color frame a wide range of relationships.

In *Juliet of the Spirits*, Federico Fellini evokes the interior life of an isolated

[2] Sven Nykvist, "A Passion for Light," *American Cinematographer* (April 1972), p. 381.

wife, alternating between her empty reality and her vivid, colorful fantasies. The light is blindingly bright throughout. Realistic scenes are lit largely from the front, giving a flat, garish hue to all the colors; fantasy scenes are lit largely from the side, rimming the colors with halations of light. The resulting character of the light creates a wild, garish effect that perfectly suits the material.

The "family reunion" scene in *Bonnie and Clyde*—an American Gothic scene in which Bonnie and her family have a get-together in the middle of a dust bowl—is illuminated by a hazy soft light that makes the scene a mock-sentimental orgy, a satiric underscoring of the "real folks" theme that lies beneath much of the film. The character of the light flattens the color, and as we view the scene we subconsciously understand its purpose in the film.

Light, then, is the substance with which the filmmaker "paints." The subtle use of light to illuminate, create mood, give character, and communicate has elevated lighting for film from its craft origins to its present artistic level.

THE TOOLS OF CINEMATOGRAPHY

Whereas the basic elements of cinematography are the characteristics of the raw stock itself, composition, and illumination, the tools of cinematography are (1) the camera, (2) the lens, and (3) the lights and lighting equipment.

Camera

The camera is, of course, the primary mechanical tool in filmmaking. Most cameras consist, first, of a magazine that houses the unexposed and exposed film in total darkness. From the magazine the film is fed into a totally enclosed chamber, usually through sprocket-driven gears that engage the perforations in the film. These gears may be part of the magazine or part of the camera chamber.

In this manner, the film is propelled forward. A claw pulls the film into a position flush behind the shutter. When the film has been placed in position, movement comes to a full stop, the shutter opens and closes, and a single image is exposed—exactly in the manner of a still photograph. This is called *intermittent motion*. The process continues at such high speed that the stop-and-go motion is all but invisible; the film seems to move continuously through the camera. This concept of the intermittent image is basic to understanding the art of the motion picture.

Once the frame has been exposed, the claw moves the film forward, bringing the next frame into position behind the shutter, and so on. The shutter closes and remains closed during movement within the chamber. At sound film speed, raw stock moves through the camera at 24 frames per second. Thus in 16mm film, with 40 frames to the foot, this operation takes place at 36 feet per minute. In 35mm film, with 16 frames to the foot, the rate is 90 feet per minute.

Fig. 19. 35mm Panaflex (Panavision). **Fig. 20.** 16mm Arriflex.

Motion picture cameras are designed for every purpose, and the type of filming dictates the type of camera. The large studio-type camera is heavy, relatively immobile, excellently tooled, and almost trouble-free. It is enclosed in a soundproof casing (a blimp) for operation during sound shooting. The camera is capable of running eleven minutes of film without reloading. Examples of this type of camera are the 16mm and 35mm Mitchell NC and BNC. The new Panaflex studio camera (Fig. 19) is lighter and more mobile.

The smaller, mobile type of camera that can be hand-held during shooting is available in a lightweight model for silent (no sound recording) shooting and a slightly heavier model that is soundproofed. It is capable of running up to eleven minutes in 16mm and four-and-one-half minutes in 35mm without reloading. Examples are the 16mm Arriflex for shooting without sound (Fig. 20), the 16mm Arriflex BL for sound shooting (Fig. 21), and the 16mm Eclair for sound shooting (Fig. 22). In 35mm, Arriflex offers the model 35 BL for sound shooting.

The small, lightweight, spring-driven camera used for newsreel or candid shooting is capable of only short runs of film. Examples are the 16mm Bolex (Fig. 23), the 35mm Eyemo, and the 16mm Filmo.

The Mitchell camera is generally employed in feature-length theatrical films shot in studios or studio-location setups. It requires a power source and is not conveniently powered by batteries. The Arriflex and Eclair models are usually powered by batteries and thus have greater mobility.

The *nouvelle vague* (or New Wave) films, so influential in the 1950s, came into being with the emergence of lightweight, hand-held cameras that enabled the cameraman to change the focus of the lens as action developed. Jean-Luc Godard's *Breathless* was one of the first films to make extensive use of the nervous, jerky images created by a freely moving camera.

In operation, the camera can be either hand-held or mounted on (1) a tripod, (2) a dolly, or (3) a crane. In mounting, the camera is usually fixed to a device called a *head* that is placed on top of the tripod and permits *panning* (lateral movement) and *tilting* (vertical movement) of the camera. The head operates hydraulically or mechanically and provides smooth, professional

Fig. 21. 16mm Arriflex BL. **Fig. 22.** 16mm Eclair. **Fig. 23.** 16mm Bolex.

movement through a series of interlocking gears. Panning and tilting are the primary movements of the camera in fixed position.

When it is necessary for the camera to move forward, backward, or diagonally during shooting, the camera and its head are placed on a *dolly*, a truck or cart that is capable of moving about noiselessly. This is called a *dolly shot*, and the camera is said to be *dollying*. The most primitive type of dolly is a simple steel platform mounted on four tires and placed on tracks. It is capable of moving only forward and backward on these tracks.

The film director's desire for a more flexible and mobile instrument that would enable the camera to move freely about the set led to more sophisticated machinery. One such device is the *crab dolly*, a steel cart mounted on heavy pneumatic tires. This type of dolly can be steered noiselessly and abruptly and contains a pedestal upon which the camera is placed. The pedestal can be raised and lowered during the shot.

From this type of dolly it is but a simple progression to the elaborate *cranes* of the "big studio" operation. The camera and camera operator sit in a cockpit, and the crane moves noiselessly forward and backward, up and down, over a wide area. Whereas the dolly is manually operated—pushed and pulled by a member of the crew—the crane is usually electrically operated.

From the 1930s to the 1950s, when most film production was confined to the large studio, tripod, dolly, and crane provided what mobility the camera possessed. The basic studio camera, the Mitchell BNC, was far too cumbersome and heavy to be moved around unless it was placed on one of these supports. The current trend in cinema, however, has been greatly influenced by the emergence of the small, lightweight, noiseless camera. More and more films contain a large amount of hand-held camera work, in which the cameraman provides his own mobility.

As has been pointed out, the art of cinema depends heavily on motion. A series of scenes photographed with the camera in fixed position will have a static quality that no amount of skillful editing can improve. Many of the standard Hollywood films produced in the 1940s contain a high percentage of such *setup shots*, in which there is little or no camera movement. This fact contributed to the decline of Hollywood as the center of the motion picture art. As the European filmmakers freed the camera from the confines of the tripod, the dolly, and the set by picking it up in their hands, the art of film gained a new vitality.

A truly mobile camera can contribute a great deal to the effect of a film on the audience. The impact of most current films is greatly heightened by the use of the moving camera. If one views the typical Hollywood film of twenty years ago and compares them with contemporary films, the fact of camera mobility is probably the single most striking difference. In the films *Z* and *State of Siege*, the filmmaker Costa Gavras gets a tremendous amount of dramatic mileage from a camera that is totally mobile, darting here and there, moving inside trucks and cars, effecting a subjective point of view when necessary, suddenly changing speeds and direction, and zooming in and out.

A final element that lends the camera mobility is the *zoom lens*. In documentary situations where repeat action is impossible, where the nature of the action will not permit the director to run through a scene several times for close-ups and alternate angles, the zoom lens is a very useful tool. Although the zoom lens frequently produces an artificial and distracting visual effect, it does permit the cameraman to change the frame *during* a scene. The film editor can then eliminate the zoom movement and use long shot and close-up as though they were photographed in two separate scenes.

The motion picture camera, then, is the basic instrument by which a film image is photographed. It is unique in that it provides motion both by photographing action (in a series of separate images) and by changing vantage points during the action. The cameraman can vary both the speed at which the film moves past the shutter and the speed at which the shutter opens and closes.

Lens

The "eye" through which the image is seen is the *lens;* this is the focal point of the camera. It is the lens that transmits the image from the real world to film. The determination of the *exact* lens needed to produce the *exact* image desired is a key factor in transmitting the image onto celluloid.

The human eye is a lens; it is, in fact, many lenses. It can enable us to see an entire scene with a peripheral vision of about 180 degrees, or it can contract to provide us with a microscopic close-up of an object. We can, at our convenience, change the focus of our eye.

The following experiment will demonstrate focus. Hold a pencil close to your eye and try to concentrate your attention on the pencil and the pencil alone. Bring the pencil into sharp and clear focus until it fills the scene. Notice how soft and fuzzy everything in the background appears. Now, without moving the pencil, shift your attention to the background — focusing on it and bringing it into sharp detail. Notice that the pencil, still large in the foreground, is fuzzy and soft in focus. Your eye has shifted its focus and has thus changed the essential character of what is seen.

Since we perceive all film through the "eye" of the art—the lens—it is essential to understand the character and properties of the wide variety of lenses with which a motion picture is created.

As a film is being made, director and cameraman view each image through a lens. They then prepare each scene, composing and lighting the image *after* they have selected the lens through which the action will be photographed. Their eye becomes the lens, and the final image is exactly what the selected lens is capable of "seeing."

The key factors in the evaluation of a lens are (1) *size of the image* (long short or close-up), (2) *depth of field* (relative sharpness throughout the scene), (3) *linear distortion* (distortion from visual reality as we perceive it), and (4) *effect of the lens on movement*. These four basic properties determine the esthetic values that will exist in the frame.

Size of the image   From a fixed point, different-sized lenses will transmit onto film images of different sizes. (For purposes of clarity, all lens sizes referred to in this section are for 16mm cameras. However, the principles discussed are identical for all cameras.) The following are the most common types of lenses: (1) wide-angle (5mm to 18mm), (2) normal (18mm to 60mm), (3) long (60mm to 90mm), and (4) telephoto (100mm and larger).

Figures 24A through 24D show the same scene photographed from a fixed camera position with four different-sized lenses. Figure 24A gives a full view of the scene, a *wide-angle* view, photographed with a 12.5mm lens. Figure 24B shows a medium view, a *normal* view, photographed with a 25mm lens. (The word "normal" is used to designate the range of lenses that most closely approximates the image size that the human eye would see without conscious effort to enlarge or contract the image.) Figure 24C shows a close view, a *long* view, photographed with a 90mm lens. Figure 24D gives an extremely close view, a *telephoto* view, photographed with a 200mm lens.

Fig. 24. A. 12.5mm, B. 25mm, C. 90mm, D. 200mm

Fig. 25. A. 12.5mm at 10 feet   B. 12.5mm at 5 feet

The first esthetic consideration in the choice of lens, then, is the desired *size* of the image. Image size is also affected by the position of the camera. Compare Figures 25A and 25B. Both were photographed with a 12.5mm wide-angle lens, yet in Figure 25B the foreground subjects are much larger. The camera was simply moved from a distance of 10 feet to a distance of 5 feet from the scene.

Why, then, should a cameraman bother to change lenses? The answer requires an examination of far more subtle esthetic differences between lenses than those of size.

Depth of field   The depth of field of a lens is traditionally defined as *the range of acceptable sharpness before and behind the plane of focus obtained in the final screened image.* This technical definition does not, however, communicate the importance of depth of field to the total esthetic values present in the image.

With the camera positioned close to the subject, a wide-angle lens will present an image of almost the same size as that obtained by a longer lens at a greater distance from the subject. Examine Figures 26A and 26B. Figure 26A was photographed with a 12.5mm lens (a wide-angle lens) at a distance of 5 feet from the foreground subject. Figure 26B was photographed with a 150mm lens (a telephoto lens) at a distance of 55 feet from the foreground subject. The *size* of the face and the boundaries of the frame are approximately the same in each case, but the visual values within the frame are quite different. It is the nature of these differences that can tell us much about the subject of cinematography.

In Figure 26A the background is relatively clear and well delineated, thus competing to some degree with the girl in the foreground. At the same time, the sense of place created by the background casts an impression over the girl's face and subtly affects our perception of the scene. Although the foreground figure dominates the scene by virtue of size alone, it does not exist in limbo; we are fully conscious of where the face is and partially aware of what is occurring in the background. Our attention is projected into the frame and our reaction to this image is strongly affected by events occurring in the background.

In Figure 26B the face commands the entire stage. The background,

Fig. 26. A. 12.5mm at 5 feet   B. 150mm at 55 feet

though closer, is a blur that creates only a mood of softness around the face. Nothing distracts us, nothing divides our attention, nothing competes for our minds or hearts.

Thus size is only the most superficial of differences between lenses, and depth of field, a characteristic that varies with the size of the lens, is a key factor in the ultimate impact of the image. *The wider the lens, the greater the depth of field. The longer the lens, the shallower the depth of field.*

In the death scene of Charles Foster Kane in Orson Welles' masterpiece we see: the giant head of Kane in the foreground, in sharp focus, dominating the frame; the glass of water huge in size in the ever-nearing foreground, also sharp; and far, far into the frame, the door. The nurse enters, in sharp focus, carrying our eye deep into an almost endless frame, until we are, as audience, almost between Kane and the nurse. When Kane dies, we feel a dramatic intensity and immediacy—an effect that could not have been achieved with a normal lens. Our traditional "observer" role has been broken down through use of the wide-angle lens.

Lenses of large focal length produce much shallower depth relationships. The close-up scenes in *Elvira Madigan* are excellent examples of long-lens photography. The camera dwells on the beautiful face of Pia Degermark. Grass, leaves, sky, and water frame her image with blurred softness, creating the kind of idealized romantic haze through which a lover sees his beloved. The significant factor here is not the repeated use of close-ups, which could have been effected simply by moving the camera toward the subject, but rather the repeated use of soft-focus backgrounds and foregrounds that fill a large portion of the frame and surround the actress with a gauze of color and undelineated shapes. The mood of the audience is formed by the repeated use of the long lens. Indeed, the effect of the film depends almost entirely on this technique.

Everything related to depth of field—the relationship of elements in sharp focus to elements in soft focus, the use of these elements in depth, and the decision of whether foreground or background is to be sharp or soft—helps to determine the effect of the image upon the audience.

The artistic use of depth of field is a subject too often misunderstood by many professional directors and cameramen, yet it is an essential element in the making of a film.

Linear distortion   To reproduce reality with one hundred percent accuracy, a photograph should be completely free of linear distortion. This presupposes a lens that can reduce the size of the image without altering the course of the individual rays of light that transfer the image from the real world to film. Such a lens, of course, does not exist. As light rays are refracted (or bent) through the optical system of a lens, changes occur in relationships.

The normal lens provides an image most free of linear distortion. Look carefully at Figure 27A, which was photographed with a 25mm lens, a normal lens. To the eye it seems in all respects to be a "true" reproduction of the scene. Relative sizes look normal and in proportion. Relationships within the frame appear to be free of distortion. The slight changes that did occur in the process of reducing the scene in size are proportional changes and cannot be noticed by the human eye. Horizontal and vertical lines are almost completely straight.

Now examine Figure 27B, which shows the same scene photographed with an extreme wide-angle lens, the 5.6mm. The distortion from reality is obvious. Horizontal and vertical planes are noticeably bent and depth relationships are broadly inaccurate.

Extreme wide-angle lenses (Fig. 28), sometimes called *fish-eyes*, are excellent for dream sequences, fantasies, "drunk" scenes, and scenes of ominous foreboding. In the film *Seconds*, John Frankenheimer made excellent use of an extreme wide-angle lens to depict a patient's view of his own operation.

The wider the lens, the greater the linear distortion. The *linear distortion factor* is thus an important consideration in the selection of a lens. Creative use of the linear distortion factor depends largely on an intuitive judgment of the effect of the distortion on the audience. There are times when an image must be as accurately and faithfully rendered as possible, and times when a distorted image is the key to a sequence.

Fig. 27.

Fig. 28. *The Odds Against* (Lee R. Bobker)

The effect of the lens on movement   The effect of each lens on how movement within the frame is perceived is a strange optical phenomenon. Again, the more normal the lens (18mm to 50mm), the more faithfully movement is reproduced. The greater the departure at either extreme from the normal lens, the greater the distortion of movement.

This distortion of movement is called the *telescopic effect.* As the focal length of a lens increases, movement toward or away from the camera seems to contract, or telescope inward. Conversely, as the focal length of a lens decreases, movement seems to increase, or telescope outward. The most dramatic effects are generally obtained with lenses of large focal length, or long lenses. When a subject coming toward the camera is photographed with a long lens, his motion is generally so contracted that he appears to be moving very slowly, or indeed not at all. This is *not* because his legs are not moving—they may be moving furiously. It is, very simply, because the overall size of the subject within the frame remains almost constant. It is the disparity between the subject's obvious effort to move toward the camera and his apparent lack of success that yields the dramatic effect.

Figures 29 through 31 demonstrate the telescopic effect. In the scene, the actor ran about 35 feet down a street. The director did three takes of the same action—with normal, telephoto, and wide-angle lenses. Reproduced here are the first, middle, and last frames of each take. In the first take, shot with a normal lens, the actor does seem to move about 35 feet between the first and last frames (Figs. 29A–29C). In the second take, shot with a telephoto lens, the actor seems to move much less between the first and last frames (Figs. 30A–30C). In the last take, shot with a wide-angle lens, the actor seems to move considerably more than 35 feet between the first and last frames (Figs. 31A–31C). Keep in mind that all three takes required the same shooting time and the same screening time. The only difference was in the focal length of the lens.

This phenomenon, though striking, is really just another instance of the optical effects of long lenses described earlier. In Figure 26B, the people in the background are more than 50 feet behind the girl in the foreground. Because they are almost the same size, they appear to be in the same plane, or at least very near to each other. Since the distances in depth have been greatly foreshortened, movement toward or away from the camera is also distorted. A figure observed through a long lens moving from background to foreground changes very little in size and thus does not appear to cover much ground.

The lens, then, does more than simply record the image. It affects the audience's perception of that image by changing the appearance of (1) relationships between objects in the frame and (2) motion.

Size of the image from a fixed vantage point, *depth of field* (relative sharpness of objects within the frame), and *linear distortion* (departure from reality) are the elements contributed by the lens, the "eye" of the cinematic art.

Lighting and lighting equipment

It has already been established that all artificial light has a particular quality and character. Essentially, there are only two kinds of artificial light by which the filmmaker illuminates the set: the spotlight and the floodlight.

The *spotlight* provides a focused beam of light that is usually harsh in character. It is projected through a lens and can be focused and directed. Because of the shape of the lens, the light forms a circular pattern on the object on which it falls. The *floodlight* provides diffuse light that is soft in character. It usually consists of a bulb surrounded by reflective material that diffuses the light and projects it in the desired direction.

Spotlights and floodlights, used in combination, have for years been the traditional tools of the cinematographer. Both types of light come in several intensities and sizes. *The larger the light (the bulb), the greater the intensity.* The Hollywood set contains all types and sizes of arc and incandescent bulbs — from the great *brutes,* the arc lights that illuminate large studio sets, to the tiny *inkies,* the 100-watt spots that light the eyes of the star.

The range of incandescent spots in common use includes:

type	common name
10,000-watt spot	ten
5,000-watt spot	five
2,000-watt spot	deuce
750-watt spot	keg or baby
100-watt spot	inkie

Fig. 29. A   B   C

Fig. 30. A   B   C

Fig. 31. A   B   C

Floodlights are also available in a wide range of sizes and types:

type	common name
5,000-watt flood	five cone
2,000-watt flood	deuce cone
1,000-watt flood	cone
750-watt flood	750 cone
2- or 4-bulb flood	broad

These lights are used primarily in studio lighting or in large feature-film productions. The advent in the 1950s of a lighter, more mobile bulb and frame made popular the *cine-kings,* which emit a powerful light of much the same character as the studio lights. In the 1960s, the crystal quartz bulb revolutionized film production. A variety of quartz lights is currently available. These very small bulbs, mounted in a lightweight frame, emit 500, 750, 1,000, and more watts of light, facilitating all types of location photography and greatly speeding up the lighting process. Currently any desired level of lighting can be achieved with a combination of photoflood bulbs and quartz lights. Lightweight xenon arc lamps are also currently in wide use.

The other major tools of the art of illumination include (1) cloth (silks), (2) metal (such as copper screen and aluminum strips), and (3) reflectors. With these materials the character and quality of the light can be adjusted, and sections of light can be shaded or eliminated. The control of subtle gradations of light intensity is, in the final analysis, the ultimate art of illumination. The more control that the cameraman exerts, the greater his possibilities for capturing images artistically. These materials enable the cameraman to pinpoint any element within a frame and to vary in minute ways the intensity of all light that falls within the boundaries of the image.

In outdoor filming, the cameraman can use silk screens to soften the harsh rays of the sun and reflectors to direct and change the character of sunlight. These materials extend his control and leave him less at the mercy of random light. With a light meter, he can measure the intensity of the light in any part of the frame and can control relative intensities in the most subtle gradations. Another light gauge, the contrast glass, reveals the relationships between light and dark that the processed film will show and enables the cameraman to "paint his canvas with light."

The trend in filmmaking today is to use less and less artificial light. Because new film stocks have much higher ASA ratings (greater sensitivity to light), the cameraman can illuminate his scene — in color or in black and white — at a much lower light intensity. In addition, the smaller, lightweight lights emit the same intensity as comparable heavy studio lights.

Compare in size the 2,000-watt incandescent bulb used in a studio deuce with two 1,000-watt quartz bulbs, which give in effect the same amount of light. The quartz bulb is approximately the size of a fountain pen cap, whereas the 2,000-watt incandescent is the size of a basketball. This difference in size and mobility, plus the increased sensitivity of color and black-and-white film, has enabled the filmmaker to move away from unrealistic, static methods of lighting.

The camera, the lens, and lighting are the tools of cinematographic art, the instruments with which the filmmaker composes and illuminates the image.

FILMS FOR STUDY

> *Breathless*, Jean-Luc Godard. Brandon Films, Inc., 200 West 57 Street, New York, New York 10019.

> *Citizen Kane*, Orson Welles. Janus Films, 24 West 58 Street, New York, New York 10019.

The Seventh Seal, Ingmar Bergman. Janus Films, 24 West 58 Street, New York, New York 10019.

Wild Strawberries, Ingmar Bergman. Janus Films, 24 West 58 Street, New York, New York 10019.

The Magician, Ingmar Bergman. Janus Films, 24 West 58 Street, New York, New York 10019.

SUPPLEMENTARY READING

Bobker, Lee R., with Louise Marinis, *Making Movies.* New York: Harcourt Brace Jovanovich, 1973.

Clarke, Charles G. *Professional Cinematography.* Hollywood, Calif.: American Society of Cinematographers, 1964.

Rebel, Erique J., *Great Cameramen.* Cranbury, N.J.: A. S. Barnes, 1971.

SOUND

THREE

I attribute enormous importance to the sound track, and I always try to take the greatest care with it. And when I say the sound track, I am talking about the natural sounds, the background noises rather than the music. For L'Avventura, I had an enormous number of sound effects recorded: every possible quality of the sea more and less stormy, the breakers, the rumble of the waves in the grottoes. I had a hundred reels of tape filled with nothing but sound effects. Then I selected those that you hear on the film's sound track. For me, that is the true music, the music that can be adapted to images. Conventional music only rarely melts into the image; more often it does nothing but put the spectator to sleep, and it prevents him from appreciating what he is seeing. After long consideration, I am relatively opposed to "musical commentary," at least in its present form. I detect something old and rancid in it. The ideal solution would be to create a sound track out of noises and to call on an orchestra leader to conduct it. But then, wouldn't the only orchestra leader capable of doing that be the director himself?

Michelangelo Antonioni
The World of Film: Michelangelo Antonioni
by Pierre Leprohon
New York: Simon and Schuster, Inc., 1963, p. 100.

IN THE BEGINNING, THE ART OF FILM WAS LIMITED TO THE EFFECT OF THE VISUAL image upon the audience. Except for the piano that accompanied the silent film, the first motion pictures relied solely on what was seen. However, the very presence of the piano indicated a desire to add *aural* impact to the visual elements of film.

In a sense, the old-time piano provided the beginnings of film sound. The piano music served a variety of purposes. First, and most obvious, it supported and strengthened the mood of the film: a gentle romantic melody often accompanied an impassioned love scene; a switch to a few minor-key chords — a sinister rumble in the lower octaves — announced a cut to the villain lurking in the shadows. The relationship between the piano music and the film was scarcely subtle. In addition to supporting the prevailing mood, the piano music helped to establish the pace and rhythm of the film. The humor of the "Keystone Cops" sequences was greatly enhanced by a racing up and down on the keyboard; the sequences seemed to move at an even more insane pace when accompanied by an inspired pianist.

The appearance of the first sound motion picture in 1927 marked a new era in the art of film. Suddenly an entirely new element had to be considered in the making of a motion picture. Today, as the art of cinema continues to expand its techniques, the use of sound in film is increasingly important, and the impact of sound upon film cannot be overstated. Every motion picture of importance produced from 1955 to the present is accompanied by a complex and highly artistic sound track.

THE MECHANICS OF FILM SOUND

The principle of film sound began with the discovery that sound waves could be "photographed." In its simplest form, the procedure for producing film sound is as follows:

(1) Sounds projected into a microphone are translated into electrical impulses.

(2) These electrical impulses, which vary in intensity, are transmitted onto celluloid, forming a visual pattern. A section along the edge of the finished film is set aside for this "photographed" sound track.

(3) The visual pattern is read by the "sound eye" of the projector — a small light bulb that scans the track area as the film moves through the projector. The pattern is then retranslated into the original sounds that formed it.

(4) The sounds are fed into an amplifier and then through a speaker.

The sound track recorded through this photographic process is called an *optical* sound track. Until the late 1940s, all film sound was recorded directly onto celluloid in this manner.

The arrival in the early 1950s of magnetic tape revolutionized the entire process of recording sound for film. Today, almost all film sound is recorded on magnetic tape of varying types and widths. Only the final sound track that accompanies the film to the laboratory is still recorded on celluloid.

The above discussion offers a brief look at the mechanics of film sound. The art of contemporary film, however, demands a deeper understanding of the key elements of film sound and their artistic uses in filmmaking.

THE ELEMENTS OF FILM SOUND

Synchronous sound — dialogue

The simplest and most obvious type of film sound is the dialogue track re-corded at the precise moment of photography. The sound track, in order to give maximum fidelity, must be played back at the identical speed at which it is recorded. Thus all recorded film sound that is to be projected as part of the sound track on a composite print (Fig. 1) must be recorded at the same speed as the film (the tape equivalent of 24 frames per second).

To demonstrate the principle of fidelity, try the following experiment on a tape recorder. Record your voice at the speed most common to home tape re-corders — 7½ ips. Play back your recording at the same speed. Your voice will be reproduced with almost complete accuracy. Now play the recording at 15 ips. Your voice will sound like that in an animated cartoon, high-pitched and largely incomprehensible. Now switch speeds to 3¾ ips. You will hear a low, droning sound bearing little or no resemblance to your voice. Thus any variance, however slight, between the speed of the recording and the speed of the playback will distort fidelity.

Fidelity is only part of the problem of film sound. The key factor in shooting sound and film together is *synchronization*. If the film and magnetic tape are not moving at the same speed in relation to each other, lip movements and dialogue will not be coordinated and the film will be "out of sync."

Before the development of reliable synchronizing systems, most film sound recording was done on sprocketed optical film or sprocketed mag-netic tape. But tape recorders that utilized 35mm or 16mm sprocketed magnetic tape were large and cumbersome. Today almost all film sound recording is done with lightweight magnetic recorders that employ non-sprocketed quarter-inch tape. These small, portable recorders, such as the Nagra IV (Fig. 2), have revolutionized the entire process of sound recording for film by giving a new mobility to sync-sound cinematography. Since there are no sprocket holes on quarter-inch tape, a "sync signal" is used to insure

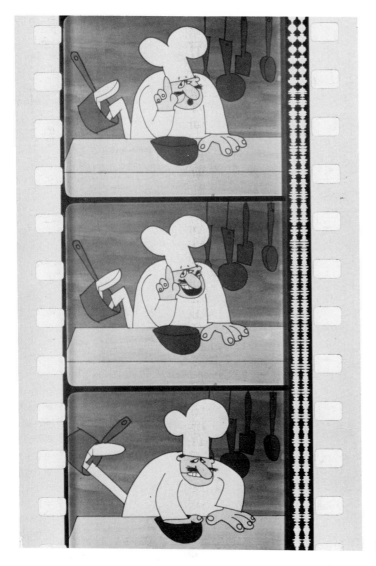

Fig. 1.

synchronization between camera and recorder. The camera and sound recorder are connected by an electric cable. The camera motor generates an audible signal of approximately 60 cycles. This *reference signal* is recorded on the quarter-inch audio tape. When the tape is played back for rerecording, the signal is reproduced at exactly the speed at which the quarter-inch tape was recorded during filming. Thus perfect sync is maintained.

As an alternative to cable-linked synchronizing systems, crystal units are now available to provide a totally cordless setup between the camera and the quarter-inch recorder. This type of operation permits maximum mobility

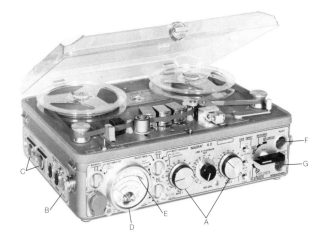

Fig. 2.

PROD. NO. 371   ROLL # 3
SCENE | TAKE | SOUND
18A | 2 | 105
DIRECTOR BOBKER
CAMERAMAN RADITSCHNIG
DATE 8|30|68 EXT. X INT.
PRODUCED BY VISION ASSOC.

Fig. 3.

for filming over a fairly wide area and enables sound and camera to be widely separated. This system is quite reliable.

Before editing begins, the sound track is transferred from the quarter-inch tape to sprocketed tape, since it is easier to handle with current editing equipment. The film editor must first align the picture and sound track in precisely the same relationship that existed at the time of photography. To accomplish this, either of two methods of marking sync on both picture and tape is used.

(1) The sound recorder and the camera are started. When both are operating at normal speed, a *clapstick* (Fig. 3) is held in front of the camera. The camera photographs the clapstick, which contains pertinent production information (usually identifying the scene number). This information is read into the microphone. The top of the clapstick is then closed, producing a hard, sharp noise. The camera photographs the closing of the sticks (Fig. 4A); at this

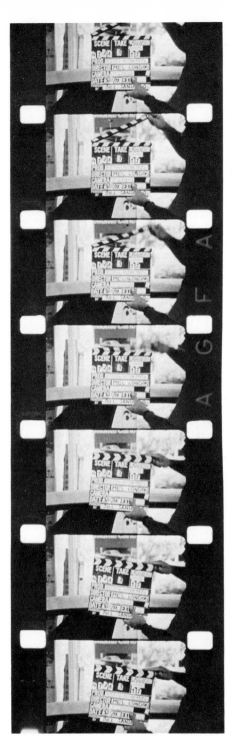

Fig. 4A.

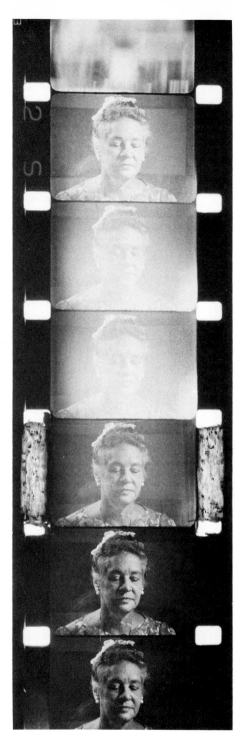

Fig. 4B.

same moment the sound of wood hitting wood is recorded on the tape. Only one frame on the film will show the sticks coming clearly together. In the editing room, the film editor lines up this frame with the exact spot on the 35mm or 16mm magnetic tape where the sound is first heard. The film is now "in sync," and the image and voice that follow will be perfectly matched. (Needless to say, neither camera nor tape recorder is shut off *after* the clapstick has been closed. The photographing of the scene must follow immediately. If there is any interruption, the clapstick must be photographed and recorded once again.) The system of marking picture and tape by matching the visual closing of the clapstick with the sound of the stick closing does not create sync; it is merely a convenient way of providing the editor with an easily identifiable reference point.

(2) The second method of marking sync is electronic. A light within the camera aperture flashes as the film starts. This fogs a frame (Fig. 4B). At the same moment an electronic "beep" is recorded on the tape. The editor uses these two reference points to line up frame and tape in the same manner as that described above.

If no marking system is used, picture and sound can be aligned by eye — by moving film and sound track back and forth until the perfect sync is found. This, however, is a slow and time-consuming task.

In films that contain dialogue (the majority of films today), photography and sound recording usually take place simultaneously. Synchronous sound, of course, is not restricted to dialogue, but includes the recording of any sound at the precise moment of photography.

Dubbing

Early in the development of the sound motion picture, many practical problems arose in connection with the recording of sync sound. Some of these problems were:

(1) The inability of an actor to deliver lines convincingly.

(2) The difficulty of obtaining high-fidelity sound outdoors.

(3) The difficulty of editing tracks with "too much" sound. (For example, on a dialogue track recorded in a noisy theater, the noise levels will vary from shot to shot. Since the noise levels are an integral part of the dialogue track, they cannot be "evened out" from cut to cut.)

(4) The difficulty of obtaining a good position for the microphone on very long or wide shots. The greater the distance between microphone and speaker, the poorer the sound. (The recent development of long-range "shotgun" microphones has minimized this problem.)

(5) Foreign actors not fluent in the language of the film.

(6) Nonsinging actors in musical roles.

These and similar problems led to the development of *dubbing*—the process of adding sound to a film after photography. There are four basic types of sound that can be added to a film through the dubbing process.

(1) Postsynchronous dialogue dubbing   In postsynchronous dialogue dubbing, the sound track recorded at the time of photography is used only as a guide. Since the track is *not* used in the final film, the quality of reproduction is not important. Dialogue need only be audible. Thus photography can proceed at a much more rapid pace, and certain scenes can be shot with lightweight cameras regardless of how much camera noise they make.

The scenes are later projected in a recording studio, where the actor watches himself on screen and listens through earphones to the sound track recorded at the time of photography. The film and track are played over and over until the actor can repeat the lines into a microphone at the speed and timing of the original recording. In effect, he matches the original track. The new recording, free of noise and delivered more convincingly, becomes the dialogue track of the film. Carefully controlled outside noises or other background sounds are added later to eliminate the sterile studio quality of the track.

Most theatrical feature films are dubbed in whole or in part. In some cases, the voices of the actors are replaced by new voices. In musical films, a kind of inverted dubbing takes place. Because it is so difficult to record sound synchronously in a musical "production" number, the music is prerecorded in a studio, insuring top-quality sound for both singer and orchestra. The track is then played in the film studio and the dancers and singers act out their motions to match what they hear. Thus the cameraman has free rein as regards movement, angles, and camera noise and can provide the best possible visual coverage without compromising the sound. This method is called *photography to playback*.

A major use of postsynchronous dialogue dubbing is in foreign films. This type of dubbing is the center of much controversy. When a foreign-language film is released in the United States, English subtitles are often superimposed on the film. The subtitles appear on the lower portion of the screen. The subtitle, however, is not a satisfactory device because the viewer must divide his attention between the entire frame and the title. Often, by the time the viewer reads the title and returns to the action, the scene is over and a cut has been made to another shot. In addition, most subtitles are oversimplified and incomplete renderings of the dialogue. They are generally written to communicate with the lowest common denominator of the audience and carry little of the flavor and quality of the dialogue in its original language.

In recent years many important films have been dubbed in several languages. Some films, such as *Cries and Whispers* and *State of Siege*, have been released in the United States in two versions: one with subtitles and another with dubbed-in English voices roughly synchronized to the lip movements seen on screen. Although synchronization in this type of dubbing can never be perfect, great technical advances have been made. Today, most dubbed films give the effect of being in sync. The translator of a foreign film must not only provide an accurate and faithful translation; he must select words that phonetically approximate the lip and mouth movements seen on screen. Thus *oui* can never quite be in sync with *yes* because of the essential difference in vocal production. The words *mon amour*, however, can be translated as *my dearest* because in both vocal production and length the two expressions come pretty close to being in sync.

The basic controversy in this type of dubbing, however, deals not with the question of technical excellence but with the artistic concern of replacing the voice of the original actor, who, after all, created the role. How much of the integrity of the original performance is lost, regardless of the technical excellence of the dubbing, is the key question here.

In any event, as modern filmmakers seek to create more mobile images and to move away from static methods of studio photography, the process of dialogue dubbing—which admittedly frees the camera—will remain an important part of film sound.

(2) Narration and voice-over   In most documentary and educational films, and in many theatrical features, a narrative track supplies information in support of the images. Often narrative is used to signal time transitions or to present information that is not provided by the film's images. In the more creative vein of contemporary cinema, narrative is also used to project the onscreen action beyond the confines of the moment. (For example, dialogue from a scene viewed early in a film may be used as narrative in a later scene.) Narration is usually recorded after the film is edited and is "laid in" alongside the scenes to which it relates. Voice-over sound can be excerpted from dialogue scenes or recorded separately; it too is placed on a track in precise relationship to the images.

Narration and voice-over tracks are recorded in a studio on magnetic tape and are edited into a sound track completely separate from the sync dialogue tracks. If the voice-over tracks are to be excerpted from sync dialogue scenes, the original recording tapes are simply rerecorded on new tapes. Since there is little if any loss of quality in duplicating magnetic tape, a piece of dialogue can be used as many times as desired.

(3) Sound effects   In direct sync dialogue recording, all sounds in the immediate environment become part of the voice track. For example, if the wind blows through the trees while someone is speaking on camera, the sound of the wind will also be heard on the track—but at a slightly lower level than the voice. When sound is recorded in a studio, only those sounds that are a desired part of the scene—a door opening, footfalls, the click of a switch— will be heard on the track. If a scene photographed in a studio needs additional sounds to create realism, or is shot without a desired sound, these *sound effects* are dubbed in later.

Most standard sound effects can be purchased on magnetic tape from a music-and-effects library. However, special sound effects, such as a plane landing, often have to be made. The sound of the plane's wheels touching the ground can be recorded separately and laid in alongside the precise frames of picture to which it relates. The net effect is that of sync sound.

As has been pointed out earlier, one of the prime advantages of dubbing is that it enables the filmmaker to control relative sound levels. In many types of on-location shooting, such as a scene in a sports arena, it is impossible to control the volume of the background sound. If dialogue is recorded synchronously, any cuts from shot to shot will create abrupt and disturbing changes in sound level. This problem can be easily handled by dubbing: the background actors silently go through the motions of talking and cheering. After the dialogue scene is recorded and edited, the sound effects of the crowd are dubbed in at a desired volume.

Most films require a carefully prepared sound effects track. This track can be used to replace poor sound effects, add sound effects that are missing, or provide a "presence," a sense of immediate reality, for films that are photographed without a sound track.

(4) Music for film   Music for film is obtained in two ways:

(1) A wide variety of musical selections can be purchased on tape from a music library. After the film is edited, the editor prepares the music track, laying the appropriate selections opposite the scenes that they are to accompany.

(2) A composer views the edited version of the film and makes a careful record of the exact length of each scene that requires music. He then composes and records the music for the film. Film music is composed in a series of short selections. Each selection is edited with the finished film as the music track or tracks are put together.

Whether the film music is a "library" or an "original" score, the film editor still must adjust the final relationships between music and picture.

Synchronous and dubbed dialogue, narration and voice-over, sound effects, and music are thus the major elements of a cinema sound track. The separate shots, scenes, and sequences are edited, and the many sound tracks — which together contain the above elements of sound — are edited to match and support the visual elements.

The mix

At the end of the editing process, the sound tracks, lined up with the visual images, are blended into a final composite sound track. The technical process by which the composite track is made is called the *mix*.

The film editor prepares for the mix by lining up the sound tracks with the picture. Each track has at the start a single frame with a hole punched in it that corresponds to a frame on the picture roll. The picture roll is threaded into a projector, and the frame with the hole in it is placed in the gate behind the lens. Each sound track is threaded onto a playback machine, and the marked frame is placed over the sound head. The projector and each playback machine are started together and played at exactly the same speed. Each sound track is projected into a central "mixing console," where it is adjusted for quality and relative volume. The sound mixer blends all the tracks (dialogue, narration, voice-over, music, and sound effects) into a composite sound track. This is the sound mix, the last creative step in filmmaking prior to submitting the film and final tracks to the laboratory for a finished composite print. If there are a large number of sound tracks, the mixer may make one or more *premixes*. In each premix, he blends several of the tracks together, thus reducing the number of separate tracks used in the final mix.

These are the key elements of film sound. The art with which these elements are used is as important to the finished film as any aspect of the visual image.

THE ART OF FILM SOUND

One of the simplest and most effective ways to demonstrate the importance of sound as a major element of cinematography is to view a scene in a film *without* the sound track. Viewed without sound, the images, however well photographed and well edited, lose their sense of reality and hence their impact. The pace of the film also seems retarded. Often, the effect is like that of a series of stills.

One of the most effective sequences in William Friedkin's suspense film *The French Connection* is the car chase. In the chase sequence, the policeman (Gene Hackman) commandeers a passing car in order to pursue a murderer who is attempting to escape on an elevated train. Hackman races through the streets below the train, trying to arrive at the next station in time to apprehend the killer. Without any sound the sequence would lose much of its immediacy and impact, but with the addition of traffic noises, tire squeals, and train sounds the entire sequence assumes a dimension that adds immeasurably to its dramatic effect.

Dialogue recording

The recording of voice at the time of photography would seem at first examination a fairly simple procedure: put a microphone in the vicinity of the person talking and shoot. But nothing could be more deceiving. There are three important factors in the recording of dialogue for film:

   (1) *The sound must accurately relate to the picture.* If the camera is shoot-

ing an extreme close-up of the speaker, and the microphone is ten feet away, the sound will be so out of perspective with the image that the audience will not believe the reality of the moment. If the camera is shooting an extreme long shot (two lonely riders on a ridge in the desert), and the microphone is a few inches from the speaker, again the result will be absurd. The sound must match in perspective what is seen.

(2) *The sound must faithfully reproduce the voice.* The sound track must be as free from distortion as possible. Even more important, each voice must be consistent from shot to shot and scene to scene. It is most distracting to hear a voice change character three or four times in the course of a film. A basic sound that *fits the character* must be created for each voice being recorded.

In a film like *The Godfather*, the textures of each voice play an important role in helping to establish mood and define character. All the harsh, guttural undertones present in the voices that Marlon Brando affected for his portrayal of Don Corleone are present on the sound track. On the other hand, the soft but menacing voice of Michael, Corleone's son, is also faithfully reproduced on the sound track and provides a contrast to the vocal quality of Don Corleone.

(3) *The sound must move with the image.* Movement, a primary element in visual composition, is also a key factor in sound recording. As characters move toward or away from camera, the sound perspective of the dialogue must change accordingly. When the camera moves in on an actor, the sound too must gradually and subtly move closer, to give the audience a better "ear" for what is being said. If the dialogue is acted out against a background of noise (as in the sports arena example discussed earlier), the actors must appear to be talking *over* the noise. In a wonderfully conceived sequence in Mike Nichols' *The Graduate*, the hero (Dustin Hoffman) is given a complete diving outfit for graduation. At his graduation party, he is asked to demonstrate the suit in the family swimming pool. The camera alternates between an objective position—a third-person or "outsider" view—and a subjective position—a first-person view through the hero's goggles. The sound obediently accompanies the camera: it is clear and understandable when the scene is viewed from the outside, but garbled and muddy or completely cut off when the scene is viewed from the hero's vantage point. As the hero waddles into the pool on his flippers and goes underwater, the sound approximates the rush of water over the hapless boy.

At first, dialogue recording was much like Samuel Johnson's dog that walked on two legs: one did not wonder how *well* it was done but simply that it was done at all. Since most films of the 1930s were studio productions, with each scene composed as a static set, sound recording consisted primarily of just picking up what was said. Generally, the dialogue was formal and staged—each person waiting for the other to finish his lines, then a reaction, then more talk. In daily life, however, conversations are never held in such an orderly fashion. Rarely are sentences thoroughly coherent or ideas clearly developed. Orson Welles was one of the first directors to use realistic dialogue on film. The overlapping dialogue, interruptions, and fragmented sentences of *Citizen Kane* transformed dialogue recording. The brilliant interrogation scene of the Mexican boy in Welles' *Touch of Evil*, with almost everyone in the room speaking simultaneously, created a reality far removed from the synthetic world of the Hollywood dramas of the thirties.

As cinema changes, the nature of dialogue recording also changes. Camera movements and movements within the frame are rapid, and tempos have greatly increased. Long-range microphones, wireless mikes, and electronic booms have greatly expanded the range of sound recording. Today, overlapping sound, voices heard simultaneously, distortions in quality for effect, and deliberate lack of clarity are all part of the art of on-set sound recording.

Voice tracks

The relationship between voice track (other than dialogue track) and picture can be either (1) direct and supportive or (2) indirect.

Direct use of voice tracks   In the vast majority of documentary and educational films, the narrative track is simply a descriptive instrument. At its worst, it duplicates what the film is saying. The following narrative excerpt is from a recent travel film about Japan.

> Looming over the vast expanse of the biggest city in the world, the Tokyo Tower beams television broadcasts from a height greater than that of the Eiffel Tower . . . to a people whose own work has lifted them to the third rank of the industrial nations of the world . . . a hundred million people dwelling in a mountainous, only partly arable land smaller than California . . . Poor in natural resources, Japan is rich in the human talents and energies that count most. . . .
>
> It's a country that like the so-called Bullet Train — the world's fastest — moves at speeds the Occidental would once have characterized as non-Oriental.
>
> Take in the countryside. Even here time has been flying. The tractor has brought technology to the age-old farmlands. . . . Then, fitting the traditional image to a T, you see bamboo growing, whole jungles of it. . . .
>
> It takes all a man and his family can do to give Japan the food her people require. . . . You plant watermelon seedlings under plastic in a barley field. You waste neither land nor space, not an inch of it.
>
> The green leaves of the green tea of Uji are part of the Japan the world thinks it knows from the hanging scrolls called *kakemono*. . . .
>
> The land gives up nothing without a fight. The sea provides Japan more than half her protein food. . . .
>
> Diving for cultured, pearl-bearing oysters dates back to the turn of the century.

No man can rush an oyster, which takes its own time in performing its own special alchemy. It takes a few years for the oyster to produce a decent pearl. . . .

Note that the narrative simply describes what the audience is already seeing on screen. This kind of one-to-one correspondence is a throwback to the early documentary and educational films of the 1930s and represents the worst possible use of narration.

All sound must make a distinct contribution to the total effect of the film. The visual elements are the central point of communication. When the viewer is subjected to a "double telling" of the material, his attention is divided between picture and sound, and the impact of the film is diminished. To be sure, there are proper uses for voice tracks that are directly related to picture. Narrative clues are often needed, for example, when the picture itself reveals only one aspect of the material, or when the material being communicated is highly complex. The following excerpt from an effective documentary film on India represents a valid use of the direct narrative track.*

It is early morning in a small village in northern India.

Govind Mandel searches the sky for signs of rain . . . for in India, rain is life.

The first meal of the day is served to Govind and his son, Ramdas, by Govind's daughter-in-law, Kamla. This first meal must be eaten early so they can work in the fields in the cool of the morning before the sun is high.

Slowly, they chew the food. Govind does not expect that this day will be different from any other day. He hopes for little and expects less.

Within the pattern of his life, we can learn much about life in rural India today.

Govind and his family live in the small village of Sehbasu in the upper Ganges Valley.

Life in this village and many other villages of India has not changed significantly for thousands of years.

Each morning the father and his son travel the dry dirt roads between their home and their fields.

With each passing minute, the heat of the sun grows more intense. With primitive tools, with little or no knowledge of modern agriculture, the Indian farmer struggles against famine and drought.

Ramdas plows his fields using the same wooden-tipped plow that his father and his father before him used.

Despite his labors, his land yields little. He scratches at the dry, barren soil . . . and in the end his harvest is meager.

One out of every seven persons in the world is Indian.

Every month, there are one million new mouths to be fed.

It is on farms like this that the struggle for food in India must be met.

The image of the farmer plowing effectively communicates India's lack of modern farm equipment and agricultural know-how. In addition, each paragraph of the narrative gives information *not* contained in the visual images

* From *India: The Struggle for Food,* courtesy of McGraw-Hill Book Company.

and at the same time supports the mood of the film. For example, the description of the farmer's dedication to tradition adds an element of hopelessness to the scene and enriches the meaning of the film for the viewer.

Voice-over tracks can also be used in direct relationship to picture. It is important to examine the *physical* placement of voice-over sound in relationship to the picture it accompanies. The film editor is usually responsible for aligning the voice track with the film. If the information carried by the track is direct, the track is usually laid in a few frames behind the key element in the scene. Generally, this type of voice-over sound is simply descriptive.

The voice track, however, can be used in a far more interesting and complex relationship to picture. In the opening scenes of *Hiroshima, Mon Amour*, the dialogue begins as direct on-camera dialogue between the man and woman in bed. It then becomes directly descriptive voice-over sound supporting the very strong scenes of the A-bomb holocaust in Hiroshima. The museum and the hospital are identified by the voice-over track on a one-to-one basis. The following is an excerpt from the opening scenes of this film.*

> SHE: The hospital, for instance, I saw it. I'm sure I did. There is a hospital in Hiroshima. How could I help seeing it?
>
> (*The hospital, hallways, stairs, patients, the camera coldly objective. [We never see her seeing.] Then we come back to the hand gripping—and not letting go of—the darker shoulder.*)
>
> HE: You did not see the hospital in Hiroshima. You saw nothing in Hiroshima.
>
> (*Then the woman's voice becomes more . . . more impersonal. Shots of the museum. The same blinding light, the same ugly light here as at the hospital. Explanatory signs, pieces of evidence from the bombardment, scale models, mutilated iron, skin, burned hair, wax models, etc.*)
>
> SHE: Four times at the museum . . .
>
> HE: What museum in Hiroshima?
>
> SHE: Four times at the museum in Hiroshima. I saw people walking around. The people walk around, lost in thought, among the photographs, the reconstructions, for want of something else, among the photographs, the photographs, the reconstructions, for want of something else, the explanations, for want of something else.
>
> Four times at the museum in Hiroshima.
>
> I looked at the people. I myself looked thoughtfully at the iron. The burned iron. The broken iron, the iron made vulnerable as flesh. I saw the bouquet of bottle caps: who would have suspected that? Human skin floating, surviving, still in the bloom of its agony. Stones. Burned stones. Shattered stones. Anonymous heads of hair that the women of Hiroshima, when they awoke in the morning, discovered had fallen out.
>
> I was hot at Peace Square. Ten thousand degrees at Peace Square. I

* From *Hiroshima, Mon Amour*, text by Marguerite Duras for the film by Alain Resnais, trans. by Richard Seaver (New York: Grove Press, Inc., 1961), pp. 15–18. Copyright © 1961 by Grove Press, Inc. Reprinted by permission of Grove Press, Inc.

know it. The temperature of the sun at Peace Square. How can you not know it? . . . The grass, it's quite simple. . . .

HE: You saw nothing in Hiroshima. Nothing.

(*More shots of the museum. Then a shot of Peace Square taken with a burned skull in the foreground. Glass display cases with burned models inside. Newsreel shots of Hiroshima.*)

Throughout the sequence, the voices continue conversing with no break in rhythm—with no concession, as it were, to their narrative purpose. The conventional editing procedure is reversed: images are edited in flow to match dialogue. The entire film, picture and sound, moves forward in a perfect rhythm that engulfs the audience.

The voices, which exist on many levels, come and go as they are needed and supply direct information concerning the visual images. At the same time, the relentless flow of conversation between the lovers provides the *external cadence* (the metronome, so to speak) by which the film is propelled.

Thus even direct voice tracks can serve many purposes. And the way they are used often determines the difference between an old-fashioned didactic motion picture, replete with descriptive narrative, and a film in which the spoken word enhances the entire work.

Indirect use of voice tracks   In indirect voice-over, the track serves a more complex purpose than that of description. It contributes an emotional value either consistent with or in counterpoint to what is seen. Often this type of voice-over sound has little or no relationship to what is being seen.

Robert Altman frequently uses indirect voice-over tracks. One of the most effective segments in his black comedy *M*A*S*H* takes place in the operating room of a mobile army hospital during the Korean War. Altman shows the chaotic bustle in the hospital tent—the grim parade of medics rushing in and out with wounded and dying soldiers. Accompanying these grizzly shots of the wounded men is the steady stream of casual banter between the surgeons and nurses. The result is a grotesquely comic blend of image and sound—the camera capturing one thing, the sound track another. The cumulative effect is highly ingenius filmmaking.

Narration too can be effectively employed in an indirect manner. Instead of describing the action, the narrative may proceed on an independent course but at the same time add to the impact and meaning of the visual images. The following narrative, from a recent documentary film on health care, was used to accompany shots of a group of healthy children playing in a park.

NARRATOR: We are a nation of over 200 million people.

Each year we suffer 396 million acute illnesses.

Each of us will spend 15 days of restricted activity a year . . . an average of six days in bed.

One-half of our population has suffered a chronic illness.

Thirteen countries in the world have a lower infant mortality rate than we do.

One person in ten requires treatment for a mental disorder. Fully one-half of of our hospital beds are being used by psychiatric patients.

The shadow of mental illness reaches into the lives of one family in three.

Almost two million of us die each year . . . two-thirds from cancer, heart disease, and stroke.

The contrast between sound and image was extremely effective and served to strengthen both elements.

Although it is far more common to photograph and edit a film and then prepare the narrative, a narrative track is sometimes prepared first and oblique or symbolic images shot *to* it. The final eighteen minutes of Joseph Strick's film of Joyce's *Ulysses* consist primarily of the famous "Molly Bloom soliloquy." The images that accompany this recitation, delivered by the fine British actress Barbara Jefford, create a stunning combination of direct and indirect relationships. At times the images quite literally portray what is being said in the narrative; at other times symbolic shots are used. In this example, the words of the narrative controlled the director's choice of images, and the pace of the narrative informed the final editing.

There are, then, two basic uses of voice tracks. Each is important and each can add a particular value to the whole. Every element of sound has an important role to play and must never be considered a subordinate or secondary contributor to the art of the motion picture.

Creative use of sound effects

It is common practice among filmmakers to add sound effects to cover everything seen on screen. Such use of sound needs little elaboration: a long shot of a city street — the lid on a garbage pail falling to the pavement — *crash* — add sound of metal against concrete. In this way the sense of reality, of place, is heightened. This is a direct use of sound, and it is usually designed to get the audience to believe the *mise en scène*.

There are several ways to enlarge and enrich this standard use of sound effects. For example, a careful selection of the *quality* of the sound effect is very important. If the above scene takes place at dusk and the film seeks to convey a mood of mystery, foreboding, and gloom, the sound of the lid can be given a slight reverberation. If the purpose of the scene is to startle or frighten the audience, volume can be added beyond normal reality. To create an effective FX (sound effects) track, the editor must make a *qualitative* evaluation of each sound as it relates to the action seen on screen. Too often, the FX track is regarded as "icing on the cake" or a finishing touch, but in reality it is one of the most important tracks in the final mix.

The sound effects track can also be used to extend the dimension of what is seen. As discussed in detail earlier, the filmmaker uses extended images to project people and objects beyond the periphery of the frame. The extended image removes the constrictive boundaries of film. The creative use of sound effects can add to and reinforce this objective. The filmmaker simply adds sounds that originate from elements *not contained in the frame*. For example, in a Western, on a lonely street at dawn just before the gunfight, the offscreen sound of a dog barking heightens the isolation of the participants and at the same time enlarges the boundaries of the frame—we can visualize the dog though the camera does not show it.

In discussing his film *Here at the Water's Edge*, the great documentarian Leo Hurwitz expounded a valid approach to film sound. He pointed out that many of the sounds we hear every day originate from *unseen* sources. These sounds, moreover, give us our sense of environment. Thus there is no reason to restrict film to sounds originating from *seen* sources. Alfred Hitchcock was an early exponent of the use of offscreen sound effects. He frequently uses sounds from beyond the frame to heighten and increase the terror of his suspense sequences. No visual clues are needed. The impact of a scene can be heightened by sound effects totally unrelated to what is on screen. For example, in a scene in a jail cell, we hear only the wings of a bat beating a furious rhythm against its body. Where? Somewhere nearby. This sound in itself makes the cell seem more gloomy and dank.

Bergman is a master in the use of offscreen sound effects to create mood. The sound effects in the opening sequence of *The Magician* add "atmosphere" to the woods through which the coach is riding. Creaking wood, croaking frogs, strange bird sounds, wind, hooves against the wet ground, all communicate the mood of the film and deepen the audience's perception of Bergman's theme—truth and illusion. Study the following script description of this sequence* and try to imagine a fully realized sound effects track— direct and indirect—that would contribute to the success of the sequence.

On a summer evening pregnant with thunder in July of the year 1846, a large coach stops beside a road just south of Stockholm. The hot sun slants down mercilessly on the marshes, the forest and the black clouds in the eastern sky.

Four travelers sit around the coach. The fifth—a small, bent old woman —walks around poking in the ground, as if searching for something.

The coachman, who is the youngest in the group, has just returned from the forest with water for the horses. Near the coach step sits a big redhaired man, eating ham. His lunchbox is open beside him.

A little to the side, by themselves, the other two sit. One is a tall, thin man with a pale face, straight black hair, a beard and black eyebrows. Bareheaded, he is dressed in a dusty traveling suit and smokes a short

* From *The Magician*, text and film by Ingmar Bergman, in *Four Screenplays of Ingmar Bergman*, trans. by Lars Malmstrom and David Kushner (New York: Simon and Schuster, Inc., 1960), pp. 245–46. Reprinted by permission of the publisher and Janus Films.

pipe, which he lights continuously. The other, smaller in height, rather delicate, also dressed in a traveling suit, seems more a boy than a man.

The coach is heavily laden with boxes and crates; it looks comfortable enough but has seen better days. The horses are strong but not very well groomed. Now the little old woman has dug a hole in the ground with a stick. She kneels and searches in the hole with her hand, looks rather satisfied, fishes up something which can best be described as a black stone. She looks carefully over her shoulder to see if the others are watching, but when no one seems to be taking notice she puts her find in a small leather bag she carries.

A remarkably large magpie stares at the old woman. She becomes angry and holds the bag close to her. The magpie remains there and sneers scornfully. The old woman spits on the ground and rushes away.

The sun burns down on the edge of the forest and it is very quiet. The travelers step into the coach while the coachman climbs up to the coach box and shouts at the horses. The coach springs creak and sigh as the heavy vehicle slowly sways up onto the narrow, rutted road.

In the forest, sunbeams tremble in the trees like hurled spears, but the twilight is heavy.

The big man — the one who was eating — grins good-humoredly as he picks his teeth. The old woman draws her breath and coughs for a moment.

The most important uses of sound effects are (1) to strengthen a sense of reality, of "being there," and (2) to enlarge the boundaries of what is seen. The sound effects track should be a major artistic factor among the elements that make up the finished film.

One of the finest examples of the total use of sound effects is the famous "island search" sequence in Antonioni's *L'Avventura*. The sequence begins on a note of idle pleasure. A boating party leaves their yacht and wanders over a small, rocky island. Suddenly, one of the party — an attractive, bored young girl — is missing. At first, her absence is interpreted as a joke, but slowly an apprehension for her safety develops. This gives way to hysteria as all members of the group clamber over the rocks in a desperate search. A priceless antique vase is found and carelessly dropped; the vase shatters against the rocks. The missing girl's lover begins to make love to her best friend. Slowly, inexorably, the entire purpose of the search is forgotten as the quest for per-personal gratification and pleasure is resumed. All these events are supported by a filmy gray photography that makes the island a kind of nether world.

A key factor in the success of this sequence is the brilliant use of sound effects. The waves crash against the rocks and rise in a crescendo as the mood of the sequence changes. Although we do not always see the waves on screen, we *hear* them constantly, beating a cacophony that at times becomes unbearable. The voices of the party come and go, shouting the name of the missing girl and calling the names of others in the party. Bits and pieces of dialogue float through an aural haze. The result is an almost symphonic orchestration of sound effects in support of the dramatic action. The emptiness of the lives of the people is clearly delineated by the sound effects—the ceaseless roar of waves beating senselessly on stone.

The art of film music

From the moment the first note was struck on the tinny piano that accompanied the silent film, music has been a constant companion of the film image. For the most part, music has been used in direct support of the on-screen action, supplying mood and pace. Allowing for variations in talent and taste, film music has traditionally been employed in the following ways:

(1) *To accompany the main titles of the film.* A main-title background theme can vary from a satiric pop tune (such as "Suicide Is Painless," the theme from *M*A*S*H*, which sets the tone for the black comedy that follows) to a grandiose, orchestrated piece (such as Handel's "Hallelujah Chorus," which accompanies the main titles of *Viridiana*).

(2) *To heighten the dramatic effect.* A piece of "musical commentary" is often used to complement a scene. For example, in Stanley Kubrick's *2001: A Space Odyssey* the use of Strauss's *Thus Spake Zarathustra* to accompany the "Dawn of Man" prologue does much to enhance the elemental power of the scenes. In *Gone with the Wind,* the title theme is employed in a dozen different orchestrations and tempos to vary mood and elicit a specific audience reaction. The uses of this type of musical accompaniment are endless.

(3) *To give a sense of locale.* The most familiar use of "locale" music is the standard Western theme, replete with pretentious orchestration and "outdoor" feeling (for example, Ferde Grofé's *Grand Canyon Suite*). Another example is the "foreign theme," which establishes the national or ethnic subject of the film (for example, a mandolin playing "O Sole Mio" as a scene shifts to Naples, or an orchestrated adaptation of "Old Man River" accompanying a cut to a riverboat on the Mississippi). Included also are the sophisticated band music that accompanies nightclub montages and the wheezy calliope music that accompanies circus or carnival scenes.

(4) *To create or support pace and movement.* Here the tail wags the dog. The music is established first and the scenes move to the rhythm of the orchestration. In *Doctor Zhivago,* the beautiful "passage of time" sequence following the reunion of the lovers—a series of "meeting" scenes in different locales, one dissolving into another—is paced by Maurice Jarre's theme music for the film. A fast-moving piece of jazz music that accompanies a chase sequence can often determine the pace of the editing.

(5) *To identify character qualities.* Here again, the music provides the audience with clues as to "who's who" in the film. Throughout the 1930s and 1940s, film music was used to blatantly *announce* character—the villain through minor-key music with sinister low-octave overtones; the heroine through ethereal sounds of violins in the distance; the hero through strong "honest" music.

(6) *To predict things to come.* Important in the traditional use of film music is the "subtle" musical announcement of what lies ahead. In the 1939 film *Dark Victory*, the heroine (Bette Davis) is dying of an incurable brain tumor. Each time plans are made for the future, an ominous chord is struck, clearly notifying the audience that for Miss Davis there will be no future. This type of musical "telegraph" was used as recently as 1973, in *Butterflies Are Free*, a sentimental story of a blind youth.

(7) *To establish, maintain, and change mood.* This, of course, is the most obvious and traditional use of music. Since the art of music is centered around the transmission of emotions through sound, music is an ideal instrument to establish, heighten, maintain, and change mood throughout a film. A gracious, romantic theme accompanying a love scene may suddenly give way to more ominous music, thereby changing the mood of the scene although nothing changes *on screen.* A scene of joy and laughter can be materially altered by a sad and foreboding musical accompaniment. The music, in effect, warns the audience not to be deceived by what is happening on screen.

These are the most common uses of film music. They will probably persist for quite a time. However, a number of more exciting and creative uses of music are now beginning to appear.

Use of musical themes Although there is nothing startlingly new about establishing a musical theme and using it throughout a film, this use of film music has grown in subtlety and creativity. Fellini's first major artistic success, *La Strada*, described in Chapter 2, uses a musical theme most effectively.

The musical theme associated with Gelsomina is a simple melody played on a circus trumpet (such as that used by Zampano and later by Gelsomina). In the joyous moments of discovery early in the film, this theme has a buoyant quality that suggests the internal awakening of Gelsomina. When she is happy in her relationship with Zampano, the theme is played more slowly and takes on a romantic quality. At the end of the film, the theme becomes the means by which Zampano discovers Gelsomina's death. Time has passed. Zampano, wandering through a town, hears the theme being sung. At first he thinks the voice is Gelsomina; then he sees that it is a woman hanging out wash. The woman tells Zampano that she learned the theme from Gelsomina, and that Gelsomina has died. The theme is heard again on the plaintive trumpet, and it becomes the messenger of a deep sadness that reaches the audience.

René Clément's *Les Jeux Interdits (Forbidden Games)* also uses a repetitive musical theme to link visual elements together. This theme, played on a guitar, is associated with the little girl who is the heroine of the film. The child's parents are killed by German planes, and she becomes involved in a macabre infatuation with death.

Claude LeLouche's *A Man and a Woman* relies heavily on the use of its now well-known title theme. This theme not only sets the romantic tone for all the meetings of the two lovers, but, since a large portion of the film carries no dialogue, it actually sets the pace and becomes the major element of communication on the sound track.

Costa Gavras in both *Z* and *State of Siege* uses highly dramatic theme music composed by Theodaraxis. The themes return over and over again during the suspense or action sequences and in *Z* the music creates its own force and momentum that helps to propel the film.

Today, film music is used in refined and subtle ways. Audiences no longer accept the heavy-handed "soap opera" music of the past. A modern musical theme must have distinction as music. When played separately, it may have an entirely different quality from that which it imparts as *film music*. The key here is that the relationship between film and music need not be obvious. A romantic scene, for example, can be subtly juxtaposed against mysterious music. The overall effect will be totally different from that of either music or image.

Music and movement   The recurrent thematic music in Alain Resnais' *Hiroshima, Mon Amour* consists in large measure of a rhythmic melody written by Giovanni Fusco. The theme is established in the opening sequence of the film. It has a motion of its own and a rhythmic undercarriage, and it is frequently tied to Resnais' favorite technique—a flowing, mobile camera. Near the end of the film, the heroine flees the teahouse where she has been reliving the past with her Japanese lover. He pursues her. As the camera moves with her, the music sets the pace and at the same time evokes in the audience a clear memory of all the torment that the woman has suffered. Since the theme is used throughout the film to signal movement, we expect movement in this scene. As the theme begins, we are ready for the night flight. In addition, the music provides us with instant memory, recapturing all the scenes in which it was previously heard. The pace of the actors, the movement of the camera, the *rhythm* of the cuts from scene to scene—all seem dictated and maintained by the music, which retains its own integrity. The mood of this sequence is thus evoked as much by the music as by any other element.

Indirect use of music   In all the above examples, the mood of the scene changes with the music. A piece of music often has changes of pace and mood built into it. Indeed, this is considered a prime necessity of *good* music for film. If a mood changes radically within a sequence, or from sequence to sequence, the filmmaker will usually dissolve, or *segue*, to another piece of music. This technique, however, is being modified as leading artists experiment with more *indirect* uses of music. In his masterpiece *Through a Glass Darkly*, Bergman employs a single piece of classical music, the Bach Cello

Suite #2. It is used sparingly throughout the film and is not employed in direct relationship to what is seen. The music itself is dark and strangely beautiful. It evokes in the audience a sense of the grandeur and awesomeness of the kingdom of heaven. But it is not without foreboding and threat. Bergman uses the music intact, and he makes no attempt to fit the film to the music. He simply permits each element to go its own way. The result is fascinating: although used only a few times, the music imparts its dark and awesome character to the entire film. Each time the bleak opening notes are sounded, a chill goes through the audience, and something of the schizophrenic world of the daughter is revealed. The music achieves this by its very nature and is used only in an oblique relationship to the action on screen. Yet the effect is as though a funeral procession had passed a block away from a Mardi Gras celebration, adding its own somber character to the festivities.

The Swedish film *Elvira Madigan*, mentioned earlier for its fine long-lens photography, utilizes Mozart's Piano Concerto #21 in much the same manner. There is little obvious consistency as to when or how the music is used. The music just seems to come and go at random, but it imparts a romantic beauty quite consistent with the film's theme and execution.

The Graduate, which goes even further in the indirect use of music, deserves careful study. The music consists primarily of three songs written by Paul Simon and Art Garfunkel. These pieces, "The Sounds of Silence," "Scarborough Fair/Canticle," and "April Come She Will," were composed and recorded before the film was made. They were *not* written for the film.

The mood of the songs is stated in the lyrics, with their heavy overtones of alienation and isolation. The lyrics of the song that accompanies the main titles of the film are as follows:*

> Hello Darkness my old friend,
> I've come to talk with you again,
> Because a vision softly creeping,
> Left its seeds while I was sleeping,
> And the vision that was planted in my brain
> Still remains within the sound of silence.
>
> In restless dreams I walked alone
> Narrow streets of cobblestone,
> 'Neath the halo of a street lamp,
> I turned my collar to the cold and damp
> When my eyes were stabbed by the flash of a neon light
> That split the night
> And touched the sound of silence.
>
> And in the naked light I saw
> Ten thousand people maybe more.
> People talking without speaking,
> People hearing without listening,
> People writing songs that voices never share
> And no one dare disturb the sound of silence.

* "The Sounds of Silence" by Paul Simon. Copyright © 1964, 1965 by Charing Cross Music.

"Fools!" said I, "You do not know
Silence like a cancer grows.
Hear my words that I might teach you,
Take my arms that I might reach you."
But my words like silent raindrops fell,
And echoed in the wells of silence.

And the people bowed and prayed
To the neon god they made.
And the sign flashed out its warning.
In the words that it was forming.
And the signs said "The words of the prophets are
    written on the subway walls
And tenement halls"
And whisper'd in the sounds of silence.

There is no *direct* relationship between this song and the scenes it accompanies. It is used in the opening scenes — a series of extreme closeups of the leading character, Benjamin Braddock, walking through the Los Angeles airport and into the street. It is later used to provide continuity for a series of scenes in which Benjamin pursues his affair with his girlfriend's mother, Mrs. Robinson. In these scenes, which take place over a period of several weeks, Benjamin alternates between idle time at home and trysts in a hotel room with Mrs. Robinson. The music, with its highly communicative lyrics and elaborate guitar and rhythm scores, proceeds continuously and independently of the action of the film. The song is used several other times in the film and in the final scene.

The key to this use of music is that it expands the meaning and emotional content of the scenes. The songs in *The Graduate* do not simply accompany the film; they are an equal partner to it and add specific qualities of their own.

Lindsay Anderson's recent film *O, Lucky Man!* provides an example of how a sound track can alternate between direct and indirect relationships to the film images. The film was conceived as an epic satire of the capitalist success story, as revealed through the struggles of an ambitious but hapless young innocent (Malcolm McDowell). The form of the film is episodic: the hero's efforts to make his fortune are presented through a great number of brief vignettes separated from each other by "black-outs" (momentary periods of total blackness on the screen). The musical sound track consists of a group of rock songs written for the film by Alan Price. The songs, in keeping with the intent of the film, have somewhat satirical lyrics that are underscored by up-tempo rock rhythms. However, the songs do not always correspond directly to the scenes they accompany — at times the songs mesh with the images being shown, while at other times they provide ironic counterpoint related not to the on-screen action but to the ideas inherent in that action. Because the story is composed of so many episodic fragments, the songs also serve as bridges to hold together all the bits of the film's action.

Another example of an effective music track is the banjo accompaniment in *Bonnie and Clyde*. This simple musical idea achieves several positive results: it adds to the satiric aspects of the film, keeps the audience in a mood of laughter until the scenes of horror and violence, and evokes the mood of the thirties in an "old-time movie" vein.

Music, in itself a major art form, is also an important factor in the creation of the motion picture. The successful integration of music and filmed images creates *film music* and greatly enriches the complex tapestry of film.

Silence

The final element of sound is *silence*. When skillfully used, absolute silence can carry more impact than a dozen tympani crashing in unison. One of the most memorable examples of the creative use of silence occurs in Jules Dassin's famous suspense film *Rififi*. During the climax of the film, the burglary sequence, not a single sound is heard. The impact of this silence mounts with each movement, until the suspense is almost unbearable. The use of silence here is not a gimmick: the success of the burglary depends entirely on the ability of the thieves to function without making a single sound.

Silence has been effectively employed in many modern films. By eliminating all footfalls from the sound track of *The Silence*, Bergman transmitted a feeling of horror to the halls of the strange hotel. The shriek of the reed instrument that heralds the death of the daughter in Satyajit Ray's *Pather Panchali* is preceded by a moment of absolute silence. The shattering outburst of guns in the finale of *Bonnie and Clyde* is also preceded by silence as Bonnie and Clyde Barrow gaze at each other. The impact of the sound that follows is multiplied tenfold by this use of dead track.

These are the basic elements from which the sound track of a film is created. The careful and creative use of each element, and the skillful blending at the final mix, are essential to the artistic success of the film.

FILMS FOR STUDY

L'Avventura, Michelangelo Antonioni. Janus Films, 24 West 58th Street, New York, New York 10019.

The Language of Faces, John Korty, Contemporary Films, McGraw-Hill Book Company, 330 West 42 Street, New York, New York 10036.

Citizen Kane, Orson Welles. Janus Films, 24 West 58 Street, New York, New York 10019.

Forbidden Games, René Clément. Janus Films, 24 West 58 Street, New York, New York 10019.

Through a Glass Darkly, Ingmar Bergman. Janus Films, 24 West 58 Street, New York, New York 10019.

Dylan Thomas. Janus Films, 24 West 58 Street, New York, New York 10019.

Wings to Japan. Pan American World Airways, 200 Park Avenue, New York, New York 10017.

India: Urban Conditions; India: The Struggle for Food. McGraw-Hill Book Company, 330 West 42 Street, New York, New York 10036.

SUPPLEMENTARY READING

Happé, L. Bernard, *Basic Motion Picture Technology.* New York: Hastings House, 1971.

Nisbett, Alec, *The Technique of the Sound Studio.* New York: Hastings House, 1970.

Tremaine, Howard M., *Audio Cyclopedia.* Indianapolis: Howard M. Sams, 1969.

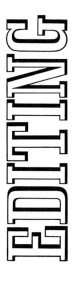

EDITING

FOUR

We'll save it in editing. . . . Though true of James Cruze, Griffith, Stroheim, this maxim was hardly any longer true of Murnau, Chaplin, and becomes irretrievably untrue with sound film. Why? Because in a film such as October *(and still more so with* Qué Viva México) *editing is above all the supreme touch of direction. The two cannot be separated without rhythm and melody. Elena, just as Mr. Aradkin, is a model of editing because each in its class is a model of directing. . . .*

"We will save it in editing," is, then, a typical producer's statement. The most that good editing will bring to a film otherwise devoid of all interest is precisely, first, the impression of having been directed. It will restore to the lifelike the ephemeral grace which the snob and amateur disregard; or it will transform chance into destiny. Is there greater praise than that the public rightly confuses editing with cutting?

Jean-Luc Godard
"Montage, Mon Beau Souci,"
in *Film Culture*, No. 22–23 (Summer 1961),
pp. 37–38. Originally published in
Cahiers du Cinéma.

The very essence of film, that which makes film unique . . . is the rhythm, or intuitive putting together of the pieces of film. I have never yet seen a movie that I enjoyed that was ineptly or crudely cut. This enjoyment is not simply a question of speed or slickness. Rather I should compare good montage with good style—as in, for instance, a poem where the style evolves from the choice of words in relation to the poem's music or meter.

John Bernard Meyers
"A Letter to Gregory Battcock,"
in *The New American Cinema*,
ed. by Gregory Battcock
(New York: Dutton, 1967), p. 139.

O NE OF THE MANY ASPECTS OF FILM IS THE FACT THAT IT IS SUBJECT TO SEVERAL "beginnings." At least three times on the road to completion a film is reevaluated and often remade. First, the film is conceived in the mind of the writer. A script is written. At that moment, the whole film exists — on paper — as a completed work. Then, the director takes the work and transfers it from paper to film. In doing so, the director is "making the film." Whether he follows the script rigidly or strays a long distance from it, the director applies the cinematic art in transferring the basic material from paper to screen. Once the scenes have been photographed and the sound tracks recorded, the third major creative act of filmmaking takes place — film editing.

THE MECHANICS OF FILM EDITING

Editing is in many ways a new beginning, a reevaluation of everything that has gone before. On a purely mechanical level, the editing process is not difficult or complicated. At the time of photography, each scene and each sound track is identified by a simple code number. The scenes are numbered in order, from the beginning of the script to the end. The *master number* covers the basic or central action. Any *coverage* (or variation) given the master scene — through camera movement, change of camera position, or change of lens — is assigned a letter designation. Thus, if scene 32 is the master scene, 32A, 32B, and 32C are details or variations of that scene. Successive take numbers are assigned each time a scene is shot. If scene 32 is shot three times from the same camera position, the code numbers will appear as follows: scene 32 take 1, scene 32 take 2, scene 32 take 3.

When a scene is photographed with sync sound, a sound number is also added for purposes of identification. Each "sound take" is given a successive number.

The following are some sample codings:

Scene 1 take 1 sound 1 identifies the first scene in the film on its first run-through, shot with sync sound.

Scene 1A take 2 sound 2 identifies an insert (such as a close-up) for scene 1 shot for the second time, also with sync sound.

Scene 2 take 1 sound 3 identifies the second scene in the film shot for the first time, also with sync sound.

Scene 2A take 4 identifies an insert for scene 2 shot for the fourth time, *without* sound.

109

Scene 2B take 1 sound 4 identifies another insert for scene 2 shot for the first time, *with* sync sound. (*Note:* Since the preceding insert has no sound, the next sound number is applied to the sound accompanying this scene.)

This system of coding was developed primarily for the convenience of the film editor. It enables him to match scenes with sound and to place sound and picture in proper order prior to actual editing.

The editing process begins even before the editor receives the film. If a scene is shot several times, the director will order a print of only those takes that he wants the editor to work with. In a sense, he is editing the film. If a scene is shot four times, for example, the director may choose only takes 2 and 4. The editor will never see or work with takes 1 and 3. After the director has made his selection, the process of film editing begins.

The steps in film editing are as follows:

(1) A duplicate print of the scenes selected by the director is made from the original film. The duplicate is a cheap, low-quality print and is used by the editor for working purposes only. This is called a *work print.*

(2) A duplicate sound track of all the sound from the selected scenes plus all sound that is recorded "wild" (without accompanying picture) is made from the original tracks. These are called *work tracks.*

(3) The editor aligns the scenes photographed with sync sound. He then assembles all scenes and sound in the order of the original script. Usually, the editor and director view this assemblage and exchange opinions on how best to edit the film.

(4) The editor runs the film through a machine that permits him to view picture and listen to sound separately or synchronously. He arranges and juxtaposes those takes that he feels will create the most effective film. His first draft is called a *rough cut.* Traditionally the Moviola (Figure 1A) was the editing machine in greatest use in the filmmaking industry. Recently, however, a variety of tabletop editing devices such as the Kem (Fig. 1B), the Steenbeck, and the Moviola tabletop editing machines have come onto the market. Because they are easier to use and combine all editing equipment into a single machine, they now threaten to make the Moviola obsolete. One of the greatest advantages of these tabletop editing consoles is the fact that the work print does not have to be separated into individual scenes but can be kept in large rolls to be viewed and selected as needed.

(5) After the director has commented on the rough cut, the editor refines his first draft and completes what he considers to be the best version of the film. This is called a *fine cut.*

(6) The editor adds all the major supportive elements—narration and

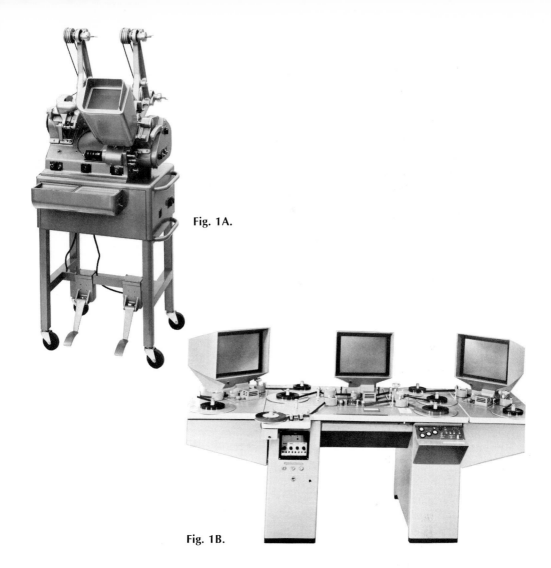

Fig. 1A.

Fig. 1B.

voice-over tracks, sound effects, and music — and orders his optical effects from the optical laboratory. This completes the editorial process. (Normally, the editor also supervises the sound mix.)

(7) The work print is now used as a blueprint to which the original film — untouched since photography — is matched. The original film and the sound mix track are then sent to the laboratory where the final composite (picture and track) prints are made.

This description of the mechanics of editing gives only a basic outline of the immensely complex art of film editing. The film editor's contribution is as crucial to the quality of the finished film as any other factor in the filmmaking process.

THE ART OF FILM EDITING

Film editing begins when the editor is given a script to read and analyze. As mentioned above, each day on set the director chooses several takes of each scene and orders a print made of these takes. Editor and director then view the selected takes, called *rushes* or *dailies*, and determine how the finished film should look and sound. During this screening, the editor gets his first glimpse of the film. As he looks over all the elements that the director has given him, he considers the following points:

(1) *Variety of coverage.* From how many angles and viewpoints has the director photographed the scene?

(2) *Quality of performance.* From which angle or in which take or section of the scene is performance most effective?

(3) *Number of supportive elements available.* How many silent "detail" shots are included? What additional "atmosphere" sound is available? What else in the way of image and sound has the director provided in support of the scene?

As the editor views the footage, he forms his own ideas as to the most effective way to assemble the material. He eliminates those scenes, angles, and sections of film that are obviously substandard and works with the best (in his own judgment) of what was shot and recorded. Some directors maintain an authoritarian control of the editing process; often, however, the editor is left on his own during this stage. As he works with the material, running the film back and forth in the Moviola, he formulates and imposes his own esthetic judgments on the film. In this process, he functions as a creative artist.

The film editor's role is distinct from that of the director or cameraman. The director deals with structure and performance, with mood and philosophical ideas; the cameraman deals with composition and light, with images that move and change. The editor, however, is concerned with the following elements: (1) time, (2) rhythm and pace, and (3) visual and aural relationships.

Time

As we view a motion picture; we are, for the time spent in the darkened theater, totally under the influence of the film we are watching. In two hours, one film may cover a lifetime; another, only ten minutes. Arthur Penn's film *Little Big Man* spans almost one hundred years in the life of the leading character and *The Godfather* gives the audience several years of action and events in the life of its leading figure, Don Corleone. We sense the passage of time, watching Corleone's son grow older and change before our eyes. On the other hand, the award-winning French short subject based on Ambrose Bierce's

Incident at Owl Creek Bridge expands the action of a split second (the moment a man is hanged) into a thirty-minute motion picture.

Time is the dominant factor in the art of editing. The editor, in effect, controls time. He can so extend a scene that action supposedly taking place in one minute will feel like an hour; and he can, by means of fragmented flash-cutting, compress an hour's action into a minute.

An early example of the ability of the film editor to manipulate time is the famous sequence on the steps of Odessa in Eisenstein's *Potemkin*. This sequence has been much studied and copied by other filmmakers. The action itself, the people of Odessa running up the steps into the guns of the Czarist soldiers, actually takes place in a few minutes. But because of the many "detail shots" cut into the action — feet, faces, guns, and falling bodies — the sequence seems to go on for a much longer period of time.

An excellent example of the film editor's total control of time is the editorial architecture of the final sequence of *Bonnie and Clyde*. The ambush is prepared. Bonnie and Clyde agree to assist the old man with his car. The action seems to proceed at a snail's pace because of the many detail shots edited into the sequence. The basic action, if allowed to run without interruption, would happen briefly and quickly. The editor, however, continually intercuts other shots: the bushes behind which the police hide, trees, birds flying by, and faces. Finally, just before the dénouement, there is a superb extension of time — the exchange of looks between Bonnie and Clyde, held just a beat or two too long and suspending the audience for what seems to be forever. This is followed by a fusillade of gunfire that also goes on and on. Nothing in the sequence takes place in realistic time duration. Everything is manipulated for effect. Throughout the sequence, the film editor controls time on an absolute scale, accelerating or retarding it to achieve a desired end.

The film editor controls time in two ways: (1) by expanding or contracting the normal time of an action through the use of intercuts, and (2) by using optical effects to link scenes and sequences.

The use of intercuts   By using a single intercut, the editor can eliminate large segments of time from the action. For example, at a key moment in a fast-moving dialogue scene, the leading character gets up and walks across the room to get a glass of water. If the editor feels that this pause slows down the pace, he simply adds a close-up of someone watching the walker. The intercut of the face can be shown on screen for a split second, followed by a shot of the leading character already at the water cooler (thereby eliminating the entire walk). We accept this artificial tampering with time because we are involved in the action. The shift of attention produced by the intercut distracts us momentarily, and we are no longer able to judge how much time the walk should take. We accept the unreal acceleration of time simply because it is done. The man is already at the water cooler — our eyes do not lie.

Conversely, if the editor wishes to retard the pace of the action, he can insert a sequence of intercuts that actually uses up more screen time than the offscreen walk to the water cooler could possibly take. Again, because we are momentarily distracted by the intercuts, we do not question this manipulation of time.

This type of manipulation is like a cinematic "shell game." We see only what the editor wishes us to see, whatever he chooses to put on screen. Since we cannot judge offscreen action in terms of elapsed time, the editor becomes the sole arbiter of the time of such action. Thus the editor is in complete control of the time of a scene or sequence. When his selection of intercuts is skillful and well handled, the audience is completely in his hands.

From our own experience we know how long it usually takes a person to mount a flight of stairs. If we view this action through a single shot, the time element is totally within our own experience. The scene is simply a shot of a man mounting steps. Once the film editor begins to manipulate such a scene, however, we become subject to an artificially created time segment. For example, if the editor fragments the scene by adding carefully selected shots that are slowly and languidly paced, the normal time sequence will begin to expand. Columns A and B, shown below, represent two ways to edit this scene. Each creates a totally different sense of elapsed time.

In example A, the normal flow of time is retarded. The action is constantly interrupted—we are taken away from the main action and presented with shots that are in themselves static in character. Each time we return to the main action, the man has not advanced sufficiently to account for the time that our attention was diverted. Thus time is expanded.

A	B
Long shot: Man ascending stairs	*Close-up:* Feet mounting stairs
Close-up: Feet mounting stairs	*Close-up:* Hand sliding up banister
Close-up: Clock	*Close-up:* Face
Close-up: Candles burning	*Long-shot:* Man halfway up
Medium shot: Face	*Close-up:* Feet
Close-up: Hand gripping banister	*Askew angle shot:* Man coming at camera
Long shot: Man continuing to climb	*Long shot:* Man at top of stairs
Reverse angle shot: Man viewed from above	
Close-up: Feet	
Medium shot: Face	
Close-up: Clock	
Close-up: Candles flickering	
Slow dolly shot following the man	

In example B, fewer intercuts are used, and they simply cover gaps in the main action. When we return to the main action, the man has advanced much farther than he possibly could have during the short time of the intercuts. In addition, the sharp angle of the intercuts heightens the pace of the central action. Thus time is compressed.

There are few general rules concerning the way time can be manipulated. Editing is largely an intuitive process. The editor simply cuts a scene until it "feels" right. He is bound by no rules other than the very pragmatic one, *Does it work?*

The film editor should also recognize that every image has its own "feeling" as to time, and he should select his intercuts with careful attention to the desired effect. In the above sequence, the editor's selection of a clock or candle shot is based on his own feeling about the effect of such a shot on the audience. A clock without a second hand shows no movement at all—time seems to be standing still. A flickering candle is also normally a "still" shot. By inserting such shots within a sequence, the editor can retard time, and the "feeling" of the inserted shots will carry over into subsequent shots of the main action.

The editor's control of time has an important effect on the entire film. For example, if the central dramatic unit of a film is a long and difficult journey, as in David Lean's film *Bridge on the River Kwai,* the editor must convey a sense of the hardship of that journey. It does not matter whether the audience is told, via dialogue, how long the trip will take. The audience must still *feel* the length of the journey in viewing the film. Thus the film editor's sense of time must be perfect. If the audience feels that the journey is too short to be really difficult, the central dramatic structure of the film will falter. If the journey is so drawn out that the audience cannot accept the attrition, again the film will falter. The editor must decide how many days and nights should be shown on screen and how long each day should seem.

In *Bridge on the River Kwai,* the long, difficult trek into the jungle is shown through a series of long shots freely mixed with close-ups. Some days are covered in two or three shots; others are covered in fifty shots. The audience does not question this uneven distribution of time. The days following the injury to the leader's foot are extended by the repeated use of shots of his bandages and bleeding leg, of the sun glinting through the trees, and the faces of the crew. As the journey nears its end, time is drawn out and extended— just as it must have seemed drawn out to the participants in the journey.

To achieve the opposite effect, the compression of time, the editor often utilizes *flash-cutting,* the insertion of split-second fragments of scenes between direct cuts from scene to scene. Excellent examples of this type of compression occur in many television commercials and in many mystery and suspense films. Costa Gavras uses the technique in both *Z* and *State of Siege* to heighten tension as well as to compress time.

The use of optical effects   Optical effects can be used to link scenes and sequences. These effects include (1) *flip frames,* the "flipping" of frames to reveal a new scene, (2) *wipes,* the horizontal or vertical crossing on screen of an outgoing and incoming scene, and (3) *supers,* the imposition of one scene over another. These effects create changes from scene to scene within seconds and propel the audience into another place in time. It is the film editor who selects and designs these optical effects and who must decide how each pair of scenes will be altered by the optical effect that joins them.

Every optical has its own effect on the pace of the film, an effect related directly to the audience's conception of time. Long, slow dissolves usually retard time. Good examples of this are the long dissolves joining a series of sequences in George Steven's *A Place in the Sun* and the dissolves joining the "reunion" scenes of Lara and Zhivago in *Doctor Zhivago*. Flips and wipes usually speed up time, linking scenes that occur weeks or even months apart by means of an abrupt optical trick that erases the missing time segment from the consciousness of the audience. The audience becomes involved in the incoming scene while the outgoing scene is still on screen and thus has no chance to consider the time gap.

Rhythm

Every film contains unique internal and external cadences. Indeed, these cadences—or rhythms—impart to the film much of its quality and character. The control of internal and external cadences lies largely in the province of the film editor.

Internal rhythm   In addition to mood and impact of performance, every scene has an inherent quality of movement, an *internal rhythm*. In viewing a film, we are often aware of individual scenes that seem especially slow or fast. As obvious examples, a scene photographed from a speeding motorcycle imparts a feeling of fast movement; a scene photographed from a gondola in Venice imparts a sense of languor and slow movement.

The editor, relying chiefly on his intuitive sense, must recognize the particular rhythm of each scene. This rhythm is determined by everything happening within the scene—the movement of the camera, the pace of the action, the speed of the dialogue, the number of events occurring at the same time. Once the film editor understands the rhythmic quality of a scene (for example, "dreary," "interminable," or "frenetic"), he can determine where to place the scene, how long it should run, and which scenes it should follow or precede. The editor must select scenes that both in themselves and in relation to preceding and following scenes will achieve the desired effect.

Consider the "health spa sequence" in the early part of Fellini's *8½*. The film deals with the life—past, present, and future—of a film director who has lost both purpose and commitment to his art. The action takes place during a period of time when he is about to begin a major new film. Overwhelmed by many pressures, he goes to a health spa with his wife, his writer, and other assorted members of the crew. The sequence is meant to be in part satirical commentary on that useless, idle life lived by the Italian aristocracy, but more important, it is meant to reflect the torpor that grips and paralyzes the central figure in the film, the director Guido. This sequence was edited to the fast-moving overture to Giacomo Rossini's *La Gazza Ladra*. The scenes themselves, however, contain slow and languid rhythms that transmit a sense of slothful purposelessness—a mood that gives this sequence its brilliant satiric quality. Thus, even though the music moves swiftly, filled with mercurial configurations typical of Rossini, the scenes convey a feeling of torpor—figures float by, the camera pans lazily past the guests, hands reach slowly for mineral water, and the camera dollies at an almost artificially retarded pace. In all, it is in the internal rhythm of each scene that carries the mood and pace of the sequence. Despite the frantic pace of the music, the entire sequence transmits a mood of somnolence and death.

The opposite effect—rapid pace—is achieved in *Bonnie and Clyde* in one of the most violent sequences ever created by an American filmmaker. As the sequence begins, Bonnie, Clyde, Clyde's brother and sister-in-law, and C. J. Moss are enjoying one of their many "just folks" recreational respites from the law in a Texas motel. Suddenly they are surrounded by the police. From the moment they break out of the motel room until the brother dies in the field, this sequence has an incredibly frantic pace. The cinematic elements that give this sequence its power were created in the film editing. There is little of the flash-cutting so common in contemporary films; rather, the editor has selected scenes that contain in themselves a high degree of rapid physical movement: the escape from the motel, the leap into the cars, the overturned car bursting into flame, the race through the night, the spin of the cars into the open field, the bodies falling and twisting, and finally, the camera circling around the dying man. The editor keeps each scene in high movement, rarely pausing for a static close-up.

The mood of each sequence—so essential to the film—is created largely by the editing, by the *use* of the material. The editor determines the length of each scene, the transitions from scene to scene, the order of the scenes, and all supporting elements (sound, music, voices) that will be used. These creative decisions make the sequence work.

External rhythm   The external rhythm of a film often depends on the length of time most of the individual scenes in the film run. A film that contains many single scenes that begin, develop, and end over a period of several minutes, will transmit to the audience a slow, deliberate, external rhythm. For example, a film such as Joseph Losey's *The Go-Between* contained many long scenes that ran for 4, 5, or even 8 minutes. On the other hand, a film in which scenes are short, fragmented and constantly interrupted with unmotivated and oblique cuts exhibits a much faster jarring external rhythm. A film such as Costa-Gavras' *State of Siege* uses successive short cuts, that grow even shorter, as sequences proceed to communicate a great deal of tension.

The external rhythm of a film is also strongly affected by the editorial choice of *how* to interrupt movement. In other words, *What do we cut to?* Again, in traditional practice, the editor cuts to elements that are contained within the scene or cued by the sound track. Modern film editors, however, frequently utilize the totally *unrelated* cut to heighten impact and greatly increase pace. For example, in a scene from *Hiroshima, Mon Amour*, the camera follows a baby carriage through a park. Suddenly the camera cuts to a peace demonstration in Tokyo. We, as audience, are totally unprepared for the scene and are barely able to get our bearings when the scene is over and we are back in the park. Our disorientation is so great that the action seems to be greatly accelerated.

In every motion picture of artistic merit, careful attention is given to the cadences, or "pulse," of the film. We remember a film as being "fast moving" or "poetic," as having "tremendous punch," or as conveying "a sense of peace and beauty." These phrases are the articulated descriptions of the cadences created by the film editor.

Visual and aural relationships

In the editing of a motion picture, there are three important relationships to be considered: (1) image to image, (2) sound to sound, and (3) image to sound.

Image to image   Every scene is affected by the scenes that precede and follow it. To demonstrate the effect of scene upon scene, consider the following:

Scene 1: Close-up of a man smiling

Scene 2: Close-up of a gun going off

Scene 3: A body falling

Scene 4: Close-up of a sad face

If these scenes are edited in the order 1 2 3 4, they tell the story of a happy man shooting someone who is then mourned by a third person. If the scenes are edited in the order 4 2 3 1, they tell the story of someone regretfully shooting someone else to the joy of a third party. Thus the ordering of the scenes determines the audience's reaction to the shooting.

In a well-edited film we are never aware of the cuts themselves; we sense only the continuity of the film as a whole. Thus we are often unaware that our emotional response to a scene is carefully conditioned by a preceding scene. As each shot leads to the next, it imparts emotional and intellectual "memories" that often change the values in the following scene.

The film editor has the power to change the character and purpose of a scene. Since there are no immutable laws governing his choices, the film editor can transcend the boundaries of time and space to achieve a desired effect. A party can be given somber overtones by a cut to a funeral shot—a casket being lowered into a grave. It is not necessary for the audience to know whose funeral or whose casket it is. The shot is simply an *effect shot;* it makes a comment and achieves a desired result. If the funeral shot is used with a realistic script (for example, while the party is going on, miles away the hero's mother dies), the shot will change the character of the party scenes. We become angry or ashamed at the participants, and the very gaiety of the party becomes depressing. If the editor chooses to run an entire party sequence before proceeding to the funeral sequence, the party scenes will retain their inherent gaiety until the funeral. If, however, the funeral and the party are intercut—a shot of laughter followed by a shot of gloom—the party shots will be destroyed by the funeral shots.

The relationship of image to image is a prime factor in the editing of a film. It is through this relationship that communication is achieved and that the mood of each sequence is established. One of the best examples of the relationship between images can be seen in the "flagellants sequence" from *The Seventh Seal*. The plot "line" of the film concerns itself with a knight returning home from a crusade in the Middle Ages. Threatened with death, he challenges the figure of Death to play chess with him on the agreement that he will live until the game is resolved. During his journey from the edge of the sea toward his home many miles away, he encounters many people, among them a beautiful young couple (symbolic of the Holy Family), Jof and Mia, who are actors and travel from town to town giving performances. The countryside has been ravaged by the plague, and groups of flagellants provide a bizarre and threatening background to the main action of the film. In this scene, Jof and Mia begin their performance. The following is the script description of this sequence.*

> *Jof stands in the hot sun with a flickering lantern in his hand. Mia pretends to be asleep on a bench which has been pulled forward on the stage.*
>
> JOF: Night and moonlight now prevail
>   Here sleeps my wife so frail . . .
>
> VOICE FROM THE PUBLIC: Does she snore?
>
> JOF: May I point out that this is a tragedy, and in tragedies one doesn't snore.
>
> VOICE FROM THE PUBLIC: I think she should snore anyhow.
>
> *This opinion causes mirth in the audience. Jof becomes slightly confused and goes out of character, but Mia keeps her head and begins snoring.*
>
> JOF: Night and moonlight now prevail.
>   There snores—I mean sleeps—my wife so frail.
>   Jealous I am, as never before,
>   I hide myself behind this door.
>   Faithful is she
>   To her lover—not me.
>   He soon comes a-stealing
>   To awaken her lusty feeling.
>   I shall now kill him dead
>   For cuckolding me in my bed.
>   There he comes in the moonlight,
>   His white legs shining bright.
>   Quiet as a mouse, here I'll lie,
>   Tell him not that he's about to die.

* From *The Seventh Seal*, text and film by Ingmar Bergman, in *Four Screenplays of Ingmar Bergman*, trans. by Lars Malmstrom and David Kushner (New York: Simon and Schuster, Inc., 1960), pp. 121–25. Reprinted by permission of the publisher and Janus Films.

Jof hides himself. Mia immediately ends her snoring and sits up, looking to the left.

MIA: Look, there he comes in the night
    My lover, my heart's delight.

She becomes silent and looks wide-eyed in front of her.

The mood in the yard in front of the inn has, up to now, been rather lighthearted despite the heat.

Now a rapid change occurs. People who had been laughing and chattering fall silent. Their faces seem to pale under their sunbrowned skins, the children stop their games and stand with gaping mouths and frightened eyes. Jof steps out in front of the curtain. His painted face bears an expression of horror. Mia has risen with Mikael in her arms. Some of the women in the yard have fallen on their knees, others hide their faces, many begin to mutter half-forgotten prayers.

All have turned their faces toward the white road. Now a shrill song is heard. It is frenzied, almost a scream.

A crucified Christ sways above the hilltop.

The cross-bearers soon come into sight. They are Dominican monks, their hoods pulled down over their faces. More and more of them follow, carrying litters with heavy coffins or clutching holy relics, their hands stretched out spasmodically. The dust wells up around their black hoods; the censers sway and emit a thick, ashen smoke which smells of rancid herbs.

After the line of monks comes another procession. It is a column of men, boys, old men, women, girls, children. All of them have steel-edged scourges in their hands with which they whip themselves and each other, howling ecstatically. They twist in pain; their eyes bulge wildly; their lips are gnawed to shreds and dripping with foam. They have been seized by madness. They bite their own hands and arms, whip each other in violent, almost rhythmic outbursts. Throughout it all the shrill song howls from their bursting throats. Many sway and fall, lift themselves up again, support each other and help each other to intensify the scourging.

Now the procession pauses at the crossroads in front of the inn. The monks fall on their knees, hiding their faces with clenched hands, arms pressed tightly together. Their song never stops. The Christ figure on its timbered cross is raised above the heads of the crowd. It is not Christ triumphant, but the suffering Jesus with the sores, the blood, the hammered nails and the face in convulsive pain. The Son of God, nailed on the wood of the cross, suffering scorn and shame.

The penitents have now sunk down in the dirt of the road. They collapse where they stood like slaughtered cattle. Their screams rise with the song of the monks, through misty clouds of incense, toward the white fire of the sun.

A large square monk rises from his knees and reveals his face, which is red-brown from the sun. His eyes glitter; his voice is thick with impotent scorn.

MONK: God has sentenced us to punishment. We shall all perish in the black death. You, standing there like gaping cattle, you who sit there in your glutted complacency, do you know that this may be your last hour? Death stands right behind you. I can see how his crown gleams in the sun. His scythe flashes as he raises it above your heads. Which one of you shall he strike first? You there, who stands staring like a goat, will your mouth be twisted into the last unfinished gasp before nightfall? And you, woman, who bloom with life and self-satisfaction, will you pale and become extinguished before the morning dawns? You back there, with your swollen nose and stupid grin, do you have another year left to dirty the earth with your refuse? Do you know, you insensible fools, that you shall die today or tomorrow, or the next day, because all of you have been sentenced? Do you hear what I say? Do you hear the word? You have been sentenced, sentenced!

The monk falls silent, looking around with a bitter face and a cold, scornful glance. Now he clenches his hands, straddles the ground and turns his face upward.

MONK: Lord have mercy on us in our humiliation! Don't turn your face from us in loathing and contempt, but be merciful to us for the sake of your son, Jesus Christ.

He makes the sign of the cross over the crowd and then begins a new song in a strong voice. The monks rise and join in the song. As if driven by some superhuman force, the penitents begin to whip themselves again, still wailing and moaning.

The procession continues. New members have joined the rear of the column; others who were unable to go on lie weeping in the dust of the road.

The early part of the sequence consists of the strolling players' performance. These images proceed at a brisk pace, assisted by the drum and flute music of the players. As the players act out the story of the cuckolded husband, each shot imparts to the next a lighthearted warmth and humor. Suddenly the flagellants appear—a grotesque parade of hysterical human beings carrying incense, irons, whips, and a wooden cross. This succession of images is so powerful and frightening that all memory of the delightfully comic play vanishes. It is the image-to-image relationship that creates the full impact of horror. The effect is cumulative: each image derives strength from the preceding image and passes on power to the following image.

The same editorial effect is achieved in the "tavern scene" in *The Seventh Seal.* The later action of the film takes place in a local tavern where the townspeople sit terrified, discussing the plague. Jof joins them and is threatened by Raval, a defrocked priest. Plog is a slow-witted smith whose wife is cuckolding him. The scene is described in the screenplay as follows:*

The smith sighs sadly and goes inside.
The inn is very small and full of people eating and drinking to forget their newly aroused fear of eternity. In the open fireplace a roasting pig turns on an iron spit. The sun shines outside the casement window, its sharp rays piercing the darkness of the room, which is thick with fumes and perspiration.

MERCHANT: Yes, it's true! The plague is spreading along the west coast. People are dying like flies. Usually business would be good at this time of year, but damn it, I've still got my whole stock unsold.

* From *The Seventh Seal*, pp. 126–31.

WOMAN: They speak of the judgment day. And all these omens are terrible. Worms, chopped-off hands and other monstrosities began pouring out of an old woman, and down in the village another woman gave birth to a calf's head.

OLD MAN: The day of judgment. Imagine.

FARMER: It hasn't rained here for a month. We'll surely lose our crops.

MERCHANT: And people are acting crazy, I'd say. They flee the country and carry the plague with them wherever they go.

OLD MAN: The day of judgment. Just think, just think!

FARMER: If it's as they say, I suppose a person should look after his house and try to enjoy life as long as he can.

WOMAN: But there have been other things too, such things that can't even be spoken of. (*Whispers*) Things that mustn't be named — but the priests say that the woman carries it between her legs and that's why she must cleanse herself.

OLD MAN: Judgment day. And the Riders of the Apocalypse stand at the bend in the village road. I imagine they'll come on judgment night, at sundown.

WOMAN: There are many who have purged themselves with fire and died from it, but the priests say it's better to die pure than to live for hell.

MERCHANT: This is the end, yes, it is. No one says it out loud, but all of us know that it's the end. And people are going mad from fear.

FARMER: So you're afraid too.

MERCHANT: Of course I'm afraid.

OLD MAN: The judgment day becomes night, and the angels descend and the graves open. It will be terrible to see.

They whisper in low tones and sit close to each other. Plog, the smith, shoves his way into a place next to Jof, who is still dressed in his costume. Opposite him sits Raval, leaning slightly forward, his face perspiring heavily. Raval rolls an armlet out on the table.

RAVAL: Do you want this armlet? You can have it cheap.

JOF: I can't afford it.

RAVAL: It's real silver.

JOF: It's nice. But it's surely too expensive for me.

PLOG: Excuse me, but has anyone here seen my wife?

JOF: Has she disappeared?

PLOG: They say she's run away.

JOF: Has she deserted you?

PLOG: With an actor.

JOF: An actor! If she's got such bad taste, then I think you should let her go.

PLOG: You're right. My first thought, of course, was to kill her.

JOF: Oh. But to murder her, that's a terrible thing to do.

PLOG: I'm also going to kill the actor.

JOF: The actor?

PLOG: Of course, the one she eloped with.

JOF: What has he done to deserve that?

PLOG: Are you stupid?

JOF: The actor! Now I understand. There are too many of them, so even if he hasn't done anything in particular you ought to kill him merely because he's an actor.

PLOG: You see, my wife has always been interested in the tricks of the theater.

JOF: And that turned out to be her misfortune.

PLOG: Her misfortune, but not mine, because a person who's born unfortunate can hardly suffer from any further misfortune. Isn't that true?

Now Raval enters the discussion. He is slightly drunk and his voice is shrill and evil.

RAVAL: Listen, you! You sit there and lie to the smith.

JOF: I! A liar!

RAVAL: You're an actor too and it's probably your partner who's run off with Plog's old lady.

PLOG: Are you an actor too?

JOF: An actor! Me! I wouldn't quite call myself that!

RAVAL: We ought to kill you; it's only logical.

JOF (*laughs*): You're really funny.

RAVAL: How strange — you've turned pale. Have you anything on your conscience?

JOF: You're funny. Don't you think he's funny? (*To Plog*) Oh, you don't.

RAVAL: Maybe we should mark you up a little with a knife, like they do petty scoundrels of your kind.

Plog bangs his hands down on the table so that the dishes jump. He gets up.

PLOG (*shouting*): What have you done with my wife?

The room becomes silent. Jof looks around, but there is no exit, no way to escape. He puts his hands on the table. Suddenly a knife flashes through the air and sinks into the table top between his fingers.
Jof snatches away his hands and raises his head. He looks half surprised, as if the truth had just become apparent to him.

JOF: Do you want to hurt me? Why? Have I provoked someone, or got in the way? I'll leave right now and never come back.

Jof looks from one face to another, but no one seems ready to help him or come to his defense.

RAVAL: Get up so everyone can hear you. Talk louder.

Trembling, Jof rises. He opens his mouth as if to say something, but not a word comes out.

RAVAL: Stand on your head so that we can see how good an actor you are.

Jof gets up on the table and stands on his head. A hand pushes him forward so that he collapses on the floor. Plog rises, pulls him to his feet with one hand.

PLOG (*shouts*): What have you done with my wife?

The smith beats him so furiously that Jof flies across the table. Raval leans over.

RAVAL: Don't lie there moaning. Get up and dance.

JOF: I don't want to. I can't.

RAVAL: Show us how you imitate a bear.

JOF: I can't play a bear.

RAVAL: Let's see if you can't after all.

Raval prods Jof lightly with the knife point. Jof gets up with cold sweat on his cheeks and forehead, frightened half to death. He begins to jump and hop on top of the tables, swinging his arms and legs and making grotesque faces. Some laugh, but most of the people sit silently. Jof gasps as if his lungs were about to burst. He sinks to his knees, and someone pours beer over him.

RAVAL: Up again! Be a good bear.

JOF: I haven't done any harm. I haven't got the strength to play a bear any more.

At that moment the door opens and Jöns enters. Jof sees his chance and steals out. Raval intends to follow him, but suddenly stops. Jöns and Raval look at each other.

JÖNS: Do you remember what I was going to do to you if we met again?

Raval steps back without speaking.

JÖNS: I'm a man who keeps his word.

Jöns raises his knife and cuts Raval from forehead to cheek. Raval staggers toward the wall.

In the beginning of this sequence, the editor cuts together all the shots containing "atmosphere": the craggy faces of the men, the tired women, the coarse food, the fire, the architecture of the period. These shots build a fine sense of place (one of the leading attributes of the film). The editor then builds a sense of fear and foreboding by intercutting bits and pieces of dialogue shots — shots of the diners talking about the plague and its effects. Here, the editor has specifically selected shots that contain the mood of fear and images that evoke terror: shadows flickering on the wall, hands violently tearing at food, drooling mouths, darting eyes. The tavern is subtly transformed into a terror-ridden cave of superstitious, frightened people. Jof's dance begins, and each successive image, feeding upon its predecessors, builds up an atmosphere of hate and fear. The final rescue of Jof by Jöns is a welcome relief. This sequence is an excellent example of the editor's art in controlling the impact of scene upon scene.

Sound to sound   The second major relationship that the editor works with is the relationship of sound track to sound track. In the two sequences examined above, the use of sound and the relationship of each section of sound track to each succeeding section play a key role in the final artistic achievement. In the first sequence, the initial comic quality of the strolling players' performance is greatly heightened by the drum and fife music and by the exaggerated delivery of the players. Suddenly, just as Jof is whipping up a mood of fun and joy, the sound of his drum dissolves into the sound of the *Te Deum* of the flagellants. As we hear this sound, the gaiety of the original music is lost. In turn, the gloom of the religious requiem is greatly heightened by our memory of the music that precedes it. The editor has carefully structured the sound tracks to blend, with rising intensity, all the sounds in the scene: the voices, drums, whips, moans, cries, and — soaring above all — the *Te Deum*. This sound begins faintly in the distance, reaches a crescendo, and finally fades away into a moment of silence.

In the second sequence examined above, the tavern sequence, the sound relationships also play a key role. The boisterous sounds of the tavern in the early part of the sequence give way to a sinister, rhythmic rumble as the defrocked priest forces Jof to dance on the table. The sound of everyone slowly beating time builds a sense of threat. The fact that it follows hard upon the realistic sounds of the tavern extends the sense of danger. The sudden silence that follows and attends Jöns' entry and fight with the priest is also magnified.

The relationship between sound tracks can be *vertical* or *horizontal*. In vertical relationship, each sound track prepares us for what is to follow and affects the sounds that come before and after it. In horizontal relationship, several sound tracks are mixed in a single scene.

As has been noted earlier, it is possible to accommodate a great variety of sounds in a single scene. The film editor usually determines how many tracks will be employed. He begins with the basic sound track, the sync dialogue track, and builds outward from that point. The sync dialogue track contains all the environmental noises that occurred as the dialogue was being recorded. After the initial editing of this track, the editor creates the basic sounds of each scene — sounds that in many cases originate from unseen, off-screen sources. The editor creates, out of all the sounds available, several tracks containing general environmental sounds. He then adds sound effects. In the tavern sequence described earlier, for example, the editor might add the crackle of the fire, the noises of people eating, footsteps on the wooden floor, and dialogue from characters not seen. Finally, the editor can add music with and under the dialogue. The horizontal relationship of the sound tracks is determined by director, editor, and sound mixer at the final mix. Volume is raised and lowered, and the tracks are put in creative relationship to one another.

Often, an editor must build the sounds of a scene from scratch. For example, he may be working with a documentary film that contains a lengthy montage showing conditions in American jails. If these scenes have been shot without sound, the editor must supply realistic sounds — such as voices, doors clanging, and cups banging on bars. These sounds are recorded separately (nonsynchronously). The editor can also add music and narration. Throughout his work, he must carefully and creatively control the relationships among the tracks. At what point should only effects be heard? When should the music come in, and when should it dominate the track? How much narration is desirable, and where should it be placed? How much space for other sounds can be left between narrative sentences? At what point should all the tracks be heard, and when should one or more be inaudible? All these questions must be answered by the editor as he works with sound-to-sound relationships.

Image to sound   The third major relationship that the film editor works with is the relationship of image to sound. Every sound affects the audience's reaction to what is seen, and every image conditions the audience's response to what is heard. A simple scene of a man walking down a city street can become a tense, nerve-wracking experience by the addition of confused traffic noises. The same scene can become an exercise in isolation and loneliness if all realistic sound is removed and we hear only the wind. In the opening scene of Fellini's *8½*, the hero, Guido, is caught in a car in a traffic jam. By using silence, Fellini presents the scene as a nightmare. In David Lean's *Lawrence of Arabia*, the sense of loneliness and alienation conveyed by the desert images is immeasurably heightened by the soft, monotonous sounds of the wind in almost every scene. In turn, the desert images impart to the sounds a vividness that makes the audience aware of even the most subtle noises originating from both onscreen and offscreen sources. An imaginative editor does not rely exclusively on sounds that are already a part of the sync track; rather, he adds sounds that have no direct visual cues but that serve to enrich the scene.

Current editing techniques have made exciting use of the *overlap sound cut*, in which the sound accompanying one scene overlaps into a preceding or following scene. The editor uses this technique to alter or enrich unrelated visual images, to link action from scene to scene, and to heighten the pace of the film.

Excellent use of the overlap sound cut appears in the film *The Graduate*. The middle section of the film, from Benjamin's seduction by Mrs. Robinson to his meeting with Elaine, consists of a time-flow segment. Benjamin's meetings with Mrs. Robinson are juxtaposed against his idle, almost paralytic life by the swimming pool at home. The images flow into one another without traditional optical connecting devices. Thus Benjamin, lying by the pool, gets up and walks into the cabana; as he crosses the doorway, he is walking into Mrs. Robinson's hotel room. In another scene, Benjamin hoists himself out of the pool onto a rubber raft; as he makes this move, a cut is made and he is rolling over on top of Mrs. Robinson in bed.

In traditional editing practice, each picture cut is generally accompanied by a sound cut. In *The Graduate*, however, the editor permits the sound of the outgoing scene to extend briefly into the incoming scene, the sound of the incoming scene to overlap the final seconds of the outgoing scene. In some instances, a sentence is cut in half and joined with part of a sentence from the new scene. The sound affects the new scene by sustaining the intellectual and emotional overtones of the scene to which it belongs. This deliberate mismatching of sound unifies, in impact and idea, a sequence that would otherwise consist of disparate elements. The imaginative use of sound-to-image relationships successfully contrasts Benjamin's comatose existence at home with his emotional affair with Mrs. Robinson.

In the films of 1930s and 1940s, the relationships between picture and sound were relatively unimaginative and mechanical. Since that time, film editing has undergone a number of changes. Today, the creative film editor, through the skillful and imaginative employment of image and sound relationships, adds richness to the finished film.

As the director becomes more freewheeling in his execution, and as film becomes less tied down to the studio, the film editor will continue to experiment. One major weapon in the editor's arsenal is the *montage*, a series of images and sounds joined only by internal relationships and capable of transporting the viewer just about anywhere.

Montage

Over the past two decades, no term in cinema has been more distorted or abused than "montage." Every time a film editor puts two or more scenes together in a series of short cuts, he claims to have created a montage. Nonetheless, montage can be a key creative term in the filmmaker's lexicon. Practically speaking, cinematic montage is *the use of a succession of visual images and/or sounds to create emotional impact*. Generally, the montage is used to compress or expand time or space and to create special moods. Several basic types of montage are discussed below.

The time-transition montage   The pool game between Paul Newman and Jackie Gleason in *The Hustler* (directed by Robert Rossen) is a good example of the time-transition montage. The audience watches a series of fragmented scenes of two men playing a tense game of pool. The screen shows only bits and pieces of scenes linked by long, lingering dissolves. Each scene is superimposed on the next, yet from this succession of images we feel that we have been through the entire game.

The mood montage   The opening scenes of Fred Zinnemann's historical drama *A Man for All seasons* illustrate the effect of mood montage. The departure of Sir Thomas More (Paul Scofield) to London is shown through a series of images of the Thames in early morning. These images create a mood of time and place. This opening montage permeates the entire film and helps to expand this chamber play into an exciting motion picture.

The impact montage   Lindsay Anderson's first feature film, *This Sporting Life* (1963), deals with the life of a professional rugby football player. To delineate the effect of this vicious body-contact sport on the hero, Anderson uses several impact montages of the game. These montages consist of fragmented long-lens shots of the body-contact aspects of the sport, coupled with the sounds of the game—thuds, groans, and bone-crunching noises. The audience is thus propelled *into* the game.

There are, of course, an endless variety of uses for the montage. Indeed, it is one of the real refinements of the editor's art. The montage involves crucial picture-to-picture relationships. Every scene chosen must be exactly right in position and length. The sound too—whether dialogue, effects, or music—must be carefully chosen. The flow of images propels the audience to a desired destination. One wrong scene and the entire "visual train" will be derailed. There are no restrictions in the art of cinematic montage. The film editor edits viscerally—instinctively—and makes decisions based on what he feels will do the job.

EFFECTIVE EDITING

As the film editor organizes the finished film, he achieves many of the writer's and/or the director's goals. In effective film editing, control of the audience's attention must be absolute. The editor must carefully manipulate each element—time, rhythm, and visual and aural relationships—and must structure these elements to convey the meaning and emotional content of the film.

Alain Resnais' film *Hiroshima, Mon Amour* is a good example of effective editing. The film contains, in both script design and execution, some of the most complicated elements ever attended on screen. Although the action takes place in a single day, the film spans several years (the history of a complex and profound woman) and examines timeless themes—the effect of war on man, the nature of the relationship between two people in love.

As the film begins, the two lovers are in bed conversing about Hiroshima. The editor leaves this scene, permitting the dialogue to continue, and creates a montage—a flow of images giving a memorable view of the bomb in action. These images are edited in brilliant counterpoint to the continuing dialogue. The editor moves freely between past and present. The woman looks from the terrace at her sleeping lover, and the camera cuts to a jolting fragment from another time and place: the hand of her dead German lover, followed by a swift pan to his head. Suddenly, there is another cut, and we are back in the present.

The film is designed like a fantastic jigsaw puzzle. The editor selects key episodes from the heroine's past and pieces fragments of these episodes into the onscreen action. In effect, the editor is duplicating the very process that is going on in the heroine's mind. Her past is thrusting itself into her present, building up a pressure that even she is not aware of. The film editor makes this process the very substance of the cutting. The fragmented scenes become meaningful as the heroine begins to remember things she had sought to repress. The past forces its way to the surface. As the action continues, the editor permits us to see entire sequences, still moving freely between past and present while retaining control of every element. Images and dialogue overlap; music provides clues and pace. The editorial choices are so appropriate that we are hardly aware of them. We know and understand. The film communicates to us because the editor has used each element perfectly—the first flashback cut (the hand of the German), the overlapping dialogue during the museum scenes, the steady extension of the flashback scenes (as both audience and heroine become aware of the forces that now move her), and the precise moment that the music is heard at the beginning of the woman's walk through the city.

In practicing the art of film editing, the film editor must be in complete control if he is to successfully arrange the sequence of the images and captivate the eye of the audience. He employs a variety of elements—all relating to visual and aural impressions—to build and reinforce this control. The creative film editor must have the ability to intuitively select and combine images and sounds for maximum visual impact, which means, in effect, that he must be part musician, part dramatist, part poet. At the same time, the film editor is a highly skilled technician capable of moving a dozen tracks and a picture through a multiheaded monster called an editing machine. Like the writer, the director, and the cameraman, the editor is a basic creator of the finished work of art—the film.

FILMS FOR STUDY

Potemkin, Sergei Eisenstein

Triumph of the Will, Leni Riefenstahl

Bonnie and Clyde, Arthur Penn

The Graduate, Mike Nichols

Faces, John Cassavetes

The Hustler, Robert Rossen

The French Connection, William Friedkin

State of Siege, Costa-Gavras

A Man for All Seasons, Fred Zinnemann

SUPPLEMENTARY READING

Eisenstein, Sergei. *Film Form*. New York: Harcourt Brace Jovanovich, 1969.

——. *The Film Sense*. New York: Harcourt Brace Jovanovich, 1969.

Pudovkin, V. I. "Film Technique," in *Film: An Anthology*, ed. by Daniel Talbot. Berkeley: University of California Press, 1966.

Reisz, Karel. *The Technique of Film Editing*. New York: Hastings House, 1959.

THE DIRECTOR

FIVE

I don't think a director should stand out. The audience should be unconscious that the damned thing's been filmed at all. There's a fashion now to give too much freedom to the director; people fought hard for that. But there was never any need to fight: If you made a couple of pictures that were commercially successful, as well as artistically good, you automatically got freedom. . . . Now directors want total control even on their first picture, which is destructive for the business.

Sir Carol Reed
in *Encountering Directors*
by Charles Thomas Samuels
(New York: G. P. Putnam's Sons, 1972),
p. 165.

A director is a kind of idea and taste machine; a movie is a series of creative and technical decisions, and it's the director's job to make the right decisions as frequently as possible.

Stanley Kubrick
in *The Film Director as Superstar*
by Joseph Gelmis
(Garden City: Doubleday, 1970),
p. 314.

HE ART OF FILM DEMANDS THE CREATIVE CONTRIBUTION OF MANY INDIVIDUALS and the interaction of many artistic elements. Thus, because he is the unifying force in the making of a film, the director occupies a unique role as a creative artist. The composer, the painter, the sculptor, the novelist, and the playwright work largely alone, and from their solitary labors the work of art emerges. Although the theatrical director also deals with a variety of elements (actors, lighting, physical movement, sound effects, and music), the film director commands the largest number of complex elements in the creation of a work of art. With the emergence of film as an art form, the role of the director has undergone a subtle but vitally important evolution.

THE EMERGING ROLE OF THE CONTEMPORARY DIRECTOR

In the early days of film the director was, for the most part, a "personality" — a creative autocrat who by dint of a bravura style and a commanding disposition was able to exert an authoritarian control over the making of a film. The great directors who emerged during the infancy of film — Griffith, Lang, Murnau, Wiene — created films by involving themselves in every aspect of filmmaking. They raised money, hired actors, took part in the writing of scripts, edited, and spent much of their time and energy immersed in the wheeling and dealing that preceded the finished product. Because of this overall involvement and because of their strong personal convictions about the way films should be made, these early directors created films that bear the stamp of their personalities.

Later, in the 1930s and 1940s, as film continued to expand beyond the artistic and technical developments of its early period, the role of the director underwent a number of changes. With the rise of large film studios came a movement toward deemphasizing the director's role in favor of a more fragmented, compartmentalized kind of filmmaking. The producer, as guardian of the studio's financial interests, began to usurp much of the control and decision making traditionally handled by the director. The studios hired and supervised the writers, actors, editors, and directors. During this period the job of most directors was simply to translate the studio's scripts onto celluloid. Although some directors were allowed more creative latitude than others and were permitted to work closely with writers and editors, by and large during this period the director did not control the entire film.

Following the Second World War, the role of the director changed again. He began once more to assume most of the responsibility for the creation of the entire film, from script to screen. He began to emerge as *auteur*, as the dominant force in the creation of a film. (The term *auteur* was first used, in the context of filmmaking, by a group of French filmmakers and film critics who, during the 1950s, contributed critical and theoretical essays to the film journal *Cahiers du Cinéma*.) The important filmmakers of this period managed to regain the pivotal position and control that directors had enjoyed before the rise of the studio system. To this regained position of dominance they brought a willingness to experiment with new modes of cinematic expression and a belief that the art of film could be used to explore a greater variety of subject matter than ever before. Directors such as Buñuel, De Sica, Bergman, and Truffaut worked as creative artists in a manner quite different from that of their predecessors. These directors (and many others of the postwar period), though their films display the widest diversity, nevertheless shared certain similar characteristics: they worked very closely with their script writers on the development of the intitial concepts and themes (or else wrote the scripts themselves); they did not feel that the traditional conventions of cinematic expression were sacred, not to be broken if their creative impulses urged them to; their careful control of every element of the filmmaking process resulted in films that displayed recognizable style, but the style evident in their films was usually more a result of their esthetic convictions than a result of a domineering personality.

In the 1930s, it was common to attribute the success of a film to an actor, with less recognition given to the director. Paul Muni, for example, was praised for his performances in *Life of Emile Zola* and *The Story of Louis Pasteur*, yet few people knew the name of the director of these films (William Dieterle). Today, film is more and more becoming recognized as primarily the work of the director. When we view a film by Bergman and examine each of the creative elements separately, it becomes apparent that one man and one man alone is in control. Despite the excellent performances by Max Von Sydow in the many films he has done with Bergman, the acting style is clearly that of the director. We no longer refer to a film as an MGM film or a Bette Davis film, but rather as a Bergman film or a Kubrick film.

The contemporary film director, then, has emerged as the most important single creative force in the making of a film. The art of the motion picture has become the art of the director — or, more correctly, the art of the filmmaker. The efforts of the writer, the actor, the cameraman, the editor, and the sound man are all guided and coordinated by the director as he creates his work of art. A few earlier filmmakers — Chaplin and Welles, for instance — foresaw this trend and functioned in much the same way. But they were, at the time, exceptions to the rule. It was not until the postwar period, when the *auteur* directors arrived on the filmmaking scene, that the idea of the director as total filmmaker began to gain a widespread basis in fact.

Now that film has attained maturity as an art form, the individual artist — the director — is as independent a creator as the painter or composer. To understand, study, or make a film, it is essential that we understand the function of the director.

THE FUNCTION OF THE DIRECTOR

The director and the writer

In the creation of a major motion picture, the work of the director usually *precedes* that of the writer. Occasionally a writer approaches a director with an idea or a script and attempts to elicit his interest, but most often it is the director-filmmaker who initiates the ideas and the themes of the film. One of the earmarks of the contemporary film is the fact that it often reflects the philosophical or social viewpoint of the director. In most great films, the hand of the director is present in the "prenatal" stage.

The *conception* of the film, then, is that of the director. Seldom does he merely pick up a script and execute it. Currently (and in the foreseeable future), the great films—the films that change and influence the art—will come from directors who conceive of the entire film. The director provides the initial creative and intellectual thrust for the writer. The *theme* of the film is the director's, and the *structure* of the script must flow from his conception of the theme. Finally, the writing of the script must be compatible in every detail with the director's conception of the film.

In most major films of the past twenty years, the artistic ideas, the philosophy, and the intellectual thrust have emanated from the director. These artistic and intellectual currents appear throughout a director's work, even though each film may be scripted by a different writer. Today, the script is primarily representative of the director's approach to film and only secondarily a product of the writer's approach. Marguerite Duras' script for *Hiroshima, Mon Amour* is a masterpiece, but it is markedly the result of Resnais' desire to make a film that would philosophically explore war and the nature of its effects on humanity. In subsequent films by Resnais, such as *Last Year at Marienbad* (script by Alain Robbe-Grillet) and *La Guerre Est Finie* (script by Jorge Semprun), we can easily recognize the same elements of thought and style present in *Hiroshima, Mon Amour*. The flowing images, the narrative cadences, the flash cutting to evoke memory—all are part of the distinctive style of Resnais.

Thus the director chooses the subject and the theme of the film. He exerts a strong influence on the writing of the script in order to insure that it conforms to his conception of the film. Ultimately, he selects the writer who can best execute the film he envisions.

The director and the cameraman

Once the director is satisfied that a script is artistically, philosophically, and intellectually consistent with his conception of the film, he chooses the artists who will assist in the actual production. His key choice is that of cameraman. Every cameraman has a particular combination of assets and liabilities, and it is sheer folly to assume that a cameraman can execute every script equally well. The director must have in mind an image of how the finished film will look, and he must select the cameraman who is best able to capture that image on film.

A good example of a perfect choice of cameraman can be seen in Ingmar Bergman's *Through a Glass Darkly*. Bergman's films deal primarily with cold, intellectual concepts: man's eternal struggle with himself, with God, with fellow men. When Bergman set out to do three films dealing with these philosophical problems (*Through a Glass Darkly, Winter Light,* and *The Silence*), he had in mind the depiction of a bleak and barren world in which alienated and lost human beings struggle for emotional survival. *Through a Glass Darkly* required an atmosphere devoid of warmth and photography that could be evocative and artistic without falling back on "pretty" black-and-white contrasts of light and shadow. It is extremely difficult to create interesting artistic images without using high contrasts, but if a film is to deal with a cheerless atmosphere, sunlight must be eliminated and a cold, depressing sky must be the central source of illumination.

With these concepts as a motivating force, Bergman selected Sven Nykvist as his cameraman. Like James Wong Howe and Gunnar Fischer, Nykvist is a master of black-and-white cinematography. His strength lies not in the use of warmly sentimental black-and-white images, swift, imaginative camera movement, or blurred, romantic long-lens photography. Rather, it lies in his ability to convey ideas through harsh black-and-white contrasts, cold gray tones, sharp-edged silhouettes, and gloomy, foreboding shadows. In addition, Nykvist excels at composing images for maximum dramatic impact. He is thus the ideal choice for *this* director and for *this* film (Fig. 1).

In *Through a Glass Darkly,* the composition and illumination of each scene are perfectly suited to the mood and theme. For example, when the schizophrenic heroine goes into an empty room and, gripped by her madness, enacts a private religious ritual — reaching out for God with a violent sexual intensity — Nykvist creates a shadowy gray atmosphere charged with the terror that fills the girl. There are no velvet tones or false shadows; there is no glamor, no artificial darkness. This powerful scene is a key moment in the film, and the cameraman gives his director exactly the right balance of light and shadow, of fantasy and reality.

In contrast, examine Richard Brooks' *In Cold Blood,* a much-acclaimed film based on Truman Capote's controversial novel. Brooks selected a superb cameraman whose skills were nonetheless wrong for the film and basically damaging to it. The main thrust of Capote's novel derives from its semidocumentary style. Capote, after extensive prison interviews with two young men who had murdered a family in Kansas, wrote a novel that attempted to synthesize the reality of their crime. Brooks apparently saw the book as ideal material for film treatment. He selected Conrad Hall as his cameraman. Hall is particularly skilled at photographing the "beautiful" black-and-white image. Rich blacks, artificial highlights, high contrasts with noticeably arti-

Fig. 1. *Through a Glass Darkly.*
Fig. 2. *In Cold Blood.*

ficial illumination, and consciously "artistic" compositions are characteristic of Hall's style (Fig. 2). Indeed, Hall's individual frames could win prizes in still photography. But the effect of using such a "theatrical" cameraman, for whom each image is a potential masterpiece, is to diminish the sense of reality of this highly documentary material.

In viewing *In Cold Blood*, we are always aware of the "beauty" of each scene. The Kansas landscape seems almost "posed." The blacks and whites of the prison scenes with their carefully manipulated shadows, the rain (used constantly for effect), the play of light on faces—all conspire to divert our attention from what should be the reality of the film. As a result, we admire the surface effects of the photography instead of becoming deeply involved in the film's substance.

The director and the crew

The crew involved in the making of a motion picture consists of a number of professional men and women working in many crafts. They can be grouped into four categories, or units.

(1) *The management unit* consists of the assistant director, the unit manager, and the script clerk. The assistant director and the unit manager work closely with the director and help to insure the smooth management of production. The script clerk keeps all production notes and makes a careful record of every shot and all details within each scene.

(2) *The photographic unit* consists of the cameraman (discussed earlier), the operating cameraman, and the assistant cameraman. The operating cameraman runs the camera and is responsible for all camera movement. The assistant cameraman loads the camera, mounts and focuses the lenses, and generally assists in all jobs related to photography.

(3) *The sound unit* usually consists of a mixer, a recordist, and a boom man. (In many films the recordist is not necessary.) This unit is responsible for the recording of all sound during actual production.

(4) *The stagehands* consist of electricians, grips, and property men. The electricians take care of mounting, placing, and operating all lighting equipment. The grips are responsible for the movement of flats (scenery) and tripods, and the handling of dollies and cranes. The property men handle all furniture and items decorating the set.

(5) *The decorators* consist of set designers, scenic artists, makeup men, hairdressers, costume designers, and wardrobe supervisors. The set designers, working from the script, draw blueprints and sketches of every aspect of set construction. They also supervise all set decoration. The scenic artists paint the sets. The makeup men (and women) and the hairdressers, as the names imply, are in charge of makeup and hairdos for all actors in the film. The costume designers design all garments worn by the actors and control the manufacture or selection of these garments. The wardrobe supervisors take care of the garments being used.

The director's relationship to this large and diverse group of artists and artisans is an important factor in the making of the film. It is through the director that the crew receives its drive and inspiration. If the crew members believe that they are involved in an enterprise of great vitality and importance, they will put forward maximum effort to insure success.

Directors achieve control over the crew in many ways. The "martinet" director, legendary in the Hollywood of the 1930s but fast disappearing, asserts control in a military fashion. The "artist" director, the director-filmmaker of today, commands his crew by the sheer weight of his artistic insight. In either case, it is the director who creates the working atmosphere on set. He is the central creative force in the making of a film, and it is his responsibility to motivate the crew members to contribute their full talent to the production.

The director and the actor

The contemporary director-filmmaker usually casts his own films, selecting actors who can respond to *him*, in *his* way, regardless of their own style or wishes. Ingmar Bergman works with a highly flexible repertory group and uses the same actors in an immense variety of roles. For example, Max Von Sydow, who created the brilliant characterization of the Knight in *The Seventh Seal*, appears for a few brief moments in *Wild Strawberries* as a gas station attendant. To comprehend the effect of the modern director on an actor, compare Von Sydow's lifeless performance under George Stevens in *The Greatest Story Ever Told*, or his hysterical, absurd performance under George Roy Hill in *Hawaii*, with his many subtle and brilliantly varied performances under Bergman.

The performance of Ingrid Thulin in Alain Resnais' *La Guerre Est Finie* is a good example of the influence of the director on acting style. Miss Thulin, one of Bergman's key actresses, responds quite differently to the control of Resnais. Whereas Bergman deals largely in static images, with movement occurring primarily within a still frame, Resnais favors a constantly moving camera, with movement taking place both within and beyond the frame. In fashioning a performance, Bergman emphasizes the revelation of internal stress; Resnais seeks external evidence of the rhythms and cadences of life. Thus Miss Thulin responds with more warmth and vitality and less brooding introspection under Resnais than she shows under Bergman. She is far less interesting an actress in *La Guerre Est Finie* than in *Wild Strawberries*, but more fun. The parts themselves, of course, are different and to some degree dictate the differences in Miss Thulin's performances, yet much of the variation in her acting style can be attributed to the differences between the two directors.

The relationship between actor and director is highly complicated and varies greatly from director to director. Because the contemporary director is the only person who has a complete view of the film, he often imposes this view on the actors. Frequently, he asks actors to perform without understanding. Harriet Andersson, a popular Swedish actress whom Ingmar Bergman has often used to good advantage, claims that she is simply instructed on her role from scene to scene and rarely has an idea of the deeper meanings of the film. Monica Vitti, Antonioni's lead in his trilogy *L'Avventura, La Notte,* and *L'Eclisse,* has said on several occasions that she never knows what a film is about. In both cases, the director manipulates the actors, instructing them as to movement, facial expressions, inner feelings, and delivery of dialogue without necessarily confiding in them the purpose of his direction.

Directors like Sidney Lumet and Alain Resnais handle an actor quite differently (for example, Rod Steiger in Lumet's *The Pawnbroker* and Yves Montand in Resnais' *La Guerre Est Finie*). They demand that the actor conceive the role in terms of the entire film, and they spend hours and hours simply discussing the character and ideas of the film with the actor.

The director's relationship to the actor is one of the most important relationships in the making of a film, for rapport with an actor is crucial to a film's success. The writer, cameraman, and editor can be controlled by the director simply by edict; if the director does not get what he wants, these artists can be replaced. But once shooting has begun, it is very costly to replace an actor. Each director has his own method of communicating with an actor and of eliciting from that actor the performance he wants. The director must know precisely what is possible; he must understand the range of the actor and must be able to shape the desired performance.

An actor cannot, while he is before the cameras, evaluate his own performance. He is not acting in front of an audience and therefore cannot feel the rise and fall of emotion that enable him to evaluate his effectiveness. In addition, the actor is permitted little or no projection; instead, he is asked constantly to give less, for film is very unkind to overacting. Thus it is the film director, *not* the actor, who fashions the overall performance and who alone is able to evaluate the effectiveness of that performance within the context of the total film.

In addition, since films are usually shot out of sequence, the director is the only person who has a perspective on the entire performance. If the shooting schedule calls for the filming of the final scene first, and then, some three weeks later, the filming of the opening scene, the director must have in mind the quality of performance required in both scenes. In the much acclaimed documentary film *The 91st Day,* the American actor Patrick O'Neal plays the part of a mental patient. The film traces the origins of the patient's illness and follows through the various stages of his deterioration. Because of the economics of the shooting schedule, all studio (at home) scenes were shot first. In these scenes, which thread the entire film, O'Neal had to show signs of progressive mental deterioration. Then, the actor had to go on location to a mental hospital and re-create the same gradual deterioration. Only the director could keep all the details of the performance in mind. The director carefully structured the performance so that the emotional shading in each scene was appropriate.

Thus the actor acts for the director and draws from him the instructions he needs to successfully perform the role. The director, in effect, creates the role and molds the actor to his desires.

In dealing with performance, the film director must first consider the actor himself: physical features, projective ability, and ability to shade and vary dialogue. In addition, the director must consider the position of the camera, the point of view from which the audience will relate to the actor. For example, if the director lacks confidence in an actor, he may choose to play a key scene on a long shot instead of moving in for that "big" close-up. It is the director who decides when to move in close and when and how to vary the point of view from which the actor will be seen. It is the director who decides how to light the face of an actor so that delineation of character will be consistent with what is seen. Occasionally, if an actor is incapable of showing certain expressions, the director may keep the face of the actor totally in shadow so that the audience can imagine the facial expressions required. For example, George Stevens used this technique in *Giant* (1956). In a key scene in the film the character played by Elizabeth Taylor is told of the death of her father. Because Miss Taylor's facial reaction to the news was not sufficiently convincing, Stevens kept her in total shadow throughout the scene.

One of the best examples of performance as it relates to the director-actor relationship occurs in Costa-Gavras' *State of Siege*. The film deals with the kidnapping of an American official by a group of South American revolutionaries. The American, masquerading as a foreign aid official, has actually been

Fig. 3. *State of Siege.*

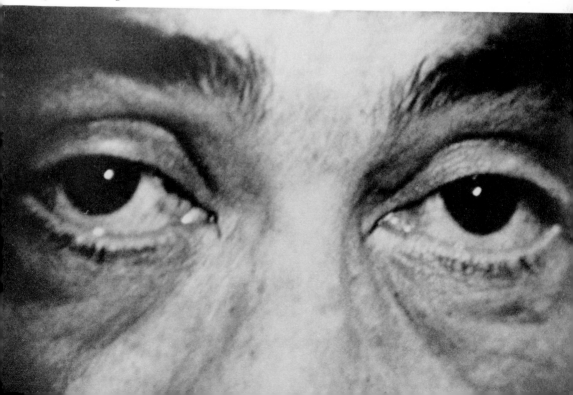

training the local police in torture and interrogation procedures in an attempt to destroy the local movement against a repressive government. In his decision to cast the French actor Yves Montand in this role, Costa-Gavras accepted Montand's existing assets and liabilities: a craggy, expressive face and a somewhat limited acting range. Costa-Gavras molded the performance by keeping Montand from "acting" at all. Throughout the film, Montand's face is relatively immobile; little change is evident from scene to scene. Dialogue is delivered in a subdued and tired fashion. Yet when loneliness, sadness, and defeat are called for, Costa-Gavras permits Montand to subtly reveal the inside of a tired man. For such moments, Costa-Gavras employs the close-up camera, and thus very small changes of expression are magnified and seem to reveal more than they really show (Fig. 3).

Another example of effective performance appears in Mike Nichols' *The Graduate*. The success of Dustin Hoffman's performance in this film can be attributed largely to Nichols' decision to create a sharp contrast between what the actor is doing and what the camera is doing. The director kept the performance on a very low key; Hoffman's face is immobile except for sudden flashes of animation. In contrast, the camera is almost frenetic in its movement. Thus the hero's alienation and isolation — a major theme in the film — is heightened. Benjy (Hoffman) moves silently and alone through a frantic, noisy world.

It is important to be able to isolate those elements that contribute to the quality of a film. The director-actor relationship is one of these elements; it is central to the effect of the finished film.

The director and the editor

The contemporary director controls every aspect of production. Usually, he views the rushes with the editor and sets the mood and tone that will guide the editing process. He has already influenced the editing by having only certain takes of each scene printed. Now he moves into the editing room and casts a large creative shadow. If the rough cut (first draft) of a film does not match the director's image, it will be recut until it conforms to that image. The "memory" flash cuts of *Hiroshima, Mon Amour* are those of Resnais, not the film editor; the "sight gags" of *What's Up Doc* are those of Peter Bogdanovich, not the film editor; and the flow of time through long dissolves in *Doctor Zhivago* is the creation of David Lean, not the editor. Contemporary filmmakers re-create a film in the editing room just as they created it on set — changing performances, adding ideas, making the film.

After the edited film has been approved by the director, the supporting elements are submitted to him for review. Bergman selected the Bach cello suite for *Through a Glass Darkly* and Mike Nichols chose the Simon and Garfunkel music for *The Graduate*. As a film begins to take shape, the hand of the director is everywhere — instructing the editor about pace and rhythm, selection of angles and intercuts, optical effects, style of title lettering, music, and sound effects. Bergman personally created the optical effects used in *Wild Strawberries* and reviewed every color print in the final stages of *Cries and Whispers*.

To be sure, the editor makes a major contribution to the film, but it is in executing the film as envisioned by the director, not by him. From start to finish, the director *is* the filmmaker. Not a single element should escape his control or find its way into the finished film without his approval. Only then will the film carry the mark that is uniquely his, a particular style.

ELEMENTS OF STYLE

It is relatively easy to identify style in literature. In each of the following excerpts, the writer has a distinctive style.

> Generous tears filled Gabriel's eyes. He had never felt like that himself towards any woman, but he knew that such feeling must be love. The tears gathered more thickly in his eyes and in the partial darkness he imagined he saw the form of a young man standing under a dripping tree. Other forms were near. His soul had approached that region where dwell the vast hosts of the dead. He was conscious of, but could not apprehend, their wayward and flickering existence. His own identity was fading out into a grey impalpable world: the solid world itself, which these dead had one time reared and lived in, was dissolving and dwindling.
>
> A few light taps upon the pane made him turn to the window. It had begun to snow again. He watched sleepily the flakes, silver and dark, falling obliquely against the lamplight. The time had come for him to set out on his journey westward. Yes, the newspapers were right, snow was general all over Ireland. It was falling on every part of the dark central plain, on the treeless hills, falling softly upon the Bog of Allen and, farther westward, softly falling into the dark mutinous Shannon waves. It was falling, too, upon every part of the lonely churchyard on the hill where Michael Furey lay buried. It lay thickly drifted on the crooked crosses and headstones, on the spears of the little gate, on the barren thorns. His soul swooned slowly as he heard the snow falling faintly through the universe and faintly falling, like the descent of their last end, upon all the living and the dead.[1]

> The bull was squared on all four feet to be killed, and Romero killed directly below us. He killed not as he had been forced to by the last bull, but as he wanted to. He profiled directly in front of the bull, drew the sword out of the folds of the muleta and sighted along the blade. The bull watched him. Romero spoke to the bull and tapped one of his feet. The bull charged and Romero waited for the charge, the muleta held low, sighting along the blade, his feet firm. Then without taking a step forward, he became one with the bull, the sword was in high between the shoulders, the bull had followed the low-swung flannel, that disappeared as Romero lurched clear to the left and it was over. The bull tried to go forward, his legs commenced to settle, he swung from side to side, hesitated, then went

[1] From *Dubliners* by James Joyce, pp. 287–88. Originally published by B. W. Huebsch, Inc., in 1916. Copyright © 1967 by the Estate of James Joyce. All rights reserved. Reprinted by permission of The Viking Press, Inc.

down on his knees, and Romero's older brother leaned forward behind him and drove a short knife into the bull's neck at the base of the horns. The first time he missed. He drove the knife in again, and the bull went over, twitching and rigid. Romero's brother, holding the bull's horn in one hand, the knife in the other, looked up at the President's box. Handkerchiefs were waving all over the bull-ring. The President looked down from the box and waved his handkerchief. The brother cut the notched black ear from the dead bull and trotted over with it to Romero. The bull lay heavy and black on the sand, his tongue out. Boys were running toward him from all parts of the arena, making a little circle around him. They were starting to dance around the bull.[2]

But as the last whelmings intermixingly poured themselves over the sunken head of the Indian at the mainmast, leaving a few inches of the erect spar yet visible, together with long streaming yards of the flag, which calmly undulated, with ironical coincidings, over the destroying billows they almost touched; — at that instant, a red arm and a hammer hovered backwardly uplifted in the open air, in the act of nailing the flag faster and yet faster to the subsiding spar. A sky-hawk that tauntingly had followed the main-truck downwards from its natural home among the stars, pecking at the flag, and incommoding Tashtego there; this bird now chanced to intercept its broad fluttering wing between the hammer and the wood; and simultaneously feeling that etherial thrill, the submerged savage beneath, in his death-gasp, kept his hammer frozen there; and so the bird of heaven, with archangelic shrieks, and his imperial beak thrust upwards, and his whole captive form folded in the flag of Ahab, went down with his ship, which, like Satan, would not sink to hell till she had dragged a living part of heaven along with her, and helmeted herself with it.

Now small fowls flew screaming over the yet yawning gulf, a sullen white surf beat against its steep sides; then all collapsed, and the great shroud of the sea rolled on as it rolled five thousand years ago.[3]

Waiting, watching the street and the gate from the dark study window, Hightower hears the distant music when it first begins. He does not know that he expects it, that on each Wednesday and Sunday night, sitting in the dark window, he waits for it to begin. He knows almost to the second when he should begin to hear it, without recourse to watch or clock. He uses neither, has needed neither for twentyfive years now. He lives dissociated from mechanical time. Yet for that reason he has never lost it. It is as though out of his subconscious he produces without volition the few crystallizations of stated instances by which his dead life in the actual world had been governed and ordered once. Without recourse to clock he could know immediately upon the thought just where, in his old life, he would be and what doing between the two fixed moments which marked the beginning and the end of Sunday morning service and Sunday evening service and prayer service on Wednesday night; just when he would have been entering the church, just when he would have been bringing to a calculated close prayer or sermon. So before twilight has completely faded he is saying to himself Now they are gathering, approaching along streets slowly and turning in, greeting one another: the groups, the couples, the

[2] Reprinted with the permission of Charles Scribner's Sons from *The Sun Also Rises* by Ernest Hemingway, pp. 229–30. Copyright 1926 by Charles Scribner's Sons; renewal copyright 1954 by Ernest Hemingway.

[3] From *Moby Dick* by Herman Melville (New York: Dell Publishing Co., Inc., 1962), p. 607.

single ones. There is a little informal talking in the church itself, low-toned, the ladies constant and a little sibilant with fans, nodding to arriving friends as they pass in the aisle. Miss Carruthers (she was his organist and she had been dead almost twenty years) is among them; soon she will rise and enter the organloft Sunday evening prayer meeting. It has seemed to him always that at that hour man approaches nearest of all to God, nearer than at any other hour of all the seven days. Then alone, of all church gatherings, is there something of that peace which is the promise and the end of the Church. The mind and the heart purged then if it is ever to be; the week and its whatever disasters finished and summed and expiated by the stern and formal fury of the morning service; the next week and its whatever disasters not yet born, the heart quiet now for a little while beneath the cool soft blowing of faith and hope.[4]

Students of English literature will recognize the four authors quoted above and, more important, will be able to separate and identify those elements that make up each writer's style. With the emergence of the director as the dominant creative artist in the making of a film, films also can be considered in terms of style. Here, of course, many more elements are involved than words on paper, yet every major director has a style that is distinctly his own.

The following elements make up a director's style:

(1) Choice of subject material

(2) Script structure

(3) Images (composition, lighting, and camera movement)

(4) Acting performances

(5) Editing (pace, cadence, and rhythm)

(6) Use of supportive elements (music, sound effects, opticals, etc.)

Subject material

Although the majority of film directors still function as technicians hired by a studio to execute a variety of scripts, the most important artists of the contemporary cinema create films out of their own philosophies and interests. As we view a film, we can often identify the director by the type of material being handled and the viewpoint from which that material is shown. For example, in the films of Alain Resnais we can see certain recurring thematic concerns (time, memory) and common choices of subject matter (war and its effects, both social and political). No one seeing *La Guerre Est Finie*, the story of an aging Spanish revolutionary, could fail to recognize its relationship to other films by Resnais such as *Night and Fog* (a short, retrospective look at Nazi concentration camps) and *Hiroshima, Mon Amour*. Without doubt, the great contemporary directors continually vary their work and expand their

[4] From *Light in August* by William Faulkner, pp. 320–21. Copyright 1932 and renewed 1960 by William Faulkner. Reprinted by permission of Random House, Inc.

interests, yet by and large each has demonstrated some pattern of consistency in his choice of subject material. Subject matter, then, provides the first recognizable signpost of style.

Script

The director's approach to the script (or story) is the second major element of style. Consistency in the choice of script material can be seen in the work of every major filmmaker—from Bergman, who writes his own scripts, to Resnais, who works with a diverse group of script writers (Marguerite Duras, Alain Robbe-Grillet, Jorge Semprun, and Jean Cayrol). The similarities in the scripts are part of the "trademark," or style, of each director.

For example, almost without exception Buñuel's scripts center about the theme of good and evil and utilize bizarre religious symbols to reveal this theme (*El, Nazarín, Viridiana, Belle de Jour*). Godard's scripts (insofar as they are scripts) are generally formless, consisting of a very sketchy story and frequent digressions that satisfy the director's penchant for diatribe (*Les Carabiniers, Weekend, La Chinoise*). Bergman's scripts rely heavily on a basic situation or event. The story is developed largely through dialogue that exposes the characters' inner lives (*Through a Glass Darkly, Persona, Cries and Whispers*).

Again, the work of Alain Resnais provides an example of consistency in approach to the script. Even though there are obvious differences between *Hiroshima, Mon Amour* and *La Guerre Est Finie*, there are important similarities in the way each story is told. In both films the internal life of the hero or heroine is revealed through fragmented scenes of the past that thrust themselves into the onscreen action. In both films the hero or heroine is tormented by a sense of the past, and all action is motivated by that past. In both films there is a simple thread of action involving physical movement: the woman in *Hiroshima, Mon Amour* walking through Hiroshima, fleeing her Japanese lover; the revolutionary in *La Guerre Est Finie* always traveling between France and Spain (Fig. 4). In both films the voice-over track is used to accompany a flow of images from another time and place. Finally, in both films the main characters are driven by love relationships to recall those elements of the past that threaten to destroy them. The similarities of these scripts are distinctive markings by which we can identify the work of Alain Resnais.

Images and movement

Images and movement are perhaps the easiest elements of style to identify, for they involve recognition at a purely visual level. Every major director approaches a film with a definite view of how the film should look. Although all the directors cited above have developed and improved their art from film to film, each has remained consistent in his basic approach to image.

Fig. 4. *La Guerre Est Finie.*

Each of the foremost contemporary directors has a unique approach to the visual image. No Bergman scene can ever be mistaken for a Fellini scene; no Resnais scene resembles a scene lit and composed by Truffaut; nor can Kubrick ever be confused for Bertolucci. The ability to recognize these differences among directors, and to appreciate the elements that create the differences, is essential to the study of the art of film.

Let us examine a group of visual images that contain elements particular to individual directors. Figures 5 through 7 present a scene from Bergman's *The Seventh Seal*, a scene from Resnais' *Hiroshima, Mon Amour*, and a scene from Antonioni's *Red Desert*. Each image contains distinctive elements of composition and lighting.

The Bergman scene (Fig. 5) is formal and dramatic in composition; it seems almost to have been composed as a still photograph. The composition of the image draws our attention deeply into the frame. The black-and-white lighting is stark and unrelieved. It is characterized by high contrast between light and dark—black and white with little or no transitional tones. As a result, the figures seem etched against the gloomy background, almost burned into the film. After carefully examining this scene, look at a series of stills selected from several Bergman films and notice the consistent elements of Bergman's approach to image (see Chapter 2, Figs. 3, 5, and 15).

In the Resnais scene (Fig. 6), the composition seems almost careless and overflows the boundaries of the frame. The lighting is so diffuse that the scene seems to be lit naturally rather than artificially. Soft gray tones fill every corner of the frame, creating that strange poetic atmosphere so typical of Resnais' work.

Fig. 5. *The Seventh Seal.*

Fig. 6. *Hiroshima, Mon Amour.*

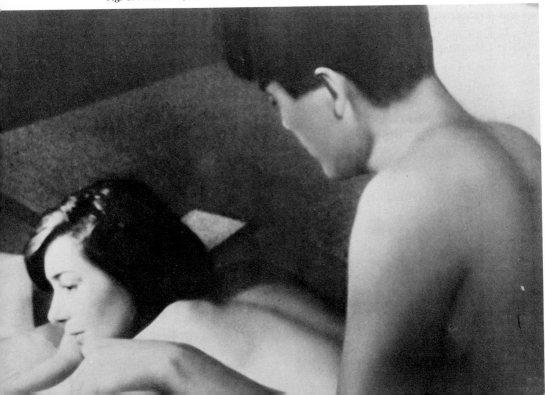

Fig. 7. *Red Desert.*

The visual style of Antonioni (Fig. 7) is very different from that of Bergman or Resnais. Contrast is almost completely gone. Sky and land blend; figures and flesh tones are equal in intensity to the elements that surround them. The composition of the scene is almost desultory, calling little or no attention to itself.

In addition to a director's approach to image is his approach to *movement*. This too is an easily identifiable element of style. Bergman works essentially with a static camera, with slow, deliberate movements that are carefully plotted and used only when motivated by specific action. For Bergman, movement is valid only when it is signaled by plot. It is never used for superfluous effect or for its own sake. In Bergman's films, every camera movement is cued to specific dialogue or action. For example, in the "flagellants" scene from *The Seventh Seal*, the camera moves among the marchers at exactly the pace of the procession itself; at no time are we aware of the camera. The music, the chorus, and the drum all set the pace at which the camera — fixed to its dolly — moves.

Resnais' use of camera movement presents a different approach. The central cinematic device of *Night and Fog*, which preceded all of Resnais' major films, is a slowly moving camera that explores, in a succession of flowing images linked by dissolves, the exteriors and interiors of deserted concentration camps. This same device appears in the opening scenes of *Hiro-*

shima, Mon Amour and *Last Year at Marienbad*. Indeed, this movement is as clear an identification of the artist as if he had signed his name at the bottom of each frame.

Antonioni's approach to movement is quite different from that of Resnais or Bergman. He prefers the use of pans and tilts. Key scenes in his films are revealed by a searching camera that moves right and left, up and down, from a fixed vantage point.

Significant and consistent elements in the style of other directors are the "nervous," hand-held camera of Jean-Luc Godard (*Breathless*); the static images of Fred Zinnemann (*A Man for All Seasons*); the fancy, complex dolly shots of Stanley Kubrick (*A Clockwork Orange*); and the rapid, evolving, straight-line dollies of David Lean (*Doctor Zhivago*) and Akira Kurosawa (*Rashomon*).

Acting performances

As noted earlier, acting performances are coming more and more to reflect the style of the director rather than the style of the actor. The way that actors perform is a clear indication of the director's view of acting. The following chapter takes up, in greater detail, the elements of film acting; here, acting will be examined solely from the director's viewpoint.

In all of Bergman's films, there is consistency in the style of the acting. Almost without exception, the actors are brooding, introspective, melancholy, and reserved. There are long silences between segments of dialogue, and the overall pace is generally slow and thoughtful. Rarely is there any bravura acting. Facial expressions, although subtle and low-key, are extremely important. Bergman maintains almost total control over every movement, every gesture. Raised voices are a rarity and are saved for special moments. There is great economy of gesture—rarely a wasted expression or movement.

Compare these trademarks with the acting in a Fellini film. Here, the actors are almost encouraged to give vent to an "Italianate" expressionism, keeping little or nothing to themselves, indulging in histrionics and a wide range of physical gestures. Performances are larger than life and dialogue is delivered with passion, even when what is being discussed is no more urgent than the breakfast menu.

In the examples cited above, the differences in acting style can be attributed to the director's approach to acting. They are part of the recognizable style—the signature—of the director.

Pace

It is part of the nature of film that when we first view a motion picture we are usually overwhelmed by it. It is difficult to isolate the elements of the film. It is particularly difficult, on first viewing a film, to grasp the "hidden" factors that affect our feeling about what we have seen. We may speak of the film as having been "powerful," "upbeat," or "slow-moving." Only after several viewings do we begin to appreciate all the elements that contribute to the overall effect.

Most of the great directors control the pace of their films by manipulating the movements of the camera and the actors, the speed of the dialogue, and the rhythm of the editing. Directors deal with pace both intellectually and intuitively. Although most films contain both slow- and fast-moving scenes, each generally conveys a single overall effect. Consider for a moment the general impression created by Bertolucci's films. Are they fast-paced, bouncy, and filled with flash-cuts, montage, and collage? Or do we remember them as slow, deliberate, thoughtful, introspective, and even melancholy? Of course, most of us will (and should) choose the latter. On the other hand, directors like William Friedkin (*The French Connection*, *The Exorcist*) and Peter Yates (*Bullitt*, *The Friends of Eddy Coyle*) are recalled as "action" directors, despite the fact that their films often contain a number of effective slow-moving sequences.

What elements contribute to the pace of a film? In most of Bergman's films, a relatively static camera is used. When the camera does move, it usually moves slowly. Scenes are played out from one camera position with few inter-cuts. Dialogue is delivered at a measured pace with little or no urgency — conversations seem to complete themselves. The dialogue of *Cries and Whispers*, for example, is delivered as though the characters intended to continue their discussions for hours.

In contrast to Bergman, Kubrick uses rapid camera movement and over-lapping dialogue. Scenes are foreshortened; action is continually interrupted by cuts that prevent the viewer from seeing the action completed. Rarely is the camera at rest. It moves at a frantic pace, capturing images from a variety of unexpected, oblique angles (Fig. 8). The eye of the audience is bombarded by a continuous succession of mobile images. Conversations are frequently interrupted and difficult to follow. Dialogue overlaps from scene to scene,

Fig. 8. *A Clockwork Orange.*

propelling the audience into the incoming scene before it has absorbed the outgoing one.

The editing

Although each editor has his own style, his own approach to film, this style is largely a reflection of the director. Editing techniques generally conform to the director's approach to a film. The use of intercuts, overlapping dialogue, brief or lengthy scenes, close-ups or long shots, fragmented visual elements — all these sign the film with a director's name. As has been noted, Resnais frequently uses flash-cuts to reveal the past. These cuts are predictably short in length (almost subliminal) and appear at unexpected moments in the film. In contrast, Antonioni uses long, uninterrupted scenes in which a moving camera follows the action. And some directors, such as Godard, fluctuate between these two techniques. Quite probably, a Resnais film has three or four times as many cuts as an Antonioni film. Some films are edited in direct chronological order (Antonioni and Bergman); others are edited in fragmented, inverted order (Resnais and Lester). In each case, the editorial style is controlled by the director.

Supportive elements

The method by which a director structures the undercarriage of a film is also a mark of his style. Truffaut, Bergman, and Buñuel usually limit their films to a Spartan simplicity. Images, dialogue, and music comprise ninety percent of their work. Rarely does a complex sound effects track, a brilliant music score, or a complicated series of voice-over dialogues play a major role in their films. To be sure, all these elements are present, but they are merely secondary elements and remain "in their place."

Stanley Kubrick, on the other hand, drenches his films with every possible supportive element, and he assigns a major role to music, sound effects, optical effects, and background noises. We can readily recognize a Kubrick film (*Dr. Strangelove, 2001, A Clockwork Orange*) by the sheer abundance and variety of aural and visual detail. Directors vary in their use of music to create emotional impact. David Lean often fills every inch of his sound tract with lush, symphonic music (*Great Expectations, Doctor Zhivago, Bridge on the River Kwai*), whereas Bergman is content in *Through a Glass Darkly* to permit the Bach cello suit to sound for a few brief moments three or four times in the film and in *Cries and Whispers* he uses the piano equally selectively.

THE DIRECTOR AS A CREATIVE ARTIST

In the final analysis, the director *is* the filmmaker. He envisions the entire film and selects the intellectual and philosophical ideas that give the film its character and power. He creates the images and adjusts their relationships to one another. He structures and creates the aural elements that support these visual images. The director deals with a variety of artistic elements — literature, visual composition, light and shade, music, and drama. In each of his artistic roles, he strives for a unified work of art.

The director must be able to conceive of the film as a whole, to envision how the finished film will look and sound long before photography is begun. He must be in complete control of every detail of the film. The director must command and control the composition of each frame, the lighting of each scene, and the pace and rhythm of each movement. He must be able to elicit a creative reevaluation of the material so that the film will come together as an artistic entity. And he must have the taste and judgment to determine what external elements should be added to the film in its final stages.

Literature

Today, as the art of film continues to evolve as the creation of a single artist, the director is moving into control earlier and earlier in the filmmaking process. No longer satisfied to work with a script over which he has had no creative control, he moves into the area of writing. Bergman writes most of his scripts and functions completely as an author. The quality of the script of *Cries and Whispers* is extraordinary in every sense, and the script can be read and appreciated as literature. Bertolucci works *with* the writer, influencing the story, the characters, and all the literary elements (such as descriptions and dialogue). He then makes on-set changes that often involve him in writing new material. In recent years, the director has become the creator of the script, and he fashions the film to explore the themes and ideas that he, the director, is interested in.

The following excerpt from a critical article by John Russell Taylor[5] demonstrates how a film critic addresses himself to the "literature" of film:

> The three films [*Through a Glass Darkly, Winter Light,* and *The Silence*] are quite separate in plot, though the same actors recur in them to some extent (as, indeed, in most of Bergman's films) and they are related in theme. The questions: Does God exist? If he exists, what is he like? What should our relations with him be? have preoccupied Bergman the pastor's son throughout his creative career, explicitly or implicitly: God is either present in the films, or his absence is in itself an important factor. As with so much of what has come after, the germ of the trilogy primarily devoted to this question is to be found in that central earlier work *Fängelse* [*Prison*]: the concept, in particular, of a Manichean world in which God may be a monster, permitting for his own unknowable ends things of (by human standards) the utmost horror and evil to occur, which recurs forcefully throughout the trilogy.

Beginning with his thematic material, Bergman shapes plot and creates

[5] From *Cinema Eye, Cinema Ear* by John Russell Taylor, p. 166. Copyright © 1964 by John Russell Taylor. Reprinted by permission of Hill and Wang, Inc.

character. He tightly structures each film, like a piece of chamber music. Simplicity is the keynote. Throughout his films, there is unity of time and place. A Bergman film is sparse in elements (usually a singleness of plot and event) but incredibly rich in personal detail. After shaping theme, plot, and character, Bergman creates dialogue that is both eloquent and revealing.

The scripts written by Bergman contain many of the characteristics of the finest literature — story ideas that reveal truths about man's estate, eloquent dialogue that reveals the essential nature of man, and poetic language that enriches our lives. Other directors are following Bergman's lead. Almost without exception, the major contemporary filmmakers control their scripts. They are becoming the creators of the literature of film.

The visual art

The portrait of the director has changed from that of an imposing "vice-admiral" to that of a working, creative artist. The contemporary director, instead of rising occasionally from his chair on set to give an order or consult with a cameraman, has become *the* filmmaker. Every visual image bears his signature. He composes each scene, controls the lighting, dictates the camera movement, and is deeply involved in every aspect of the visual art.

Most of the creative contemporary directors no longer depend on the cameraman to "okay" a scene. During rehearsals, they view the action themselves through the lens. Most important, each of the great directors of modern cinema has a distinctive style with regard to the visual image. As was noted earlier, nowhere in a film is the individuality of the director more evident than in what is seen — the image. Of course, most films are identifiable by subject matter, editing techniques, sound, and music; but by and large it is the nature of the *visual* elements that gives the film its identifying marks. The modern director no longer acts as a general major-domo, leaving technical matters to others while he deals with the actors and the *mise en scène*. The contemporary director is on center stage and he works with all the image-making elements.

Editing and sound

What has been said earlier concerning the director's emergence as writer and cameraman is equally true of the director's emergence as editor. The director influences every aspect of the editing and finishing of a film. He is involved in the creation of all the complex elements that support a film, and he impresses his personal style on these elements. In all his films, Bergman commands a static and deliberate editing. Each scene is allowed to run its course. Close-ups and intercuts are used judiciously, leaving the master scene seemingly uninterrupted. Sound is generally used in a realistic manner and is directly related to the scene it accompanies, and music is sparsely and carefully employed.

Kubrick, on the other hand, prefers a highly fragmentary style of editing—short cuts, countless interruptions of action, and total freedom in editorial treatment of time and space. Sound, too, is often totally unrelated to what is on screen and is used almost as a separate entity. Kubrick's music—drawn from a wide range of classical and contemporary sources—is often jangling, disturbing, unexpected; it changes constantly in style and usage.

Contemporary directors *are* editing, composing, and recording. They are deeply concerned that the contributions of each craftsman and technician conform in content and quality to their overall conception of the film. This deep concern has prompted directors to become more and more involved in the actual "doing" of a film, and so their influence has grown. The contemporary director is now the complete filmmaker.

FILMS FOR STUDY

Through a Glass Darkly, Ingmar Bergman. Janus Films, 24 West 58th Street, New York, New York 10019.

Winter Light, Ingmar Bergman. Janus Films, 24 West 58th Street, New York, New York 10019.

Hour of the Wolf, Ingmar Bergman. Janus Films, 24 West 58th Street, New York, New York 10019.

L'Avventura, Michelangelo Antonioni. Janus Films, 24 West 58th Street, New York, New York 10019.

Jules and Jim, François Truffaut. Janus Films, 24 West 58th Street, New York, New York 10019.

Rashomon, Akira Kurosawa. Janus Films, 24 West 58th Street, New York, New York 10019.

La Guerre Est Finie, Alain Resnais.

Pather Panchali, Satyajit Ray.

Los Olvidados, Luis Buñuel.

8½, Federico Fellini.

A Clockwork Orange, Stanley Kubrick.

SUPPLEMENTARY READING

Kyrou, Ado. *Luis Buñuel: An Introduction,* trans. by Adrienne Foulke. New York: Simon and Schuster, Inc., 1963.

Leprohon, Pierre. *The World of Film: Michelangelo Antonioni,* trans. by Scott Sullivan. New York: Simon and Schuster, 1963.

Simon, John. *Ingmar Bergman Directs.* New York: Harcourt Brace Jovanovich, 1972.

Walker, Alexander. *Stanley Kubrick Directs.* New York: Harcourt Brace Jovanovich, 1972.

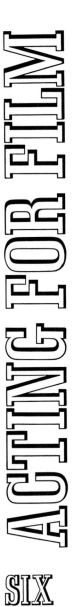

ACTING FOR FILM

SIX

The film actor ought not to understand, he ought to be. One might argue that in order to be, he needs to understand. This is not true. If it were true, the most intelligent actor would be the best actor. Reality often proves the contrary.

When an actor is intelligent, the effort he has to make to be a good actor is three times as great, for he wants to get to the bottom of everything, even the finest shades of meaning, and in trying to do so he trespasses on ground that is not his own — in fact, he creates obstacles for himself.

His reflections on the character he is playing, which, according to popular theory, should lead him to an exact characterization, end by hamstringing his work and depriving him of naturalness. The actor should arrive on the set in a virgin state. The more intuitive his work, the more spontaneous he will be.

Michelangelo Antonioni
The World of Film: Michelangelo Antonioni
by Pierre Leprohon
New York: Simon and Schuster, Inc., 1963, pp. 101–02.

The difference between film acting and stage acting is the difference between cutting a diamond and making a rather flamboyant piece of sculpture. The focus in film acting is like a laser beam, a much more specific, intense, pinpointed focus in which the camera comes to you to ferret out the little things you can show it.

Stacy Keach
"Acting for Films,"
Filmmakers Newsletter,
Vol. 6, No. 8, p. 32.

Acting is not the memorizing of lines while wear-
ing a disguise, but the clear reconstruction of the
thoughts that cause the actions and the lines. This
is not easy. In the finest sense of the word, the
actor is not only interpreter, and not only a carrier
of ideas that originate in others, but himself can
be (though not without difficulty) a good creative
artist.

Joseph von Sternberg
in *Film Culture*, I, Nos. 5–6,
(Winter 1955), pp. 1–4.

ALTHOUGH MUCH HAS BEEN SAID AND WRITTEN ABOUT ACTING FOR FILM, THE NATURE of truly great screen acting is still not clearly understood. This lack of understanding is due in part to the continued influence of the theater on screen acting as a performing art. Although the acting profession has for some time acknowledged superficial differences between stage performance and screen performance, it has only recently accepted the concept of screen acting as a separate art form.

THE HISTORICAL DEVELOPMENT OF SCREEN ACTING

In the early days of cinema, acting consisted largely of exaggerated mannerisms and gestures. The stars of the 1920s—Chaplin, Fairbanks, Pickford, Hart, and Valentino—projected larger-than-life personalities on screen and exhibited few if any subtleties of style. Since the early films were not supported by sound, the tradition of screen acting began with pantomime, in which only the most elemental emotions are communicated.

The advent of sound recording introduced a new dimension to screen acting. It enabled the actor to move away from exaggerated gesture and pantomime. However, since the majority of actors working in film learned their art on the stage, early sound films (1928–35) were still heavily overacted. The influence of the theater delayed for a long time the development of a separate and unique approach to the problems posed by the camera.

During the late 1930s and 1940s, the major development in the art of screen acting was the rise of the "screen personality." Actors like Paul Muni, Charles Laughton, Spencer Tracy, Ronald Coleman, Bette Davis, and Clark Gable were far more effective as "personalities" than as actors. They seldom

155

varied their performances from role to role and embellished every role with personal mannerisms and gestures. These mannerisms — Gable's smile, Tracy's bowed head, Davis' hands — endeared them to audiences and became the trademarks of their performance regardless of the roles they played. For example, in *The Story of Louis Pasteur* and *The Life of Emile Zola,* Paul Muni played the title roles in exactly the same way even though the two main characters were not at all alike. In both films he tugged at his beard and affected an extreme nearsightedness by squinting through small spectacles.

During this period, as directors moved the camera and microphone closer to the actor, and as lenses, cameras, and sound-recording equipment improved, actors began to render more subtle performances. Voices were lowered and conversations became more realistic, with people talking to one another instead of "performing" for an unseen audience. Facial expressions, gestures, and physical movement were reduced. Slowly, the first steps were made in the development of screen acting as a separate art form. Only after World War II, however, did the screen actor emerge as a truly consummate artist.

In the 1950s, a group of successful actors from the British stage began to adapt their art to the screen. This group of actors, including Laurence Olivier, Ralph Richardson, Michael Redgrave, Alec Guinness, Trevor Howard, and James Mason, had a strong impact on the development of acting for film. They scaled down the traditional bravura performances of the British stage while maintaining the careful attention to detail for which the British repertory theater is noted. The performances of Olivier in *Rebecca,* Mason in *Odd Man Out,* Richardson in *The Fallen Idol,* and Redgrave in *The Browning Version* are excellent examples of the contribution of British actors to the art of screen acting.

During the same period, French and Italian film directors began to strive for greater realism. They looked for actors who could project a high level of "believability" and often chose amateurs to appear in their films. In every country except America, the day of the screen personality was coming to an end. As the art of film matured, the art of film acting also grew. Today, directors as different as Fellini, Bergman, Antonioni, Kubrick and Coppola elicit from their actors performances that subtly reveal the most complex human motivations and emotions. Contemporary audiences no longer simply view a "performance"; they look deeply into inner character.

In the contemporary cinema, acting must go beyond performance. The screen personalities of the past are gone or fast disappearing, and with them, the era of the "star." Today, we often forget the actor and remember the character. The child-woman in *La Strada,* the boy in *The 400 Blows,* the woman in *Hiroshima, Mon Amour,* the reporter in *La Dolce Vita,* the Squire in *The Seventh Seal* — all these characters remain part of our experience long after we have forgotten the names of the actors. The new generation of screen actors, with creative talents such as Max Von Sydow, Harriet Andersson, Cloris Leachman, Marcello Mastroianni, Rod Steiger, Liv Ullmann, and Jean-Louis Trintignant, has given us a reality rarely achieved before in acting performance.

In casting a film, the contemporary director is no longer restricted to the same studio stockpile of box-office personalities. Performance is everything, and the contemporary filmmaker seeks actors who can reveal the role. Bergman may use Harriet Andersson in film after film and yet use Kari Sylwan in a film such as *Cries and Whispers* because she can do a very special job in a demanding, though small, role. He may never use her again. In fact, many superb performances today are fashioned by actors who appear once and then disappear. The character is far more important than the actor. One of the major artistic failures of the American cinema has been the failure to recognize this new approach to screen acting. Hollywood has held on to the "personality" for a decade too long. The appearance of Dustin Hoffman in *The Graduate* and Michael J. Pollard and Estelle Parsons in *Bonnie and Clyde* may signal the beginning of America's acceptance of this contemporary approach to the art of screen acting.

Acting on screen, then, must be considered a unique art, an art wholly separate from its past on stage and in silent film. Let us examine in greater detail the elements that contribute to the uniqueness of the art of screen acting.

THE ELEMENTS OF ACTING FOR FILM

There are five basic elements that make film acting unique:

(1) The separation of actor from audience.

(2) The camera and its effect on the actor.

(3) Performance out of sequence.

(4) Performance in small, separate units.

(5) The reconstruction of performance through editing.

The separation of actor from audience

In all the performing arts, performer and audience are essential to each other. The stage actor draws sustenance from the audience and fashions his performance according to what is happening between himself and his live audience. Film, however, separates actor from audience, and demands an entirely different approach to acting. Since every actor must relate to someone or something, the screen actor has two basic choices: either he can fix in his mind an image of an audience and reach out to it, or he can relate totally to his fellow actors and to the character he is playing. In the latter case, he momentarily drops his identity as an actor and, for the time that the camera is rolling, *becomes* the character he plays.

If the actor chooses the second approach, he can become a screen actor of merit, for film demands a higher level of reality than the stage. The film actor is separated from the audience by artificial barriers — the screen, the film itself, and the lens. The actor must reach out beyond these barriers and *project* a sense of communication with the audience. The actor who has this special ability will succeed as an artist in film.

To project successfully, an actor must be "believable." Every gesture, every expression, every line of dialogue, must be *true* — true to the situation and the character. On the stage, it is not really necessary to believe in the truth of the events we watch. Indeed, because of the limitations of the theater we are constantly reminded that we are watching a play, an acting out of an artifice. Thus we only admire; we do not believe. The entire thrust of the contemporary cinema is to make us believe, and it is to this issue that the screen actor must address himself. As the camera closes in on the actor, the audience is given an intense view of the character. If the audience feels that what it is seeing is true, communication will be established, and the actor will be projecting not himself but the reality of the character he plays.

The actor, then, must surmount the fact that he is removed from the audience when he performs, and that he is returned to the audience only as a two-dimensional figure on a screen at the end of a darkened room. To accomplish this, the actor must *be*, not act, and he must be able to project truth in every word, gesture, and expression.

The camera and its effect upon the actor

The most obvious element that makes film acting unique is the camera. In the theater, the audience sees the entire stage from a fixed vantage point. In film, the audience is given a variety of views from which to see the character portrayed: *there is no place for the actor to hide*. The camera can be on all sides of the actor; it can be far away or unbearably close. One false move, one phony gesture, one line delivered without conviction or out of character, and the illusion is destroyed. The camera can reveal age and can cast a merciless light on imperfection. It can reveal the actor either as a towering artist or as a mediocre performer.

Harriet Andersson's performance as the daughter Karin in *Through a Glass Darkly* has been called a clinically perfect portrayal of schizophrenia. Throughout the film, the camera probes the girl's personality, giving the audience a close-up view of all the intimate manifestations of her madness. Karin, seeking to hide the alarming symptoms, is forced to retreat further and further within herself. Her family is unaware of most of the symptoms, but the camera, offering intense close-ups of the girl, reveals to the audience what the other characters cannot see. Because of the intensity of the images, Miss Andersson transmits a reality that a stage performance could never reveal. When the camera looks directly into Karin's eyes, we see the reality that only cinema can show. The same is true of her superb performance as the dying girl in *Cries and Whispers*.

The actor who knows what the camera can do has taken the first step toward becoming a film actor. Because the camera can transmit a magnified reality, the actor need not "act" at all. One small tear shed in despair becomes, through the eye of the camera, more moving than all the histrionics the actor might muster.

Performance out of sequence

Most films are shot out of sequence to meet the demands of budget and locale. Since technicians and equipment outnumber actors in a film, the schedule is usually designed to accommodate the most efficient and economical method of shooting. For example, it would be uneconomical to shoot a scene on a particular set, leave the set for a week for on-location shooting, and then return to the set for another scene. Generally, scenes that take place on the same set are shot at the same time, regardless of where they fall in the script. For example, if a film contains scenes in Hong Kong, all on-location scenes will be shot before the production returns to Hollywood for the studio scenes.

Thus, whereas the stage actor usually performs his role in chronological order, the screen actor acts in small segments that are often completely out of sequence. However, if the actor has *become* the character, it will make no difference in what order the sections of the film are shot. The actor can play the scenes in any order because he *is* the character. He does not have to pretend.

In the film *Tunes of Glory*, Alec Guinness and John Mills give superb acting performances. Some of the difficulties that had to be surmounted by the two actors in performing out of sequence can be seen in a plot outline of the film. Structured like a Greek tragedy, the film deals with the conflict between two flawed men of exceptional character. "Jock" Sinclair (Alec Guinness), an old Army regular, is acting commander of the regiment in which he has served all his life. He enjoys an easy, laissez-faire relationship with the other officers and is respected by them. He fully expects to be given the post permanently. When another officer (John Mills) is given the post, Sinclair is bitter and resentful, and he sets out to destroy the intruder. The new officer also has deep ties to his regiment and has behind him an excellent war record. His prisoner-of-war experience, however, has left him in doubt of his stability. He is a rigid, unbending man who seeks to impose his will on the other officers. As we watch the slow destruction of the new commander, Mills' performance changes gradually. Mills begins the film stiff and fighting for self-control. Slowly and subtly, over an hour of screen time, he reveals his inner weaknesses, and finally he prepares to commit suicide. Concurrently, Guinness' performance changes. In destroying the commander, Sinclair also destroys himself.

Performing out of sequence in a film that requires subtle, progressive changes in character places severe demands on the actor. To cope with these demands, the actor must be so deeply immersed in the role that he can produce the *total* character at any given time. It is as though an actor playing Hamlet on the stage were asked to begin with the final scene. He must immediately be able to recall the preceding scenes even though he has not yet created them. Then, having performed the final scene, he must move directly to an earlier scene, reviving himself, retreating in time, and performing with no hint of what is to come. This factor alone, *performance out of sequence*, imposes demands on the actor's art that make film acting unlike any other kind of acting.

Performance in small, separate units

On the stage, an actor can create his entire role in a time span of two to three hours. Aside from interruptions for intermissions, the stage actor can develop his role continuously and chronologically. The screen actor, however, must work in small, separate units of time — shots and scenes that are often only a few minutes in length. When the camera is rolling, he must come instantly alive and must sustain the role for a brief moment. Then, he must be prepared to re-create that moment over and over, maintaining a consistent and convincing performance. Again, imagine a stage actor playing Hamlet being asked to repeat the opening lines of the "To be or not to be" soliloquy twenty times and afterward being expected to complete the soliloquy with freshness and spontaneity. The screen actor must sustain and nourish his art through lengthy delays and interruptions. Often, a rehearsal is held in the morning, but the actual shooting may not take place until early afternoon. Part of a scene may be shot at 9 A.M., but because of the lighting changes and preparation required for shooting the scene from a different angle, the rest of the scene may not be shot until 5 P.M.

These delays and interruptions place special demands on the screen actor. He must be able to conjure up the character he is playing at a moment's notice. If he is submerged in that character, he will be able to react consistently at all times. Again, it is the actor who *is* the character who can best cope with the demands of screen acting: performance in small, separate units.

The reconstruction of performance through editing

The final element that makes screen acting unique is the actor's awareness during filming that at some later time his performance will be re-evaluated and perhaps reconstructed. The stage actor gives his full performance each evening. When he leaves the theater, the performance is finished, and its strengths and weaknesses are consigned to the past. The screen actor, however, does not give a "complete" performance during shooting. The final performance is created in the editing room from bits and pieces of the original performance (takes) given before the camera. Details can be added or subtracted (for example, close-up reactions can be cut in or eliminated). Dialogue, expressions, and movement can be used in an order quite different from the order in which they are originally performed.

Although striving for consistency from scene to scene and from take to take, the screen actor also knows that if he is unhappy with his reading of a particular line in an otherwise excellent master scene, he will have a chance to improve that line when he does his close-ups. But if the quality of the actor's performance varies too greatly from take to take, the editor will have difficulty creating a unified and convincing performance in the final editing. However, if the actor gives a consistent performance, accurate in detail from shot to shot, the editor can make his selections motivated only by what is best. The final film will then reveal a totally convincing and consistent performance.

THE ARCHITECTURE OF A TOTAL PERFORMANCE

There are three basic elements upon which an actor builds a successful screen performance and through which his performance can be evaluated: (1) the projection of internal conviction, (2) physical performance, and (3) intellectual communication.

The projection of internal conviction

If a film is to succeed, it must be believable. In the early days of film, the wonder of cinema was in the process itself. Today, audiences want to be convinced that what they are viewing is a real part of man's experience. The world is too small, the impact of television too great, and the evidence of what is real too much a part of our daily lives for film to "get away with" the painted backdrop or the phony performance.

Styles of acting can vary greatly—from the classic style of Laurence Olivier in a music hall role in *The Entertainer,* to the method acting of Marlon Brando in *Last Tango in Paris.* These diverse performances are linked by one important element—believability consistent within the context of the film. An examination of great acting performances in contemporary films will not turn up a single false note. The accomplished actor transmits inner conviction and knowledge of the character across the barrier of celluloid and reaches directly into the consciousness of each member of the audience.

One of the finest performances achieved on screen is that of Max Von Sydow in Bergman's *Hour of the Wolf.* The film deals with an artist who is going mad. As the artist draws closer and closer to the edge of insanity, the camera moves closer and closer to him. In an early sequence in the film, the artist and his wife are invited to a dinner party. As the camera records the inanities and follies of the guests, it returns for intense close-up views of the artist, who is holding on to his sanity by a thread. Through immobile facial expressions, a variety of glances, and a few mumbled words, Von Sydow communicates the artist's inner struggle in a manner that keeps the audience in unbearable tension. The audience awaits a blow-up that never comes. Von Sydow communicates the essence of madness in so real a fashion that the audience forgets completely that it is watching a film. The actor succeeds in projecting an internal truth that not only "suspends disbelief" but that transports the audience into the world of the film, making the film a part of their lives.

There is no formula by which an actor can be taught believability. The director learns to recognize truth when he hears it. The actor must find a way to project that truth by himself. Great screen actors are very few in number. Many actors give a single fine performance and are never heard of again. But in that one performance of distinction is the projection of inner conviction.

Physical performance

Another element in successful screen acting is physical performance, or movement. Some of the best examples of the use of movement are the films of Charlie Chaplin. Without the aid of dialogue, and with flimsy and often childish plots, Chaplin creates a complex and universal character. He accomplishes this mainly through movement. Chaplin's walk, of course, is the most obvious factor, but physical gestures, facial expressions, and timing of movement in relation to plot are also key factors in his performance. Today, the technique of filmmaking is so complex that the role of physical movement in performance is often overlooked. However, as the actor seeks to structure a complete performance, movement will continue to be a major factor in communicating many hidden facets of character.

The physical element of screen acting is of considerable importance in the performance of Yves Montand in *La Guerre Est Finie*. Montand's performance suggests some of the character's internal weariness so vital to the theme of the film. His movements are deliberate, cautious, and even heavy. Since there is little physical movement in the film (much of the action consists of the endless car trips between France and Spain), it is essential that every movement of the actor reveal important information about the character. Every close-up must reveal something. In the film, even when Montand simply closes his eyes or moves a finger, the movement, magnified in close-up, communicates the thoughts or feelings of the character.

The gentle mood of romance in *Elvira Madigan* is communicated in part by the slow, languorous movements of the actors. Reactions are delayed, eyes are raised or lowered slowly, and hands are manipulated with great care. Thus, the physical performances help to extend the essential mood of the film.

Intellectual communication

The third element in a successful acting performance is intellectual communication. Whereas emotional communication is readily apparent and arises directly from the actor's internal conviction, intellectual communication must be projected by the actor. The actor must give the audience some insight into the mind of the character he is playing. If he simply creates a façade, an external view of the character, he will not project the essence of the role, which is, of course, the intellectual self.

For example, in most of the films of the 1930s and 1940s, only an external view of character is presented. The films are built largely on a single facet of personality. Thus Henry Fonda, Spencer Tracy, and James Stewart project essentially one-dimensional images, images that are lovable and honest. In *Grapes of Wrath,* we are moved emotionally by Fonda in his role as Tom Joad because Joad, an honest, loyal, and likable man, is treated badly by society. But we are not stimulated intellectually by the film. During this period, film was thought to be incapable of handling subtle and complex philosophical ideas. Thus, unlike Steinbeck's novel, the film *Grapes of Wrath* presents only the theme of social injustice, simplistically played out in a drama of good guys against bad.

The emergence after World War II of films that examined complex philosophical ideas placed new requirements on the actor. In his role as the Knight in *The Seventh Seal,* Max Von Sydow had to reveal many internal facets of character, keeping the audience involved in the film and conveying the complex personality of the character. Today, the successful screen actor must be prepared to reveal the thought processes that motivate response and must give the audience a vision beyond the obvious physical elements of acting.

THE ACTOR AS A CREATIVE ARTIST

When the camera closes in on an actor, no director can tell the actor exactly what to do or what not to do. At that moment, the actor must reach into himself and draw upon whatever inner resources will aid his creation of a convincing performance. Of course, not all actors prepare for a part in the same way. Different actors employ different techniques in working up a believable role, and some find the process more difficult than others. But regardless of the actor's methods or emotional requirements, it is essential that he receive a certain amount of guidance from the director. The director bears the primary responsibility for maintaining an overview of the entire project. The director therefore knows the relative importance of every scene in the film, and, because film actors are forced to create a role out of sequence, the director must be able to *communicate* his vision to them or else run the risk of uneven and unconvincing performances.

The ways of communicating directorial guidance and achieving effective performances are as varied as the directors themselves. Some directors exercise tight control on the set, while other directors prefer a loose climate of give-and-take. The following comments by successful directors demonstrate diverse possibilities for guiding an actor's performance. No one approach is better than another — whatever works is right.

> When an actor makes it apparent to me that it is difficult for him to say something, then we discuss the problem and I modify the thing in question somewhat. And if, while they are working, I notice that the actors are cheating on the idea of a scene, or that it is difficult for them to respect

certain movements that they find too complicated, well, then too, we discuss and I often rectify. . . .[1]

—Carl Dreyer

I give . . . [actors] a great deal of freedom and, at the same time, the feeling of precision. It's a strange combination. In other words, physically, and in the way they develop, I demand the precision of ballet. But their way of acting comes directly from their own ideas as much from mine.[2]

—Orson Welles

Very often, it is the actors themselves who suggest the action to me when they tell me their own stories, or when I see how they live off the set, during breaks. It is very important to me to permit the whole troupe . . . to live spontaneously, in order to create a very comfortable atmosphere, a playful ambience in which each one finds himself completely at ease, without ever having the feeling—paralyzing for me—that he is accomplishing a professional duty, but breathing, living, moving in a way that is most familiar to him, most congenial.[3]

—Federico Fellini

The actor must unconditionally identify himself with his part. This identification should be like a costume that is slipped on. Lengthy concentration, continuous control of feelings, and high-pressure working are completely out. The actor must be able in the purely technical sense (and if possible with the director's help) to take on and take off the character he is playing. Mental tensions and lengthy exertions are fatal to all filmic expression.[4]

—Ingmar Bergman

I could give you many instances of occasions when I had to resolve serious problems in my relationships with actors. I should like at least to mention one of them in order to return to the question of intelligence in actors: the case of my relationship with Betsy Blair [who plays Elvia in Il Grido]. She is a very intelligent actress, who demands very elaborate explanations. I must confess that it was with her that I spent one of the most agonizing times in my career as a director; it occurred when she wanted to read the scenario of Il Grido with me. She wanted me to unveil the meaning behind every speech—which was, of course, impossible. Speeches are the fruit of instinct; they are suggested by imagination, not by reason, and they often have no other reason for existing than the need felt by the author for just those words and no others. This is a perfectly natural fact, inherent in the nature of literary creation, and for that very reason often inexplicable. Thus I had to invent purely imaginary explanations for Betsy Blair, which corresponded in absolutely no way with what I meant to say in the film, and at the same time try to understand what *she* wanted to know. Only thus could I try to bring her to the point where she could play the character better than if I had explained it to her.[5]

—Michelangelo Antonioni

[1] Carl Dreyer, in Cahiers du Cinéma, No. 170. Interview by Michael Delahaye. English translation by Rose Kaplin.

[2] Orson Welles, in Cahiers du Cinéma, No. 165. Interview by Juan Cobos, Miguel Rubio and Jose Antonio Prumeda. English translation by Rose Kaplin.

[3] Federico Fellini, in Cahiers du Cinéma, No. 164. Interview by Pierre Kast. English translation by Rose Kaplin.

[4] Ingmar Bergman, "Film and Creativity," American Cinematographer (April 1972), p. 430.

[5] Michelangelo Antonioni, in Pierre Leprohon, The World of Film: Michelangelo Antonioni (New York: Simon and Schuster, Inc., 1963), pp. 104–06.

Ultimately, the actor can function as a creative artist only if he enters the role totally. In this way alone will all his responses, intellectual and emotional, emerge from the interior life of the character and not from his particular talents as an actor. This is perhaps the essence of acting for film. Although most directors exercise a broad control over the actor, the actor still has many opportunities to work creatively in this framework. Most contemporary filmmakers and actors work on a basis of mutual respect. The modern filmmaker by and large deals with complex ideas, and the actor is the chief instrument through which he communicates these ideas.

FILMS FOR STUDY

Through a Glass Darkly, Ingmar Bergman. Janus Films, 24 West 58 Street, New York, New York 10019.

The 400 Blows, François Truffaut. Janus Films, 24 West 58 Street, New York, New York 10019.

Jules and Jim, François Truffaut. Janus Films, 24 West 58 Street, New York, New York 10019.

SUPPLEMENTARY READING

American Film Institute. *Dialogues on Film*. Beverly Hills: American Film Institute, 1972.

Leprohon, Pierre. *The World of Film: Michelangelo Antonioni*, trans. by Scott Sullivan. New York: Simon and Schuster, Inc., 1963.

Simon, John. *Ingmar Bergman Directs*. New York: Harcourt Brace Jovanovich, 1972.

THE CONTEMPORARY FILMMAKER

SEVEN

People ask what are my intentions with my films —
my aims. It is a difficult and dangerous question,
and I usually give an evasive answer: I try to tell
the truth about the human condition, the truth as
I see it. This answer seems to satisfy everyone, but
it is not quite correct. I prefer to describe what I
would like my aim to be.

There is an old story of how the cathedral of
Chartres was struck by lightning and burned to the
ground. Then thousands of people came from all
points of the compass, like a giant procession of
ants, and together they began to rebuild the cathedral on its old site. They worked until the building
was completed — master builders, artists, laborers,
clowns, noblemen, priests, burghers. But they all
remained anonymous, and no one knows to this
day who built the cathedral of Chartres.

Regardless of my own beliefs and my own
doubts, which are unimportant in this connection,
it is my opinion that art lost its basic creative drive
the moment it was separated from worship. It
severed an umbilical cord and now lives its own
sterile life, generating and degenerating itself. In
former days the artist remained unknown and his
work was to the glory of God. He lived and died
without being more or less important than other
artisans; "eternal values," "immortality" and
"masterpiece" were terms not applicable in his
case. The ability to create was a gift. In such a
world flourished invulnerable assurance and
natural humility.

Today the individual has become the highest
form and the greatest bane of artistic creation. The
smallest wound or pain of the ego is examined
under a microscope as if it were of eternal im-

portance. The artist considers his isolation, his subjectivity, his individualism almost holy. Thus we finally gather in one large pen, where we stand and bleat about our loneliness without listening to each other and without realizing that we are smothering each other to death. The individualists stare into each other's eyes and yet deny the existence of each other. We walk in circles, so limited by our own anxieties that we can no longer distinguish between true and false, between the gangster's whim and the purest ideal.

Thus if I am asked what I would like the general purpose of my films to be, I would reply that I want to be one of the artists in the cathedral on the great plain. I want to make a dragon's head, an angel, a devil—or perhaps a saint—out of stone. It does not matter which; it is the sense of satisfaction that counts. Regardless of whether I believe or not, whether I am a Christian or not, I would play my part in the collective building of the cathedral.

Ingmar Bergman

in *Four Screenplays of Ingmar Bergman*
New York: Simon and Schuster, Inc., 1960, pp. xxi–xxii
Reprinted by permission of the publisher and Janus Films

THE STORY OF THE ART OF FILM MUST ULTIMATELY BE THE STORY OF THE MAJOR cinema artists of our time. Much biographical and critical material has been written about these artists; in fact, seldom has so much literature been produced about the leading figures of so young an art. This body of literature enables the student of film to closely examine the major contemporary filmmakers—such as those discussed in this chapter—while they are still at work.

THE RISE OF THE CONTEMPORARY CINEMA

Historically, the development of the art of film has seen the rise and fall of many national influences. It is difficult to account for the sudden emergence of one national group of creative and influential filmmakers. Such a group may hold sway over the art for a decade or more and then, just as suddenly, disappear from view. A country that has not produced a single creative film may suddenly, almost spontaneously, produce several interesting and creative films, thus sparking a rise in the film fortunes of that country. For example, in the 1930s Germany and Russia had a dominant influence on the art of film, giving us directors such as Fritz Lang and Sergei Eisenstein. In the early 1960s, France and Italy provided the major creative directors and cinematic innovations.

The United States was a primary influence on the art of cinema between 1938 and 1946. The films of George Stevens, John Huston, and Orson Welles were admired all over the world. However, not until 1968, with the appearance of *Bonnie and Clyde* and *The Graduate,* did the United States again produce films so original that they influenced the state of the art.

One reason for the decline of the American cinema in the postwar years was its failure to reflect the social changes of the time. No art can grow or survive without responding to the society that produces it. The slick products of the major American studios — the mass-produced epics, the glittering musicals, the ladies'-magazine dramas — did not reflect the mood of a world that was digging itself out of the rubble of years of death and destruction.

In Europe, however, film began to show small but interesting signs of change. In 1945, the Italian director Roberto Rossellini produced a devastating indictment of war in a low-budget film entitled *Open City.* Rossellini combined newsreel footage with his own photography, which he scratched to create a newsreel effect. He employed flat, realistic lighting, encouraged his actors to ad-lib, and moved his *mise en scène* into the streets of Rome. Rossellini's film struck a decisive blow against the "star" concept, the static methods of studio photography, the contrived lighting, and the slick plots that were the mainstay of an industry.

Open City revealed new possibilities for film. In the jargon of the film historian, Rossellini's film marked the beginning of *neorealism.* To be sure, many earlier films had utilized the techniques of *Open City,* but Rossellini fused them all at the right time. The neorealism of Rossellini created a new trend in filmmaking and came to mark the beginning of the contemporary cinema.

This chapter presents a brief discussion of eleven filmmakers who have produced some of the best films of the contemporary cinema and who, at the same time, have had a dynamic influence on modern film. As is true of all selections of this sort, it is impossible to list or evaluate every good film produced during this period. The filmmakers chosen are artists who have significantly extended the boundaries of the art and whose films offer the richest material for study. These filmmakers are Vittorio De Sica, Luis Buñuel, Federico Fellini, Joseph Losey, Michelangelo Antonioni, Ingmar Bergman, Akira Kurosawa, Alain Resnais, Stanley Kubrick, François Truffaut, and Jean-Luc Godard.

VITTORIO DE SICA

Vittorio De Sica was born in Sora, Italy, in 1902. As a young man he pursued an acting career, and by the 1930s he was well known to Italian cinema audiences. Although he directed his first film in 1939, it was not until 1942, when he collaborated with the writer Cesare Zavattini on *The Children Are Watching Us,* that De Sica began to influence the art of film. In 1946 De Sica again teamed with Zavattini on *Shoeshine,* a film that, like Rossellini's *Open City,* employed a neorealistic approach. *Shoeshine,* however, brought the techniques of neorealism to greater maturity and revealed powerful new possibilities for dealing with social and political problems through the use of the film medium.

Following *Shoeshine,* De Sica further extended his reputation as a humanistic director with *Bicycle Thief* (1949), *Miracle in Milan* (1950), and *Umberto D* (1952). After the release of *Umberto D,* De Sica's reputation and career suffered a somewhat lengthy decline. He turned to making slick, vapid films that enjoyed a measure of commercial success — *Gold of Naples* (1954), *Yesterday, Today, and Tomorrow* (1963), *Marriage Italian Style* (1964). With the exception of his film version of Alberto Moravia's novella *Two Women*

(1960), De Sica did little of value for almost twenty years. But suddenly in 1971, with his film *The Garden of the Finzi-Continis,* he reemerged as a filmmaker of the highest integrity and ability.

The Garden of the Finzi-Continis deals with a Jewish family in Ferrara, Italy, during the early days in the rise of Mussolini and the Fascists. The Finzi-Continis are a wealthy Sephardic family who live in a kind of self-imposed isolation, removed by choice from the mainstream of Italian life. The father is a medieval scholar who immerses himself in his studies. His daughter, Micòl (Dominique Sanda), is extremely beautiful but holds herself aloof. She is idolized by many of Ferrara's young men, and especially by Giorgio (Lino Capollichio), a Jew of middle-class background. Little by little the rising threat of action against the Jews by the government closes a circle around the family, and they, in turn, refuse to move in their own behalf, choosing rather to ignore the force of events. The film studies the effects of this artificial existence on the personal lives of Micòl and her brother Alberto (Helmut Berger) and shows the ultimate destruction of their family. Micòl ignores the love expressed by Giorgio because she considers him "beneath" her. She chooses to remain with Alberto, who is sickly, weak, and paralyzed more and more by lethargy. Overtones of incestuous love are suggested by the extremely inbred quality of their family life and by the life of the Jewish community that has been forced on them by the prejudice of the gentiles. In the final scenes the holocaust comes. The Fascist police arrest the family for deportation to a prison camp; the Finzi-Continis' way of life has been ended.

In *The Garden of the Finzi-Continis* De Sica, working in color, retained the powerful documentary realism of his first black-and-white successes and coupled it with a lyric beauty that enriched his range as a film artist. The final sequence in the film, when the police come to the house to take the family away, must stand as one of the most effective De Sica has ever created. Just as he did in *Shoeshine* and *Bicycle Thief* almost two decades earlier, De Sica integrated professional actors with others who had never acted before. Micòl's aged grandmother, for example, was played by one of De Sica's neighbors, and yet, under his control, she gives a compassionate, superbly textured performance. At the command of the Fascist police, she slowly and with great dignity descends the stairway of her house for what she knows will be the last time. When she is herded into a dark room with other deportees, she does not know how to react, having never in her ninety years had to associate with such a mixture of people. She tries to smile but can't bring it off. Finally, as she understands the full import of her situation, she rests her head on her granddaughter's shoulder and weeps like a child. Her fine performance—well-controlled, yet fresh as improvization—reflects one of the hallmarks of De Sica's directing style: the ability to portray human emotion in a sparse but evocative way. The camera movement too is minimal and uncomplicated, confined to the slow, floating dollies that De Sica uses so effectively to follow his actors. For the most part, the lighting is highly realistic (except for the purposely romantic images of the garden). Throughout the film

De Sica keeps the quantity of dialogue to an absolute minimum and the quality of speech as nontheatrical as possible. The entire final sequence contains almost no conversation, so when Micòl protests being separated from the male members of her family, her words split the silence with tremendous impact. The final scenes are accompanied only by the offscreen sound of a cantor singing the Jewish prayer for the dead (the music is sung by the great tenor Tito Schipa).

De Sica is at his best when he uses his films to explore social tragedy. His most memorable characters are victims of political injustice or social indifference: homeless shoeshine boys, an unemployed father who must steal a bicycle in order to get a job, a solitary old man about to be evicted from his apartment, a Jewish family persecuted by the Fascists. De Sica takes us deeply into the everyday lives of these characters and shows us—sometimes with humor or satire, but always with a strong sense of reality—how they go on living in the face of the harsh situations that confront them. Without resorting to artificial melodrama or postured outrage, he presents their stories and allows us to bear witness to their humanity.

Key elements in the films of Vittorio De Sica include:

1. Convincing re-creation of reality (neorealism)
2. Story lines that deal essentially with the impact of social or political upheaval on the lives of ordinary people
3. Acting performances that mirror the everyday spontaneity of common people
4. Straightforward, uncomplicated use of camera angles, composition, and movement
6. Simple, uncluttered editing style
5. Highly realistic lighting

LUIS BUÑUEL

Luis Buñuel, the grand master of contemporary filmmakers, was born in 1910 in Calanda, Spain. At Madrid University he studied with such major Spanish artists as Garcia Lorca, Salvador Dali, and Rafael Alberti. In 1925, during the repressive dictatorship of Primo de Rivera, he fled Spain and settled in France, where he entered the world of cinema by working as an assistant to the French director Jean Epstein.

Buñuel began to make his own films in 1928, when he directed the short surrealist masterpiece *Un Chien Andalou* in collaboration with Salvador Dali. He followed this short with *L' Age d' Or* (1930), his first feature-length film. These two early films remain among the most influential in the entire history of the cinema because of their pioneering use of symbols, elliptical images, and impressionistic editing. By 1932, with the completion of *Land without Bread,* Buñuel was decisively embarked on a career that was to combine his ability to produce bizarre fantasies on film with his deep concern for the social problems of mankind. With the possible exception of Bergman, Buñuel has directed more important films than any other filmmaker. His major works include *Los Olvidados* (1950), *Robinson Crusoe* (1952), *Nazarin* (1958), *Viridiana* (1961), *The Exterminating Angel* (1962), *Simon of the Desert* (1965), *Belle de Jour* (1967), *Tristana* (1970), and *The Discreet Charm of the Bourgeoisie* (1972).

Belle de Jour, a film adaptation of Joseph Kessel's 1929 novel, provides a good example of the cinema style that Buñuel has developed during his many years as a director. The film focuses on a young woman named Severine (Catherine Deneuve) who is married to Pierre (Jean Sorel), a surgeon. She is unhappy and dissatisfied with her marriage and dreams of adding some adventure to her life. When Severine hears of a woman acquaintance who is secretly working in a brothel, she too applies for a job there. She begins working at the brothel on weekday afternoons from two until five. While she is engaged in her afternoon occupation, she falls in love with a young gangster named Marcel (Pierre Clementi). As the film progresses, a friend of Pierre's discovers Severine's secret and threatens to inform her husband. Marcel, in an attempt to murder the informer, mistakenly shoots Pierre and leaves him a paralyzed cripple. Severine, overwhelmed by guilt and remorse, confesses everything to Pierre, whereupon he vows never to speak to her again. Just as the film seems about to end, there is an unexpected sequence in which Pierre suddenly rises from his wheelchair, totally recovered. All that has happened up to this point is now undercut with ambiguity. Have we simply been shown the personal mirage of a neurotic woman locked in her own fantasies and subconscious desires? Buñuel makes no attempt to answer the questions he has raised by this final twist.

Buñuel's central concern with the interplay of fantasy and reality, evident throughout *Belle de Jour,* is most easily isolated in the scenes of Severine's life in the brothel. By casting Catherine Deneuve—whose acting style is essentially low-key, even dull—in the role of Severine, Buñuel was able to subdue the main focus of the film in order to increase the contrast between Severine's commonplace home life and her clandestine visits to the brothel. During her afternoons at the brothel, Severine is surrounded by all kinds of grotesque people and violent action. The characters she meets during her harlot existence act their parts with a great degree of bizarre overstatement. The color cinematography—very reminiscent of the garish black-and-white films made early in Buñuel's career—is likewise designed to further the sense of overstatement and unreality. The composition and camera movement in the brothel sequences are unobtrusive and relatively undistinguished. The dialogue is literate but calculated to further the exaggerations that make up the film, exaggerations that are rooted in the struggle of the individual imagination against social and religious restrictions. All of the action seems larger than life and hints at meanings other than the literal. Throughout the film—even before the final revelatory sequence—we feel that we are experiencing some kind of nightmare, and we keep searching for clues to reveal whose dream world we are viewing and what meaning it offers.

The essence of Buñuel's approach to filmmaking is that all technique—acting, cinematography, and editing—should be designed to symbolically communicate his ideas and to force the viewer to reinterpret the validity of any boundaries between fantasy and reality. Buñuel has continually woven this interplay of imagination and real action into the body of his work, and although his range of subject matter has been broad, certain techniques that he employed in his early surrealist films recur in his later social satires. For example, in *L'Age d'Or* Buñuel used the jingling sound of cow bells to announce transitions from reality to carnal fantasy, a device that he again resorts to, for the same reason, in *Belle de Jour.*

The creative life of Luis Buñuel spans nearly the whole history of modern filmmaking. He has worked with distinction in a variety of genres, including avant-garde, surrealist film, documentary, comedy, and social satire. By combining his gifts for fantasy, irony, and incisive social satire, Buñuel has created films whose style and substance stress the need for liberation from deadening social and religious constraints. It is a measure of his genius that he has consistently enlarged the scope and artistry of his work for almost half a century.

Key elements in the films of Luis Buñuel include:

1. Exploration of the interplay of fantasy and reality
2. Focus on the struggle for individual freedom in the face of religious and social constraints
3. Use of symbolism and bizarre imagery to represent the world of human fantasy
4. Social satire, usually directed at the bourgeoisie, that relies heavily on irony
5. Overstated acting performances
6. Exaggerated visual contrasts and camera movement
7. Sparse use of supportive musical sound tracks

FEDERICO FELLINI

Federico Fellini was born in Rimini, Italy, in 1920 and began his film career as a gag writer in 1939. Later, in the 1940s, he worked as a writer with Rossellini on such neorealistic films as *Open City, Paisan,* and *Il Miracolo.* He made his directorial debut in 1952 with *The White Sheik,* and his first important work appeared in 1953 — *I Vitelloni.* His next film, *La Strada* (1954), captured the attention of serious filmgoers all over the world. An allegorical story concerned with a circus strong man and a gentle child-woman, *La Strada* starred Anthony Quinn, Fellini's wife Giulietta Masina, and Richard Basehart. It firmly established Fellini as a major artist and still remains one of the most beautiful films of the postwar decade. Following *La Strada,* Fellini created such major works as *Il Bidone* (1955), *Le Notti di Cabiria* (1956), and *La Dolce Vita* (1960).

Probably the most important film of Fellini's career was the autobiographical *8½* (1963), a film that marks a true departure from the neorealistic qualities of his earlier work. In *8½* Fellini shifted his emphasis from realism to the subjective realms of fantasy and obsession. Whereas his earlier films had focused on individual characters reacting to the external realities of the worlds they lived in, *8½* concerns itself primarily with the internal life of its main character and explores the ways in which that subconscious life imposes itself upon

The Contemporary Filmmaker

the character's perception of the outside world and how it influences his actions and responses.

The central character of $8\frac{1}{2}$ is Guido, a successful filmmaker who suffers a nervous breakdown while preparing to begin a film about his own life. Guido is paralyzed by fears and self-doubt that threaten to immobilize him and destroy his career. In addition, the pressures of his relationships with both his wife and mistress compound his uncertainties. He feels trapped and keeps delaying the moment when he must begin shooting the film. In the hope of regaining his confidence, Guido retires to a health spa, but his stay there proves disillusioning. Finally, he is compelled to start work again, and he finds, as the filming progresses, that his former anxieties have been relieved. His immersion in the act of creation is the liberating cure that he had been seeking all along. The film ends on an affirmative note with Guido staging a colorful fantasy carnival in which he himself, as the ringmaster, calls forth the figures of his past and present and performs in harmony with them.

Into this plot structure Fellini inserts a series of dream and fantasy sequences that reveal the nature of the inner tensions and problems with which this artist, Guido, must live. He dreams he is trapped inside a car in an endless traffic jam; he plays out a confessional sequence to a naked cardinal inside a Turkish bath; he summons all his women to a harem room where he whips them; and he relives a moment when, as a child, he watched a grotesquely fat whore do a pathetic erotic dance by the seashore. These images communicate the discord of Guido's internal life and create the film's troubling resonance.

The final sequence of the film demonstrates many of the stylistic trademarks that distinguish Fellini as a filmmaker. The *mis en scène* is grandiose and exaggerated in the Italian expressionist fashion. The scene shows a movie set of a spaceship waiting to take survivors of an atomic war to another planet, and yet the whole set appears to be inside a huge circus tent with a great ring underneath. (Fellini is infatuated with the circus, with clowns, and with the tradition of the commedia dell'arte.)

The characters in this sequence are a mixture of real people from Guido's past and present and stock circus figures complete with masks and bright costumes. The acting style is a combination of mime techniques and overblown Italian bravura. The cinematography reflects the mood of the scenes: both the lighting and composition are garish and overstated. The camera dollies continually in slow, dreamlike motion. The entire effect in this sequence is mock operatic. Guido, the director-ringmaster, shouts commands, and people appear everywhere. Real people from Guido's present mingle with characters remembered from his past and with subliminal characters from his artistic imagination. These real and unreal characters join hands and parade around the ring in a kind of circus finale. The dialogue is incessant, with everyone talking too much and simultaneously. The background music provides a circus flavor, but it too is overstated. The effect of all these elements is a brilliant evocation of the clutter and crowding that form the substance of a life.

In his films that have followed $8\frac{1}{2}$, Fellini has pushed his exploration of mental territories even further. He seems increasingly fascinated by the random correlations between the events of everyday reality and the bizarre fantasies that these events can trigger. This fascination is evident in *Juliet of the Spirits* (1965), *Fellini Satyricon* (1969), and *Fellini's Roma* (1972), in all of which Fellini continues to exploit surrealistic techniques for the purpose of demonstrating the bizarre surface textures of modern life. Although Fellini's more recent films might be considered a natural outgrowth of his earlier concentration on isolated individuals in realistic settings, there is little doubt that their subjective symbolism and distorted infatuation with surface reality make them more difficult to grasp. The danger for the filmmaker in films of this nature is that he will settle for visually dazzling the audience, in which case content and communication must suffer. Fellini's latest films — except for the beautiful documentary *Clowns* (1971) — have yet to show that he can employ his new flamboyant techniques and still create a film with *La Strada's* depth of emotion.

Key elements in the films of Federico Fellini include:
1. Exaggeration and overstatement for effect
2. Lush, romantic use of camera and music
3. Integration of symbolism and fantasy with real action
4. Striking audio and visual effects used for their own sake
5. A generally flamboyant handling of actors
6. Superb control of large groups of people and complex action
7. Integration of social satire with a genuine concern for basic human emotions

JOSEPH LOSEY

Joseph Losey—born in 1909 in LaCrosse, Wisconsin—began his filmaking career in 1937 when he supervised the production of several educational films and documentaries for the State Department and the Rockefeller Foundation. Losey came to filmmaking via earlier work as a New York drama critic in the 1930s and as a stage director for the Theater Guild. In 1939 he directed his first short film and thereafter continued to direct short films—including *A Gun in His Hand* (1945) for MGM—for the next nine years.

Losey's first feature film, *The Boy with Green Hair,* was released in 1948. The film, constructed as a childlike fable, took a moralistic look at the nature of prejudice. A young, war-orphaned boy wakes up one morning to discover that his hair has turned green overnight. Because of his green hair, a symbol of his difference, his schoolmates reject and persecute him. Losey has stated "there's no doubt that the American social structure is very simple, and often, therefore, very contradictory: sometimes very benign, sometimes very malignant, sometimes very tolerant, sometimes a lynch mob." Social injustice, very much a theme in *The Boy with Green Hair,* was also the subject of Losey's next film, *The Lawless* (1949), which examined anti-Mexican prejudice in a small Southwestern town. *The Lawless* was followed by three more films— *The Prowler* (1950); *M* (1950), a remake of Fritz Lang's classic 1917 melodrama; and *The Big Night* (1951)—that received moderately favorable critical response. After completing *The Big Night* in 1951, Losey came under the scrutiny of the House Un-American Activities Committee because of the liberal viewpoints evident in his work; he decided to leave the country. Since then he has been an expatriate, living and working primarily in Britain.

Losey's major films include *Sleeping Tiger* (1954), *The Intimate Stranger* (1956), *Time without Pity* (1957), *The Criminal* (1960), *The Damned* (1961), and *Eve* (1962). In 1963 Losey collaborated for the first time with the British playwright Harold Pinter to adapt Pinter's short play *The Servant* for the screen. This combination of script writer and film director proved to be highly effective, and Losey later returned to Pinter for the scripts of *Accident* (1967) and *The Go-Between* (1971). Other Losey films—made after *The Servant* but without Pinter as script writer—include *King and Country* (1964), *Modesty Blaise* (1966), *Boom* (1968), *Secret Ceremony* (1968), *Figures in a Landscape* (1971), and a film version of Ibsen's *A Doll's House* (1973).

With some few exceptions, Joseph Losey's films deal with philosophical dilemmas (How does man cope with guilt? Why do societies fear the intrusion of "aliens"? How does the rigidity of social structures threaten individual freedoms?) that are illuminated by a minute examination of how they affect the human relationships of his characters.

Perhaps the most "typical" of Losey's films is the recent *The Go-Between.* This film, based on a romantic novel by L. P. Hartley, deals with the themes of love, time, and memory. The opening lines of Hartley's story also open the film: "The past is a foreign country. They do things differently there." The main action of the film revolves around a grown man (played by Michael Redgrave) who recalls a time when, as a poor boy from the city, he spent the summer holidays with a rich schoolmate from the country. During her visit he becomes infatuated with his friend's older sister, Marian (Julie Christie), and is used by her as a go-between to carry clandestine messages to her secret love, a local farmer (Alan Bates). The action takes place in the early twentieth century in England, when a liaison such as Marian's would have scandalized her family. Marian's mother eventually becomes suspicious and forces the boy to reveal his secret. She then surprises Marian and her lover in the act of sexual intercourse. The next day the farmer, whom the boy had come to like and trust, kills himself. This terrible tragedy and the events that brought it on — all viewed from the young boy's vantage point — form the substance of this sensitive and often beautiful film.

Losey's strengths and failings are in full evidence throughout *The Go-Between*, particularly in the final scene between the boy and the farmer. The cinematography, as in most of Losey's work, is exquisite: the camera movement is kept slow, so as to deliberately expand the normal pacing of the film; the acting is very controlled, with little divergence from the script; and the editing is formal but uninventive. The two meet in a field and try to say something meaningful. The boy feels guilty because of his role in the mother's discovery of the lovers, and the farmer is bitter and preoccupied with his own tragedy. The scene is stretched out by hesitant, tentative dialogue and yet is curiously moving. Losey rarely rushes his action or interrupts his scenes with flash cuts or random editing. As a result, he runs the risk of inflating the length of such scenes to the point where they become pretentious or simply boring. However, when his slow pacing works, as it does in *The Go-Between*, it can totally involve the audience in emotionally charged drama that is free of "filmic" distractions.

Losey's work has been uneven in quality and difficult to neatly categorize. Still, throughout his films, he continues to explore the inner turmoil of his characters — characters presented realistically in what seem to be naturalistic settings. But Losey's visual trademark is to push naturalism a step or two beyond its boundaries by isolating certain features of his settings and subjecting them to unnaturally close scrutiny. By extracting the essence of his physical and social settings from a few closely observed elements and thereby creating a stylized naturalism, Losey has developed a more compressed, even claustrophobic, visual realism than the neorealist filmmakers. Losey is essentially an old-fashioned filmmaker. He avoids flamboyant external effects that might give his films more force. Instead, he relies on more traditional techniques but revitalizes them with his precision, judgment, and creativity.

Key elements in the films of Joseph Losey include:
1. An infatuation with detailing the events that circumscribe and eventually become critical in the lives of his individual characters
2. Lush, stylized camera work that often tends toward overstatement
3. Heavy emphasis and reliance on spoken dialogue
4. Very slow, extended pacing
5. Controlled, well-modulated acting performances
6. Generally uninventive editing and use of music

MICHELANGELO ANTONIONI

Michelangelo Antonioni was born in Ferrara, Italy, in 1912 and, like Truffaut, began his film career as a critic. His first critical articles appeared in the local Ferrara newspaper during the time of the Fascist rise to power in the late 1930s. Then, after working as a script writer for several Italian producers, he obtained a position as assistant director to Marcel Carné for the filming of *Les Visiteurs du Soir* (1942).

Following his experience with Carné, Antonioni went on to direct a series of documentary films during the 1940s, most notably *Gente del Po* (1943) and *N.U.* (1948). *Gente del Po* uses the story of a barge voyage down the Po River as the framework for examining the small villages along the river's banks and the people who live in them. The approach and the camera style are straightforward and coolly objective—trademarks that also characterize Antonioni's subsequent films. In *N.U.* Antonioni captured a single working day in the lives of a group of Roman street sweepers. The sound track of *N.U.* featured a jazz score composed by Giovanni Fusco, who Antonioni continued to collaborate with once he began directing feature films in the 1950s.

In 1950 Antonioni scripted and directed his first feature film, *Cronaca di un Amore*. He followed this film with *I Vinti* (1952), *La Signora Senza Camelie* (1953), *Le Amiche* (1955), and *Il Grido* (1957), all of which were character studies that evidenced a penetrating interest in the various forms and consequences of emotional relationships. None of these films, however, gained Antonioni a wide following outside of Italy. Then in 1960, with the release of *L'Avventura*, Antonioni's international reputation took a giant leap forward. *L'Avventura* still remains his most perfect work—one that displays the closest fusion of film style with philosophical outlook. The three films that followed *L'Avventura—La Notte* (1960), *L'Eclisse* (1962), and *Red Desert* (1964)—reaffirmed Antonioni's choice of subject matter and his willingness to experiment with a visual style that would effectively express the internal tensions of his characters.

Red Desert was Antonioni's first film in color. It tells the story of a neurotic woman (played by Monica Vitti, the star of Antonioni's two previous films) struggling to find fulfillment in an emotional setting that includes the conflicting demands of her husband, her son, and, briefly, her lover Corrado. Antonioni's use of color in this film constituted an extension of his visual experimentation—he carefully manipulated the color tone and contrasts of each scene in order to symbolically establish the changing emotional content.

Antonioni's next film, *Blow-Up* (1966), employed more garish colors and much greater contrasts than *Red Desert,* but with similar symbolic intent. *Blow-Up* is centered about a deceptively simple plot line. A bored London still photographer named Thomas (David Hemmings) takes a series of random stills of a young couple in a park. When the young woman, Jane (Vanessa Redgrave), later makes desperate attempts to obtain the negatives of the apparently innocent shots, Thomas becomes suspicious. He blows the stills up, and in the larger versions he believes he sees a body, evidence of a murder. The remainder of the film deals with Thomas' attempts to interpret the ambiguous evidence on the magnified film and provides Antonioni with a platform from which to focus on a number of philosophical and psychological questions: the nature of subjective and objective reality and the relationships of a society—and its artists—to the prevailing technology. The decadence of modern London provides Antonioni with a perfect backdrop for his story, one suited to his previously evidenced interests.

A key sequence in the film involves Jane's first visit to Thomas' studio, during which she tries to seduce him in order to obtain the negatives. As in most of Antonioni's work, the pacing here is slow and deliberate; the dialogue is simple, brief, and fragmented by long, silent pauses between sentences. The garish, high-contrast colors of the studio seem strangely muted and excellently controlled, giving the sequence an almost black-and-white realism. Few filmmakers are as successful as Antonioni in revealing, through composition and visual texture, the hidden implications and resonances submerged beneath most spoken dialogue. Just as he had previously done with the sparse dialogue of *L'Avventura* and *Red Desert,* Antonioni is able in *Blow-Up* to establish the character of the two protagonists and to suggest the sexual conflict between them.

Although the central concerns of *Blow-Up* (the question of spontaneity and reality in art and the question of the artist's role in an increasingly technological society) constitute a departure from the common themes of Antonioni's preceding films, many of his distinctive traits do carry over into this film. For instance, his earlier films emphasized the physical surroundings of the characters in such a way that inanimate objects—industrial machinery, arid sand dunes, the cold façades of modern architecture—actually became a visual commentary upon the situations in which the characters found themselves. In *Blow-Up*, the photography equipment and the unreal atmosphere created by the lights and reflectors in Thomas' studio serve to underscore the film's concern with the nature of subjective and objective reality.

In Antonioni's following film, *Zabriskie Point* (1970), the physical sur-

The Contemporary Filmmaker

roundings play an even more prominent role in the film's statement. The film attempts to capture the political conflict of American student radicals at the start of the 1970s and to portray it within the larger cultural context of America. Scene after scene shows the characters overshadowed and diminished by physical objects—billboards, skyscrapers, and ever-present automobiles—and we see that Antonioni is commenting upon the overblown status of material objects in America's affluent, technological society. *Zabriskie Point*, however, did not receive the widespread critical acclaim accorded to Antonioni's earlier films, in part because the political intent of the film seemed less suited to his style than did the cultural commentary of *Blow-Up* or the character studies of *L'Avventura* and *Red Desert*.

Throughout the body of his work, Antonioni seems primarily concerned with the struggles of individual human beings trying to relate to one another. He presents us with the facts of their situations and follows their behavior with objectivity and lucidity. His films are memorable not because they preach or offer solutions, but because they illuminate.

Key elements in the films of Michelangelo Antonioni include:

1. Scripts that explore philosophical ideas through the behavior of their characters
2. Complex, lengthy, slow-moving camera shots with little reliance on close-ups or other "filmic" techniques
3. Generally slow pacing that allows for the gradual development of ideas and events over long periods of screen time
4. Use of very brief—almost telegraphic—dialogue that is frequently punctuated by extended periods of silence
5. Great control over acting performance; Antonioni tends to restrict and mute his actors, forcing them to express internal conflicts and attitudes with a minimum of external effects
6. Little emphasis on the traditional supportive elements of film (such as music or optical effects); Antonioni tends to put his faith in the scene itself: many of his most effective scenes are played out in long master shots with only natural sound in support of dialogue.

INGMAR BERGMAN

Ingmar Bergman, one of the most influential figures in contemporary film-making, was born in Uppsala, Sweden, in 1918. The son of a pastor, he spent his early creative years in the Swedish theater and opera. His initial work in the film medium was as a script writer, and his script for the Swedish film *Torment* (directed by Alf Sjöberg, 1944) attracted a great deal of favorable attention. In the decade after the Second World War, Bergman emerged as an interesting filmmaker with such films as *The Devil's Wanton* (1948), *Illicit Interlude* (1951), *The Naked Night* (1953), and *Smiles of a Summer Night* (1955), but these films did not really evidence the intellectual and creative force that was clearly present in his next work, *The Seventh Seal* (1956).

The Seventh Seal is a powerfully intellectual examination of man's search for meaning in life and of man's relationship to God. The film, a triumph of directorial control, features a great range of excellent characterization created by an ensemble of then unknown Swedish actors. It remains the touchstone of Bergman's career.

Bergman's film output after *The Seventh Seal* constitutes the largest body of important work by any filmmaker in the history of the art. His major films include *Wild Strawberries* (1957), *The Magician* (1958), *The Virgin Spring* (1959), the trilogy *Through a Glass Darkly* (1960), *Winter Light* (1961), and *The Silence* (1963), *Persona* (1966), *Hour of the Wolf* (1967), *Shame* (1968), *The Passion of Anna* (1969), and *Cries and Whispers* (1972). These films have explored such complex and problematic themes as man's relationship to God (*Winter Light, Virgin Spring*), to love (*Through a Glass Darkly, Wild Straw-berries*), and to his fellow men (*Shame, The Passion of Anna*). He has also looked at the nature of madness (*Hour of the Wolf*) and at death (*Cries and Whispers*). Despite the diversity of their themes, Bergman's films demonstrate a remarkable consistency of philosophic insight and artistic control. He has created the first real repertory company of film actors and also, with the aid of cameramen Gunnar Fischer and Sven Nykvist, has managed to master both black-and-white and color cinematography.

An analysis of Bergman's recent *Cries and Whispers* can reveal much about his work as a filmmaker. This film, essentially a study of life in the presence of death, portrays the thwarted and disintegrating lives of three sisters. The plot turns upon the suffering of a young woman, Karin, who is dying of cancer. She awaits her death at home, surrounded by her two sisters and a woman servant who has looked after her since her childhood. In the course of the film, the lives of the two sisters and the servant are revealed through wish-fulfillment sequences that portray their fantasies. The older sister is frigid and has deadened herself to human emotion. In her fantasy she revenges herself against men (specifically her husband) by slashing her vagina with broken glass and smearing the blood on her face while her husband looks on. The younger sister, who is superficial and promiscuous, fantasizes her husband's suicide. And Anna, the maid, has a nightmare in which Karin awakens after death and calls for her, not the sisters. In the dream, Anna tries to comfort Karin, cradling her in an embrace that echoes Michelangelo's *Piéta*. (See Color Plate V.)

Near the end of the film Karin dies. The final fantasy Bergman shows is hers. As Karin describes in her diary the "happiest day" of her life, we see an idyllic scene—the sisters, all dressed in white lace and carrying parasols, strolling together over a lush, green lawn (see Color Plate III). The agony of reality (the end of life) has been forcefully presented, and Bergman's final words, in the form of a title, end the film: "and the cries and whispers die away." These final words expose Karin's fantasy as just another unrealized wish, not much different than the fantasies of the others.

The sequence in which Karin dies and Anna's fantasy emerges contains all those elements that characterize the art of Ingmar Bergman. Harriet Andersson, as Karin, delivers an incredibly intense performance. Under Bergman's direction, she so completely enters into the part that her death becomes almost unbearable for the audience to witness. The dialogue is minimal and tightly compressed, with each word important to the scene's development. The muted quality of Karin's voice and the long periods of silence between her bits of dialogue lend tremendous dramatic impact to the scene. Sven Nykvist's color photography in this sequence adds to the stifling, claustrophobic atmosphere within the old house that is symptomatic of the women's lives. Bergman keeps the camera movement simple but manages to intensify the audience's involvement with the characters through a combination of striking color values, high-contrast lighting, and unexpected compositions. Sound effects in this scene, as throughout the film, are used very selectively—usually for specific dramatic effects rather than to create "atmosphere." The total effect produced by the combination of these elements is flawlessly consistent with the film's main theme, the pervasive influence of death upon the living. Karin's death fills the house like a dark shadow. The fear it evokes and the self-examination it forces upon the women become the central focus of the film.

Bergman, more than any other filmmaker, has displayed a persistent ability to expand the creative boundaries of his art. He continues to concern himself with the universal questions raised by man's journey through life; if his films often seem philosophically open-ended, it is because he chooses to confront these questions from a variety of vantage points. Ingmar Bergman is not an experimental filmmaker, at least not in the usual sense—his basic style has a disarming simplicity about it. And yet, this very simplicity that characterizes Bergman's work is in large part the result of his willingness to experiment with the technical possibilities of the medium and his desire to make film a precise instrument for probing the human situation.

Key elements in the films of Ingmar Bergman include:
1. Philosophically complex scripts
2. Dialogue that is minimal in quantity but integrally important
3. Excellent cinematography that features unusual composition and high contrasts between light and shadow
4. Generally slow, thoughtful pacing—often lyric or musical in form
5. Controlled but intense performances by an ensemble of actors organized

by Bergman as an authentic repertory group
6. Simplicity of editing techniques; little use of unexpected cuts or elaborate montage
7. Restrained and highly selective use of music and sound effects (effective use of silences)

AKIRA KUROSAWA

Akira Kurosawa, the first Japanese film director to achieve international recognition, was born in Tokyo in 1910. Originally a student painter, he worked in film to support himself and became assistant director to one of the most successful Japanese directors, Kajiro Yamamoto. During this period Kurosawa also wrote several scripts. In 1943 he directed his first film, *Sanshiro Sugata,* which was well received in Japan. Following the Second World War, he made a series of films that dealt with the effects of the war upon Japan. These included *Drunken Angel* (1948), *The Silent Duel* (1948), and *Stray Dog* (1949). After *Stray Dog,* Kurosawa directed the masterpiece *Rashomon* (1950), which was praised by critics and enthusiastically applauded by audiences in film centers around the world. He followed this great success with *The Idiot* (1951), a brilliant adaptation of the Dostoevski novel, and with *Ikiru* (1952), a film thought by many to be one of the finest motion pictures ever made.

Joseph Anderson and Donald Richie, in their comprehensive study of Japanese film, have this to say about *Ikiru:*

> In it Kurosawa explored almost every potentiality of the film medium in illustrating his relatively simple story. A minor bureaucrat, upon learning that he has only six months to live, realizes that he has done nothing during his life which offers him the slightest hope of personal immortality. So in his last half-year he searches for the meaning of life, finding the solution in pushing a playground project through the local bureaucracy. In this film Kurosawa's humanism was at its height. This discursive film is long and varied; it winds and unwinds; it shifts from mood to mood, from present to past, from silence to a deafening roar — and all in the most unabashed and absorbing fashion. Its greatest success may be in its revitalization of film technique. It, together with Kinoshita's *A Japanese Tragedy (Nihon no Kigeki)* and *Carmen's Pure Love (Karumen Junjosu)*, shows that when it wants to, Japanese film technique can be among the most dynamic in the world.[1]

The Seven Samurai (1954), a film deeply influenced by the whole genre of the Hollywood Western, followed *Ikiru* and was probably Kurosawa's greatest commercial success. Among this director's important films are included *Throne of Blood* (1957), an interesting version of *Macbeth; The Lower Depths* (1957), an adaptation of the Gorky novel; *The Hidden Fortress* (1958); and a return to humanistic and unsentimental themes with *High and Low* (1963), *Red Beard* (1965), and *Dodeskaden* (1970).

Although his total body of work is impressive, so far it is still *Rashomon* that gives Kurosawa his ultimate stature as a filmmaker. *Rashomon* is a perfect film, unflawed and impressive in its cinematic achievement. The film's story takes place in medieval Japan and concerns a single violent event that is related by the three participants and by an observer, in four different versions. In its basic form, the story tells of a samurai and his bride who are attacked by a bandit while they are traveling through a forest. The result of the encounter is that the samurai is killed. As the film opens, an inquest is being conducted to determine the facts of the case, and the three participants are being questioned. In the wife's version of the attack, she claims that the bandit overpowered her husband, tied him up, and then raped her. She testifies that after raping her, the bandit killed her husband. The bandit, in his version, maintains that he set out to rape the woman but did not have to because she succumbed to his masculine charm. He says that the wife then insisted that he fight a duel with her husband because she felt that one of the men must die to preserve her honor. The bandit says that he killed the samurai while dueling. The third version, the dead husband's, is presented through the mouth of a spiritual medium. In this bizarre sequence, the samurai testifies that, following the rape, his wife begged the bandit to murder him. When the bandit refuses to kill the samurai, the wife runs away. The bandit sets the samurai

[1] Joseph L. Anderson and Donald Richie, *The Japanese Film: Art and Industry* (New York: Grove Press, 1960), pp. 187–88.

free and leaves him alone in the forest, where he then commits suicide because of the shame his wife's actions have brought him. In the final version, an old woodcutter who observed the incident claims that after the wife had been raped, her husband at first refused to fight for her, since he felt that the rape had rendered her worthless. The bandit, however, finally succeeds in goading the husband into a duel and kills him during the fighting.

In *Rashomon*, Kurosawa has created a highly original exploration of the nature of objective truth and its relationship to subjective reality. The sequence in which the spiritual medium, a woman, sits cross-legged in an open court and transmits the voice of the dead husband is a superb example of Kurosawa's technical mastery. As the dead man's words come through the woman's lips, the camera stalks the court in continuous motion, accompanied by the strange rattling of sticks and bones. The high-contrast black-and-white photography is expressive and complements the fluid camera movement. The acting performances, overstated in Kabuki fashion, are larger than life and yet totally believable. The music and sound effects provide pacing and an undercurrent of tension that heighten the drama of the situation. Within this single sequence Kurosawa exercises control over the whole range of elements that go into the creation of a film and successfully conveys the many complex and interconnected aspects of his thematic material.

Key elements in the films of Akira Kurosawa include:

1. Emphasis on deeply humanistic themes
2. A large degree of influence by the American Western (e.g., use of landscapes as a prominent dramatic element; simplistic plots; easily identifiable, black-and-white characters)
3. A willingness to permit overacting for dramatic effect
4. Highly mobile, fluid camera movement and high-contrast, dramatic lighting
5. An insistence on letting scenes and sequences continue at great length until a variety of perspectives have revealed themselves; the pace of his films is generally deliberate, even slow.

ALAIN RESNAIS

Alain Resnais was born in 1922 at Vannes, Brittany, where he later studied at the college of Saint François Xavier. At the age of fourteen he began to experiment with 8mm filmmaking and four years later studied acting with Rene Simon. In 1945, after completing his military service, he joined a travelling acting troup known as Les Arlinquins.

At the end of 1945, Resnais began to work as a cameraman on documentary and advertising films. For the next ten years he worked as both director and editor of a wide range of short films shot in 16mm and 35mm. Resnais' short film *Guernica* (1950), about Picasso and his famous fresco, showed early signs of the stylistic elements and thematic concerns that came to mark his subsequent work: a flair for combining visually disparate elements to create strong emotional statements and innovative editing techniques that pushed his films beyond the traditional confines of narrative and temporal continuity. By the mid-1950s Resnais was already a complete filmmaker who controlled an ever increasing portion of the creative process. His short film *Night and Fog* (1955) gave further evidence of Resnais' continuing determination to explore the destructiveness of war. The film is a brief retrospective study of Nazi concentration camps that effectively contrasts historical scenes of the camps in operation (shot in black-and-white) with present-day scenes from the unoccupied camps (shot in color). The effect of the editing and camera work is to turn even tranquil shots of the abandoned camp buildings into chilling evocations of the horrors that they once housed.

In 1959 Resnais made his first 35mm feature film, *Hiroshima, Mon Amour,* one of the most important and influential films of the decade. Based on an interesting but complex script by Marguerite Duras, this film was among the first to successfully employ the editing technique of the brief, subliminal flash cut as an integral part of its basic theme. Drawing much philosophical and literary inspiration from Henri Bergson and Marcel Proust, Resnais further pursued his early interest in the theme of time and the influence of memory on present reality. In *Hiroshima, Mon Amour,* Resnais revealed an unusual ability to integrate major thematic material (the effects of war on the human spirit) with highly personal themes (the effect the lovers and their pasts have on each other). His control over the lighting and composition of the visual images was exceptional, and his own approach to camera movement made this film one of the more innovative of the postwar period. The editing technique, of course, was the foremost element that accounted for the film's great influence. By inserting *unmotivated* fragments of scenes from the girl's past into present action, Resnais not only revealed to the audience the impact of past events on present action, but gave visual form to subconscious motives that affect personal relationships. In addition, the use of rhythmic voice-over commentary by the participants gave the film an exceptionally lyric cadence that further strengthened its thematic ideas. The contrast between the stark horror of the newsreel scenes of devastated Hiroshima juxtaposed with the lovemaking scenes of the protagonists suggested to other filmmakers possibilities inherent in the film form but not really exploited prior to this film.

Following *Hiroshima, Mon Amour*, Resnais moved even further into a cinematic exploration of the Proustian world of memory with his productions of *Last Year at Marienbad* (1961) and *Muriel, ou le Temps d'un Retour* (1963). These films were characterized by greater experimentation with subliminal flash-cutting, multiple repetitions of identical shots, flared and flashed scenes, and free association of seemingly unrelated visual elements—all in an effort to communicate the nature of his characters' internal lives.

Three years after *Muriel*, Resnais completed what can be considered his *chef d' oeuvre*, his most complete and perfect work, *La Guerre Est Finie*. This film centers about an aging Spanish revolutionary, Diego (Yves Montand), who travels back and forth between France and Spain working for the overthrow of General Franco's government. Again, the theme of the effect of the past on the present is dominant, but this time Resnais treats the theme in a totally realistic fashion. The script by the Spanish writer Jorge Semprun shows us Diego caught between his romantic memories of his revolutionary past and the harsh, cynical realities of the present in which, in effect, the revolution (*La Guerre*) is long since over. The Spain of which Diego and his aging compatriots dream no longer exists. Their chances of overthrowing Franco's government are almost equally nonexistent. These men are engaged in a hopeless charade, and yet they continue to endanger their lives because they cannot accept the reality of the situation. Resnais reveals Diego for what he is: a prisoner of his past. Despite warnings that he will be arrested by the Spanish police if he makes one more trip to Madrid, he goes. Diego's mistress Marienne, who has learned that he is heading into a trap, follows Diego to Spain in the hope of alerting him. But Diego's past, and his inability to accept the present, destroy them both.

Resnais' whole approach to filmmaking can be seen in the opening sequence of the film as Diego and his friend Carlos (who will die during the course of the film) are returning to France from a clandestine trip to Spain. (Resnais usually establishes his technique and rhythms at the very outset of his films.)

The acting is very low-key and underplayed; the dialogue is delivered almost in monotones, with little sense of "performance." Resnais chooses his actors for their ability to project *internal* emotions and thoughts with a minimum of external theatrics. Montand is, of course, a master at this style of acting. The dialogue itself is brief and fragmentary, filled with repetitions and overlaid with first-person narration that is used not to reveal any information but to evoke the internal feelings of the leading character. It is no coincidence that each of Resnais' major films contain this type of voice-over commentary.

The camera style in this sequence relies heavily on a combination of subtle movement and intense close-ups. There is little or no "arty" composition, so the camera rarely calls attention to itself. Tensions are created by sudden stops in the camera motion that coincide with silences on the sound track. The lighting tone is highly realistic and devoid of obvious effects. Only when Resnais deals with unreality does he introduce unreal lighting effects. (The scene, later in the film, in which Diego makes love to his young mistress Nadine is deliberately overexposed to demonstrate the delusory romantic quality of their relationship.) Finally, the cumulative effect of the endless driving (purposeless, with no clear destination), the external danger (the border guards who question Diego), and the implied intimacy of his relationship with Carlos combine to establish the roots of all the major themes in the film.

Resnais is thoroughly concerned with time and its effects on the ability of people to maintain control over their own lives. His great strength lies in his ability to cinematically fuse reality with the facts and distortions of memory. More than any other contemporary filmmaker, his work suggests elements inherent in the film form that can be used, beyond direct story-telling, for narrative communication.

Key elements in the films of Alain Resnais include:

1. The theme of time—the effect of the past upon the present
2. Highly literate and complex scripts written by major literary talents (Duras, Robbe-Grillet, Semprun)
3. Simplicity of basic plot lines combined with complex thematic explorations
4. Great reliance on visual images and a corresponding low dependence on explicit spoken dialogue
5. Tight control over rhythm and pacing
6. Highly effective editorial use of subliminal flash cuts, especially to provide visual contrasts

STANLEY KUBRICK

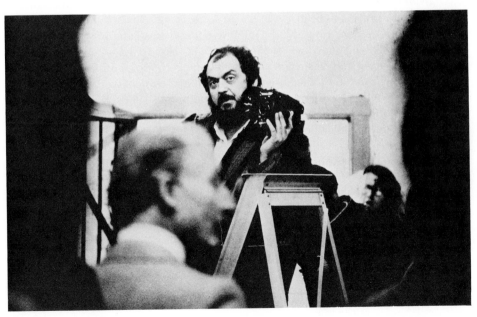

Stanley Kubrick, born in New York City in 1928, began his career as a photo journalist for *Look* magazine before shifting into filmmaking as a director of two short documentaries that he sold to RKO. His first feature film, *Fear and Desire* (1953), was a low-budget effort that received some praise from critics but was not widely distributed. Kubrick's next film, *Killer's Kiss* (1955), was a crime film shot in the streets of New York that evoked an almost documentary-style sense of realism. The experience that Kubrick gained while directing these first two features was well used in his following production, *The Killing* (1956). *The Killing*, another crime-suspense film, made brilliant use of flash cuts to show the events of a race-track robbery from the points of view of several different characters. The acclaim that this film received from the critics marked Kubrick as a young filmmaker of exceptional promise.

The technical virtuosity that Kubrick displayed in *The Killing* was even more apparent in his first major film, *Paths of Glory* (1957). The film, based on a novel by Humphrey Cobb, deals with an incident that occurred in the French army during the First World War. Three soldiers, whose superiors had saddled them with an impossible military mission, were made the scapegoats for official stupidity and corruption and were executed. The film, shot in Germany, was noteworthy for its honesty, power, and stylistic originality. *Paths of Glory* was Kubrick's first opportunity to direct well-established actors — Kirk Douglas and Adolphe Menjou — and he proved equal to the challenge, eliciting fully developed characterizations from his entire cast.

Following *Paths of Glory*, Kubrick was asked to take over the direction of *Spartacus* (1960) after the original director had been fired during the early filming. Kubrick accepted the job but was hampered because he was not given complete control of the production. He was unhappy with the finished film and now disowns it.

Kubrick's next film, *Lolita* (1962), was based on Vladimir Nabokov's novel and scripted by the novelist himself. *Lolita*, like *Spartacus*, was a film that thwarted Kubrick's desire for total filmmaking control, and as a result it is a seriously flawed film. Because the novel's erotic content would not have been tolerated in the prevailing moral climate of the mid-1960s, Kubrick was forced to adapt the book quite differently than he would today.

The three films that followed *Lolita* — *Dr. Strangelove* (1964), *2001: A Space Odyssey* (1968), and *A Clockwork Orange* (1972) — display the remarkable diversity of Kubrick's creative interests, and each of the three demonstrates a growing mastery of the technical aspects of the art. In *Dr. Strangelove* Kubrick created a grim satire of the technological and human possibilities for nuclear holocaust. *2001: A Space Odyssey*, which the director has described as a "mythological documentary," offers a poetic exploration of man's odyssey through a universe unbounded by time or space. And in *A Clockwork Orange* Kubrick gives us a frightening vision of the not-too-distant future that predicts a society dominated by man's most violent and savage instincts.

A Clockwork Orange embodies the distinctive elements that characterize the filmmaking of Stanley Kubrick. The film, adapted from a novel by Anthony

Burgess, projects human society into the near future to show the results of the moral and spiritual decay so evident in contemporary life. Senseless violence and pointless crime abound in this future world; the majority of the population lead purposeless lives, soothed by tranquilizing drugs and mindless entertainments. The plot deals with a young thug named Alex (Malcolm MacDowell), who is arrested and imprisoned for a violent crime. Once captured, he is forced to become the subject of a government experiment designed to brainwash him and recondition his behavior so as to create a placid, docile, law-abiding citizen. The cynical approach of the officials and the dehumanizing effects of their methods become evident as Alex, deprived of free will, comes away from the treatment no more than a robot. Through the events of the film, Kubrick forcefully examines the problem of the individual struggling to maintain personal identity in a totalitarian society. The film's visual design, the clever use of electronically rendered classical music, and the stylized performance of the actors are all elements that contribute to the unique character of A Clockwork Orange.

One of the most shocking and effective scenes in the film is a rape scene in which Alex and his *droogs* (gang) break into the home of a writer and proceed to cripple him and rape his wife. The set design of the home, with its suggestions of a sterile future, and the sleek but impersonal futuristic costumes visually create an environment in which violence seems expected — a symbol of a society stripped of its humanity. The dialogue in the scene is cruel but witty — perhaps too clever but quite effective. The gang members speak to each other in their own teen-age language, *Nadsat*, that is made up of a violent vocabulary derived from a variety of roots, including Russian and cockney. Using a mobile, hand-held camera, Kubrick follows the rape action closely, heightening the tension and the brutality of the crime. The brutal force and violence are in brilliant counterpoint to the sardonic humor of the criminals. Kubrick's special talents enable him to blend bizarre visual effects and a realistic camera style with music and dialogue that are strangely at odds with the mood of the scene. The result is very effective and highly original.

The key to the art of Stanley Kubrick is his continued ability to change subject matter and style while retaining his control over all visual and aural elements. He is one of the few current filmmakers whose philosophical interests seem to be constantly expanding to a larger and more interesting canvas with each new film, and his insistence on total filmmaking independence should continue to ensure him the freedom to explore those interests.

Key elements in the films of Stanley Kubrick include:

1. Intense, humanistic interest in broad philosophical questions inherent in the evolution of society
2. Carefully planned, meticulous scripts that contain a strong narrative core and are worked out in full detail
3. Highly imaginative visual design and use of special effects
4. Mobile, complex camera work
5. Intelligent acting performances that reflect the director's ability to

communicate to his cast the ideas behind each scene

6. Effective use of many styles of music (classical, country-Western, pop)

FRANÇOIS TRUFFAUT

François Truffaut, born in Paris in 1932, began his film career as a critic for *Cahiers du Cinéma* in the 1950s and came to be known as one of the most influential critics in France. In 1954 he made a 16mm short subject called *Une Visite* and followed this with two more shorts: *Les Mistons* (1957) and *Histoire d' Eau* (1958), which was completed by Jean-Luc Godard.

In 1959, Truffaut made *The 400 Blows*, the first of his films to achieve worldwide recognition. *The 400 Blows* is an autobiographical film that delves deeply into the life of a young juvenile delinquent, Antoine Doinel. The film starred a child actor, Jean-Pierre Léaud, who went on to become Truffaut's screen alter ego in many subsequent films. Stylistically, *The 400 Blows* affects a pseudo-documentary approach that succeeds in imparting to the story a feeling of truth. The film is honest and deeply moving in its insights. In the final scene, Antoine, rejected by his mother, runs away from the reformatory where he has been confined. This scene ends with the final blow as Antoine's escape is blocked by the sea. He turns away from the water and casts a forlorn gaze directly at the camera. Truffaut freezes (or arrests) the frame, capturing forever a moment of almost unbearable sorrow and impact. Although the film-making style of *The 400 Blows* was not particularly innovative, the depth of insight and pervading humanity that motivated the film gave it a distinction that propelled Truffaut into the forefront of the French "new wave."

Truffaut followed *The 400 Blows* with *Shoot the Piano Player* (1960), a comic triumph that starred Charles Aznavour as a barroom piano player, Charlie, who had once been a concert pianist. *Shoot the Piano Player* works variations on the traditional form of the American gangster film as it tells the story of Charlie's life and disastrous love affairs. For example, the customary chase scene involving the gangsters is not used for suspense but rather as a comic element; and the interlocking stories of Charlie, his wife, and the gangsters are structured so as to keep the viewer at a distance that prevents any close emotional identification with the characters. After *Shoot the Piano Player*, Truffaut made his masterpiece, *Jules and Jim* (1961).

Jules and Jim became the pinnacle of Truffaut's work up to that time—it contained all the elements of the director's genius that were never again completely present in any of his subsequent films. The film tells the story of a young Parisian woman, Catherine (Jeanne Moreau), and the two men who fall in love with her: Jules (Henri Serre), an Austrian, and Jim (Oskar Werner), a Frenchman. In the years since its release, there has been much debate about the layers of meaning and theme in *Jules and Jim*, but Truffaut himself has said "there are two themes . . . that of the friendship between the two men which tries to remain alive, and that of the impossibility of living á trois. The central idea of the film is that the couple is not really satisfactory, but there is no alternative." The film successfully alternated between a light spirit of comedy and romance and a more forbidding sense of the inevitable tragedy that must befall the relationship, a tragedy that takes shape in Catherine's impulsive decision to drive her car off a bridge, drowning both Jules and herself.

The precise evocation of Paris before the First World War and the magnificent performances by Moreau, Werner, and Serre give the film its character, but its greatness comes from Truffaut's keen understanding of the male-female relationship and from his ability to reveal the constantly changing moods that make up the pattern of these three lives.

Half-way through the film, there occurs a sequence in which Jules, Jim, and Catherine spend an idyllic summer at a chalet in Switzerland. This sequence capsulizes all of Truffaut's stylistic trademarks. The black-and-white images are pastoral and lovely, re-creating the essence of the period not only by prop and costume but by the very style of photography. The lighting is soft, with low contrast between light and shade. The camera movement is fluid, relying on long, leisurely dollying; the action is never hurried. The dialogue is fragmentary and supported by music. The acting is understated but never really muted — Truffaut allows the personalities of the three actors to dominate the mise-en-scene. The editing, too, is natural and unhurried, free of any sudden shifts of emphasis or point of view. The sequence successfully reveals the deep affection these three people have for each other and yet, at the same time, presents glimpses of the imperfect nature of their affair — the unavoidable doubts, jealousy, and insecurity. These thoroughly human shortcomings undermine the trust and spontaneity of the lovers' relationship and foreshadow the self-destructiveness that brings an end to the affair.

Truffaut's films after *Jules and Jim* continued to evidence his human warmth and sense of humor but, for the most part, lacked the solid philosophic core of his best work. His major films of this later period include *The Soft Skin* (1964), *Farenheit 451* (1966), *The Bride Wore Black* (1967), *Stolen Kisses* (1968), *The Siren of Mississippi* (1969), *Bed and Board* (1970), *The Wild Child* (1970), *Two English Girls* (1972), and *Day for Night* (1973). In many of these later films, Truffaut's concern with exploring the possibilities for romantic relationships reappears. Two of the films, for example, focus on different kinds of love triangle: *Soft Skin* concerns a middle-class husband who is murdered by his wife when she discovers that he has been keeping a stewardess as his mistress; *Two English Girls* tells the story of a young Frenchman who goes to England on a holiday and falls in love with two sisters. Truffaut's attitude toward the romantic relationships he portrays in these later films fluctuates between harsh cynicism and pointed satire, but the cynicism and satire are always tempered by the director's sense of humor and deep understanding of the emotional conflicts that motivate his characters' actions — two qualities that make him a master director.

Key elements in the films of François Truffaut include:
1. Scripts that stress the humanity of the leading characters
2. A superb sense of humor used to reveal the foibles of his characters
3. Great versatility of camera style that allows the careful re-creation of different times and places without excessive reliance on props and costumes
4. Acting performances that are tightly controlled, even down to the smallest, inconsequential nuances
5. A naturalistic editing style that creates films that look almost unedited

JEAN-LUC GODARD

Jean-Luc Godard, born in Paris in 1930, is one of the most difficult of contemporary filmmakers to analyze or evaluate. Originally a film critic, he established himself as a strong, highly opinionated voice on the subject of modern film with critical articles that he wrote between 1950 and 1954. In 1959, Godard directed his first feature film, *Breathless*, which had a vital impact on the art of film. Utilizing a freewheeling, highly mobile camera, he gave the film a feeling of spontaneity and improvization. Instead of being confined to the formal dolly set-ups and carefully rehearsed, static scenes so prevalent in Hollywood films, *Breathless* seemed totally free of restriction and inhibition. This "new" style was perfectly suited to this story of a young American journalism student living in Paris and her affair with a cheap gangster. Following *Breathless*, Godard's style became increasingly abstract and often didactic. He became a political and social polemicist, but his control of film as a creative medium continued to expand impressively. His major works include *Le Petit Soldat* (1960), *A Woman Is a Woman* (1961), *Les Carabiniers* (1963), *Contempt* (1963), *Alphaville* (1965), *Pierrot le Fou* (1965), *Masculin-Féminin* (1966), *La Chinoisie* (1967), *Weekend* (1967), *Le Gai Savoir* (1968), and *One Plus One* (*Sympathy for the Devil*) (1969).

As his films became totally involved with social and political themes, Godard's style became more and more free, to the point where many of his sequences seemed almost nonfilm. For example, in *Weekend* he stops the action for almost seven minutes while two garbage men talk directly to a static camera. In the early part of this film a young woman, clad only in a bra and panties, sits on a desk in half-shadow and talks directly to a camera that simply zooms in and out. This sequence too runs for many minutes while the woman tells, in great detail, of an orgy in which she participated. *Weekend* contains almost all Godard's ideas about how the film medium should be used. The plot, such as it is, is loosely concerned with a couple whose marriage is in the process of breaking up. They fight, leave for a holiday, separate, come back together again, and so on. Murder and other acts of violence that seem almost improvised intrude upon the action. *Weekend* is constantly interrupted by fragmentary and extraneous sequences that seem to have little or no relationship to the main thrust of the film but serve merely to permit Godard to express his views on some form of political or social injustice. This technique of inserting disjointed sequences reappears throughout Godard's films.

One of the most brilliant sequences in all Godard's body of film appears in *Weekend*. The married couple, on their way to the wife's aunt's house for the weekend, become trapped in a monumental traffic jam. At the beginning of the sequence we see them sitting stolidly immobile in their car, seemingly paralyzed. Then the camera begins what appears to be an endless dolly past literally hundreds of cars. As the camera moves slowly past the stalled cars, it focuses on acts of hostility and violence taking place at random along the road. The sequence is extremely drawn-out and potentially boring, but Godard's masterful control brings it off. As is typical in a Godard film, the actors improvise, making up dialogue motivated by impulse. They convey an exaggerated, frenetic quality that Godard encourages with his camera work, so that the actors are seldom shown in any posture other than anger or hysteria. The perpetual motion of the camera, with its disregard for conventional standards of professional excellence (Godard employs soft-focus, random pans and uneven zooms) gives the scene the look of a newsreel but certainly heightens its impact. All the artificial residue of filmmaking is gone. The audience believes in this traffic jam and forgets completely that it is contrived and controlled by the director—the audience is made to feel that it is seeing the world in microcosm, and yet the symbolism of the scene is not permitted to diminish the sense of reality.

In recent years, Godard has begun to experiment with filmmaking "en groupe." He is still changing and seeking new ways to use the medium. Godard is as mercurial as his camera and expresses little regard for the traditional "rules" of filmmaking. Critic Pauline Kael aptly summarized Godard's contribution to the development of contemporary film by comparing him to the novelist James Joyce. She maintains that Godard has "paralyzed other filmmakers by shaking their confidence. He has obviously opened doors, but when others try to go through, they're trapped." Whether or not Godard's experiments have in fact paralyzed other filmmakers is open to debate, but he remains an important source of artistic innovation.

Key elements in the films of Jean-Luc Godard include:
1. Total freedom from conventional forms of narrative storytelling
2. Oblique and unexpected methods of social commentary
3. Camera style that is closely matched to the subject matter
4. Innovative techniques of camera movement
5. Editing that ignores traditional concern for continuity and logical progression

In addition to these eleven filmmakers who have contributed substantively to the evolution of film art, there are, of course, others who merit study and analysis. Directors such as Bernardo Bertolucci, Robert Altman, Lindsay Anderson, and Eric Rohmer all have several original, creative films to their credit, and promising young directors such as George Lucas (*American Graffiti*) and Martin Scorcese (*Mean Streets*) are beginning to emerge. As filmmakers keep exploring the potential of their art, the decade ahead should witness continued expansion of the creative base achieved so far.

❧

FILMS FOR STUDY

Shoeshine, Vittorio De Sica.

Bicycle Thief, Vittorio De Sica. Brandon Films, Inc., 200 West 57 Street, New York, New York 10019.

Umberto D, Vittorio De Sica.

The Garden of the Finzi-Continis, Vittorio De Sica.

Los Olvidados, Luis Buñuel.

El, Luis Buñuel.

Nazarin, Luis Buñuel.

Viridiana, Luis Buñuel.

The Discreet Charm of the Bourgeoisie, Luis Buñuel.

La Strada, Federico Fellini. Brandon Films, Inc., 200 West 57 Street, New York, New York 10019.

La Dolce Vita, Federico Fellini.

8½, Federico Fellini.

Fellini Satyricon, Federico Fellini.

The Boy with Green Hair, Joseph Losey.

The Servant, Joseph Losey.

King and Country, Joseph Losey.

Accident, Joseph Losey.

The Go-Between, Joseph Losey.

L'Avventura, Michelangelo Antonioni. Janus Films, 24 West 58 Street, New York, New York 10019.

Red Desert, Michelangelo Antonioni.

Blow-Up, Michelangelo Antonioni.

Zabriskie Point, Michelangelo Antonioni.

The Seventh Seal, Ingmar Bergman. Janus Films, 24 West 58 Street, New York, New York 10019.

Wild Strawberries, Ingmar Bergman. Janus Films, 24 West 58 Street, New York, New York 10019.

The Magician, Ingmar Bergman. Janus Films, 24 West 58 Street, New York, New York 10019.

Through a Glass Darkly, Ingmar Bergman. Janus Films, 24 West 58 Street, New York, New York 10019.

Shame, Ingmar Bergman. Janus Films, 24 West 58 Street, New York, New York 10019.

Cries and Whispers, Ingmar Bergman.

Seven Samurai, Akira Kurosawa.

Rashomon, Akira Kurosawa. Janus Films, 24 West 58 Street, New York, New York 10019.

Ikiru, Akira Kurosawa.

Red Beard, Akira Kurosawa.

Hiroshima, Mon Amour, Alain Resnais.

Last Year at Marienbad, Alain Resnais.

Muriel, Alain Resnais.

La Guerre Est Finie, Alain Resnais.

Paths of Glory, Stanley Kubrick.

Dr. Strangelove, Stanley Kubrick.

2001: A Space Odyssey, Stanley Kubrick.

A Clockwork Orange, Stanley Kubrick.

The 400 Blows, François Truffaut. Janus Films, 24 West 58 Street, New York, New York 10019.

Jules and Jim, François Truffaut. Janus Films, 24 West 58 Street, New York, New York 10019.

The Wild Child, François Truffaut.

Day for Night, François Truffaut.

Breathless, Jean-Luc Godard. Brandon Films, Inc., 200 West 57 Street, New York, New York 10019.

Les Carabiniers, Jean-Luc Godard.

Pierrot le Fou, Jean-Luc Godard.

Weekend, Jean-Luc Godard.

Le Gai Savoir, Jean-Luc Godard.

One Plus One (Sympathy for the Devil), Jean-Luc Godard.

SUPPLEMENTARY READING

Graham, Peter. *The Cinema of François Truffaut.* New York: A. S. Barnes, 1970.

Kyrou, Ado. *Luis Buñuel: An Introduction,* trans. by Adrienne Foulke. New York: Simon and Schuster, 1963.

Leahy, James. *The Cinema of Joseph Losey.* New York: A. S. Barnes, 1967.

Leprohon, Pierre. *Michelangelo Antonioni.* New York: Simon and Schuster, 1963.

Richie, Donald. *The Films of Akira Kurosawa.* Berkeley and Los Angeles: University of California Press, 1965.

Riondi, Gian L. *Italian Cinema Today.* New York: Hill and Wang, 1966.

Roud, Richard. *Jean-Luc Godard.* Garden City, N.Y.: Doubleday and Company, 1968.

Simon, John. *Ingmar Bergman Directs.* New York: Harcourt Brace Jovanovich, 1973.

Solmi, Angelo. *Fellini.* New York: Humanities Press, 1968.

Walker, Alexander. *Stanley Kubrick Directs.* New York: Harcourt Brace Jovanovich, 1971.

Ward, John. *Alain Resnais and the Theme of Time.* Garden City, N.Y.: Doubleday and Company, 1968.

FILM CRITICISM

EIGHT

Somebody has sent me a cutting from which I gather that a proposal to form a critics' club has reached the very elementary stage of being discussed in the papers in August. Now clearly a critic should not belong to a club at all. He should not know anybody: his hand should be against every man, and every man's hand against his. Artists insatiable by the richest and most frequent doses of praise; entrepreneurs greedy for advertisement; people without reputations who want to beg or buy them ready made; the rivals of the praised; the friends, relatives, partisans, and patrons of the damned: all these have their grudge against the unlucky Minos in the stalls, who is himself criticized in the most absurd fashion.

People have pointed out evidences of personal feeling in my notices as if they were accusing me of a misdemeanor, not knowing that a criticism written without personal feeling is not worth reading. It is the capacity for making good or bad art a personal matter that makes a man a critic. The artist who accounts for my disparagement by alleging personal animosity on my part is quite right: when people do less than their best, and do that less at once badly and self-complacently, I hate them, loathe them, detest them, long to tear them limb from limb and strew them in gobbets about the stage or platform. (At the Opera, the temptation to go out and ask one of the sentinels for the loan of his Martini, with a round or two of ammunition, that I might rid the earth of an incompetent conductor or a conceited and careless artist, has come upon me so strongly that I have been withheld only by my fear that, being no marksman, I might hit the wrong person and incur the guilt of slaying a meritorious singer.)

In the same way, really fine artists inspire me with the warmest personal regard, which I gratify in writing my notices without the smallest reference to such monstrous conceits as justice, impartiality, and the rest of the ideals. When my critical mood is at its height, personal feeling is not the word: it is passion: the passion for artistic perfection—for the noblest beauty of sound, sight, and action—that rages in me. Let all young artists look to it, and pay no heed to the idiots who declare that criticism should be free from personal feeling. The true critic, I repeat, is the man who becomes your personal enemy on the sole provocation of a bad performance, and will only be appeased by good performances. Now this, though well for art and for the people, means that the critics are, from the social or clubable point of view, veritable fiends. They can only fit themselves for other people's clubs by allowing themselves to be corrupted by kindly feelings foreign to the purpose of art, unless, indeed, they join Philistine clubs, wherein neither the library nor the social economy of the place will suit their nocturnal, predatory habits. If they must have a club, let them have a pandemonium of their own, furnished with all the engines of literary vivisection. But its first and most sacred rule must be the exclusion of the criticized, except those few stalwarts who regularly and publicly turn upon and criticize their critics. (No critics' club would have any right to the name unless it included—but the printer warns me that I have reached the limit of my allotted space.)

George Bernard Shaw
in Eric Bentley, ed., *Shaw on Music*
Garden City, N.Y.: Doubleday & Co., Inc., 1955,
pp. 34–36
Reprinted by permission of The Public Trustee and
The Society of Authors

AS FILM DEVELOPS INTO A MATURE ART FORM, A KIND OF "AUXILIARY" ART emerges, the art of film criticism. In the early days of the motion picture, when film was oriented in large part toward entertainment, critics in the daily news-

201

papers and periodicals reviewed new films as they might review a musical comedy or an ice show at Madison Square Garden. Their key concern was whether the film was entertaining. The critics who occupied the film desks at the major newspapers (for example, Kate Cameron, Rose Pelswick, and Bosley Crowther) were, by and large, exreporters commissioned by their publications to provide the reading public with a guide to good and entertaining film viewing.

However, as films became intellectually more demanding, and as film techniques became more sophisticated and complex, the need for serious and thoughtful criticism arose. A critic who could easily tell his readers whether the latest Doris Day film was "funny and delightful" had difficulty explaining the character and quality of a complex film like *The Seventh Seal*.

Music, painting, literature, and theater have for many years been subject to the scrutiny of critics who have created in their thoughtful commentaries a large body of scholarship. Such eminent writers as Edmund Wilson, Eric Bentley, Harold Schonberg, Brian O'Doherty, Lionel Trilling, Jacques Barzun, and Alfred Kazin have produced short critiques and important books on a variety of art forms.

THE FUNCTION OF CRITICISM

It is essential to understand the relationship between art and criticism. The critic must not be confused with the reporter, who tells his readers how he "liked" the work and provides only a brief retelling of the story. The thoughtful and scholarly critic dissects and analyzes the work in both a historical and a contemporary context. He seeks to give his reader useful insights into the author's technique and purpose, and to direct the reader to those elements in the work that are meaningful and worthy of special consideration. Above all, the critic seeks to inform, enlighten, and stimulate the reader.

The critic must also *care*. He must have a passionate commitment to the art about which he writes. When he rejoices in work well done, the committed critic does so in appreciation of creative talent and craftsmanship; and when he damns, he does so in anger about shoddy or dishonest work.

The following selection is an example of criticism at its best. It is an excerpt from a critique of Puccini by George Bernard Shaw, writing under the whimsical name of Corno di Bassetto.[1]

> And when you come to Puccini, the composer of the latest *Manon Lescaut*, then indeed the ground is so transformed that you could almost think yourself in a new country. In *Cavalleria* and *Pagliacci* I can find nothing but Donizettian opera rationalized, condensed, filled in, and thoroughly

---

[1] From *Shaw on Music*, ed. by Eric Bentley (Garden City, N.Y.: Doubleday & Co., Inc., 1955), pp. 183–85. Reprinted by permission of The Public Trustee and The Society of Authors.

brought up to date; but in *Manon Lescaut* the domain of Italian opera is enlarged by an annexation of German territory. The first act, which is as gay and effective and romantic as the opening of any version of *Manon* need be, is also unmistakably symphonic in its treatment. There is genuine symphonic modification, development, and occasionally combination of the thematic material, all in a dramatic way, but also in a musically homogeneous way, so that the act is really a single movement with episodes instead of being a succession of separate numbers, linked together, to conform to the modern fashion, by substituting interrupted cadences for full closes and parading a Leitmotif occasionally.

Further, the experiments in harmony and syncopation, reminding one often of the intellectual curiosities which abound in Schumann's less popular pianoforte works, shew a strong technical interest which is, in Italian music, a most refreshing symptom of mental vigor, even when it is not strictly to the real artistic point. The less studied harmonies are of the most modern and stimulating kind. When one thinks of the old school, in which a dominant seventh, or at most a minor ninth, was the extreme of permissible discord, only to be tolerated in the harsher inversions when there was a murder or a ghost on hand, one gets a rousing sense of getting along from hearing young Italy beginning its most light-hearted melodies to the chord of the thirteenth on the tonic.

Puccini is particularly fond of this chord; and it may be taken as a general technical criticism of the young Italian school that its free use of tonic discords, and its reckless prodigality of orchestral resources, give its music a robustness and variety that reduce the limited tonic and dominant harmonic technique of Donizetti and Bellini, by contrast, to mere Christy minstrelsy. No doubt this very poverty of the old masters made them so utterly dependent on the invention of tunes that they invented them better than the new men, who, with a good drama to work on, can turn out vigorous, imposing, and even enthralling operas without a bar that is their own in the sense in which *Casta diva* is Bellini's own; but Puccini, at least, shews no signs of atrophy of the melodic faculty: he breaks out into catching melodies quite in the vein of Verdi: for example, *Tra voi, belle,* in the first act of *Manon,* has all the charm of the tunes beloved by the old operatic guard.

On that and other accounts, Puccini looks to me more like the heir of Verdi than any of his rivals. He has arranged his own libretto from Prevost d'Exiles' novel; and though the miserable end of poor Manon has compelled him to fall back on a rather conventional operatic death scene in which the prima donna at Covent Garden failed to make anyone believe, his third act, with the roll-call of the female convicts and the embarkation, is admirably contrived and carried out: he has served himself in this as well as Scribe ever served Meyerbeer, or Boito Verdi.

Shaw's commentary provides the reader with specific information about both opera and composer. For example, in the third paragraph, Shaw calls attention to Puccini's fondness for a specific chord, provides a basis for comparison with two lesser composers, and discusses one of Puccini's arias as an example of the composer's debt to Verdi.

As a critic, Shaw assumes the role of teacher and extends the knowledge and background of the reader. His erudition, scholarship, wit, and style provide enjoyable reading and engage the reader intellectually.

Preeminent among contemporary theater critics is Robert Brustein, Dean of the Yale School of Drama. The following excerpt from Brustein's critique of a controversial modern play, *The Deputy*, is another example of good criticism.[2]

[A]   Rolf Hochhuth's *The Deputy* reads like a German doctoral dissertation in verse: two or three epigraphs precede each of the five acts, the acts themselves are divided into discrete sections and titled as if they were chapters, discursive passages and author's asides are generously mixed in with the dialogue, and sixty pages of prose, called "Historical Sidelights," are appended at the end, accompanied by footnotes. The presence of so much scholarly paraphernalia in a published dramatic work suggests, for one thing, that the author has prepared himself for trouble ahead. And since *The Deputy* deals with an extremely inflammatory subject—the failure of Pope Pius XII to condemn unequivocally Hitler's extermination of the Jews—he has acted wisely: the work is born unto trouble, as the sparks fly upward. There is no need to rehearse here the controversy that *The Deputy* has provoked in Europe and America; the slanders, the innuendo, the protests, the riots. Suffice it to say that the customary conditions following the publication of an unpleasant truth have prevailed, and humanity has managed to disgrace itself again.

[B]   Hochhuth's painstaking research, on the other hand, does raise difficulties of a quite different kind, for although *The Deputy* is a remarkable work in many ways, it is an *animal amphibium*—a compound of fiction and fact which can be classified neither as good history nor as good literature. While Hochhuth's historical facts are unassailable, for example, some interesting questions have recently been raised about his interpretation of these facts, particularly his assumption that the silence of the Vatican—though partially determined by Church policy, which held the Bolsheviks to be the greater danger than the Nazis—would have been broken had another Pope (say, Pius XI) been in power. Guenter Lewy, in *Commentary*, has suggested that, on the contrary, Vatican policy was the logical culmination of Catholic anti-Semitism, while Hannah Arendt, in *The New York Herald Tribune*, has emphasized that it was Pacelli's predecessor who first praised Hitler and signed the Concordat with Nazi Germany. The temporizing of Pacelli over the fate of the Jews, even as they were being rounded up under his window, then, was not an isolated instance of passivity in the face of evil, but rather reflected the general moral and spiritual collapse of European Christianity, Protestant and Catholic alike.

[C]   Hochhuth's tendency to make the individual accountable for the failures of the institution is a heritage of his German idealism, an influence which can also be seen in the shape and substance of his play. *The Deputy* is written in the ponderous heroic style of Schiller, full of vaunting speeches, generous sacrifices, and externalized emotions—angry confrontations dominate each scene, the verse pitches and rolls, and indignation keeps the tone at a high boil. As for the characters, they are larger than scale, and, therefore, not always very convincing. When the author permits himself artistic license, he can create an interesting and complex individual—the Doctor, for example, whose fatigued cynicism, experimental cruelty, and intellectual arrogance make him a figure of absolute evil, a creation worthy of Sartre or Camus. But more often, Hochhuth's characters are members of a cardboard nobility: Gerstein, for example, the compassionate German who joined the SS, risking his own life to help the victims of Hitler, or Father Riccardo Fontana, the anguished Jesuit priest, who pinned the Jewish star to his cassock when the Pope refused to protest, and accompanied the Jews to Auschwitz.

[D]   Although Father Fontana is fictional, Kurt Gerstein is based on an actual figure whose heroism Hochhuth wished to celebrate in his play. But this is one of the difficulties: historical fact does not always make for very profound art, unless it is supported by a good deal of invention. This is even more obvious in Hochhuth's characterization of Pacelli who appears, a cold, forbidding diplomat, in a climactic obligatory scene, endorsing checks from the Society of Jesus, discussing the various financial holdings of the Church, condemning the Allied bombing of San Lorenzo, and composing a highly ineffectual Article against suffering and misfortune which never once mentions the Jews by name. By adhering so faithfully to contemporary accounts of the Pope, Hochhuth has protected himself, as he must, against charges of tampering with history, but he has left us with a superficial and shadowy character, whose motives remain unplumbed. Unlike Hannah Arendt, who was able to create an extraordinarily complex portrait of Eichmann because the materials were so abundant and her insight so acute, Hochhuth is limited by a scarcity of information about his subject, and by his own apparent lack of interest in the inner workings of character. Cataloguing his personages almost exclusively according to their attitudes towards the Pope's silence, Hochhuth preserves the moral integrity of his work, but at the cost of its aesthetic weight and complexity.

[E]   The New York production of his play, however, preserves no integrity at all, and I have confined my discussion to the printed text because the Broadway performance is beneath discussion. The adaptor, first of all, has confused the need to cut this six-hour work with the license to butcher it, for he has hacked away at the most interesting feature—its intellectual heart—exposing the weakest part of the anatomy—its melodramatic bones. Aside from excising four whole scenes, two of them essential to the theme, decimating characters (the Doctor and Gerstein are mere shadows now), and cutting out just about every literary, historical, political, and religious reference in the text, the adaptor has also methodically proceeded to soften the horror of the work and weaken the accusation of the author, sometimes by rewriting whole portions of dialogue. What the adaptor has left undone in the way of carnage, the director and actors have completed. Were it not so sloppy and unfinished, Herman Shumlin's direction might remind one of certain Hollywood Nazi movies of the forties, because it features exactly the same clichés: the jagged line of prisoners, rags carefully arranged, moving stagily behind barbed wire, threatened by guards; the immaculate Nazis, cracking whips against their boots and curling their lips contemptuously at their victims; the idealistic martyr-heroes, striking lofty postures, pumping up emotion, and spilling righteous rhetoric. Except for Emlyn Williams, whose characterization of Pacelli is suitably frozen and fastidious, none of the actors gives more than a stock performance, and they are using so many different styles that everyone seems to be performing in a separate play. Broadway may have had the initial courage to produce *The Deputy*, but it has not finally been able to transcend its ingrained cowardice and artistic inadequacy.

[F]   Still, the play is available in published form — a document of power and persuasiveness, whatever its aesthetic and interpretive shortcomings. If Hochhuth has not entirely proven himself yet as either an historian or a dramatist, he has certainly proven himself as a man of discriminating moral intelligence and outstanding courage, which makes him rare and valuable enough in the modern world. Appearing at this time, *The Deputy* may, as one American religious group complained, endanger the cause of "harmonious interfaith relations," but if such a cause is contingent on the suppressions of truth, then we are better off without it. As Hannah Arendt has observed, after suffering her own ordeal at the hands of groups with special interests, the truth *always* seems to come at the wrong psychological moment, but in the words of the Catholic historian whom she quotes at the conclusion of her article, "Only the truth will make us free. The truth which is always awful." I am not so certain that the truth will make us free, but a courageous confrontation of the terrible is still the most exhilarating thing I know, and the greatest source of metaphysical joy.

Note how carefully Brustein organizes his material. He presents first a brief historical discussion important to any consideration of *The Deputy* (paragraph A), then a commentary on other interpretations of the political controversy of the play (paragraph B), and finally, a consideration of the play itself through comparison with other writers (paragraph C).

Having provided the reader with the necessary background, Brustein then evaluates the play (paragraphs D and E), liberally lacing his retelling of the plot with his own judgments. After evaluating the performance itself, he comments provocatively on the play as a document of historical importance (paragraph F). In these few paragraphs, he presents many facts and opinions about the play that should stimulate both the casual playgoer and the student of the theater.

Using these examples from the worlds of music and theater as models of the art of criticism, let us now turn to the subject of film criticism.

FILM CRITICISM

To be effective, film criticism should contain the interpretation and evaluation of the following elements:

(1) Theme of the film

(2) Quality of technical execution

(3) Quality and nature of ideas in the film

(4) Validity of ideas in the film

(5) Individual contributions (for example, acting)

(6) Relationship of the film to other works by the same filmmaker

The film critic bears a great responsibility to the art of cinema because in a sense he helps to shape the future of that art. If he writes thoughtful and intelligent criticism, he can widen the periphery of all current dialogue about film and can serve as a catalyst for present and future filmmakers. His role is not, and should not be, one of simply guiding the public to or away from films. Through good film criticism the audience is better equipped to view a film, and the actor and director are stimulated to agree or disagree and thus to fortify or change their approach.

Qualifications of the film critic

The film critic must come to his work with three important tools.

(1) *A thorough knowledge of the art form.* Just as critics of art and music approach their work with erudition and knowledge in their fields, so the film critic must approach his work with a thorough background in film. Contemporary films, with their complexities of style and technique, yield far more readily to analysis if the critic has done his homework. The literary critic is best equipped to write about a complex novel like Thomas Mann's *Dr. Faustus* if he has read the earlier works of the novelist. Similarly, the film critic is best able to review *Hour of the Wolf* if he understands its relationship to Bergman's earlier films *Through a Glass Darkly* and *Persona*.

(2) *A belief in film art.* Many critics write from the vantage point of film as entertainment. They are reporters rather than critics and are usually writing for daily newspapers or monthly periodicals. Their primary function is to provide the reading public with a "preview" opinion about a specific film and a comment on the film's entertainment value. They do not provide an in-depth study of the film as art. But because many contemporary films lend themselves to thoughtful critical analysis, more and more critics are evaluating film as an art form. The conviction that film *is* art is an essential part of the critic's attitude toward contemporary cinema.

(3) *An understanding and appreciation of the other arts.* Contemporary films contain so many references to the other arts that it is no longer possible to write about film without some knowledge of music, painting, literature, and theater. For example, the *commedia dell'arte* tradition of the Italian theater, with its standard mime figures and symbols, influenced the final sequence of Antonioni's *Blow-Up* and Fellini's *La Strada*. An interpretation of these films would be incomplete without an understanding of this theatrical tradition.

Criticism and reportage

To demonstrate the basic difference between the film critic and the reporter, we need only compare the following excerpts from reviews of two of Bergman's films.

The first excerpt is from a review by Bosley Crowther written for *The New York Times*. Working under the pressure of a daily deadline, and forced by the diversity of his audience to seek a common denominator of education and background, Crowther writes commentaries that are, for the most part, reportage. He is concerned with assessing the *entertainment value* of a film rather than with analyzing the complexities of the director's art. Thus his comments lack the depth and scholarship of a review by a critic writing for a more specialized audience. The excerpt below is from Crowther's review of *The Magician*.[3]

> These are a few of the mysteries that rise from the shadows and the glooms of this eerie and Rabelaisian study of the susceptibility of the human mind to the powerful sway of illusion and of the ephemeral nature of Truth.
>
> But never mind about those details that may be vaporous and vague. The important thing is that this picture is full of extraordinary thrills that flow and collide on several levels of emotion and intellect. And it swarms with sufficient melodrama of the blood-chilling, flesh-creeping sort to tingle the hide of the least brainy addict of outright monster films.
>
> Is it something supremely contemplative of the marginal regions between reality and unreality that you would care to cogitate? Then watch the subtle inquisition of the pitifully tawdry little troupe when, in its travels through the country in the mid-nineteenth century, it is strangely incarcerated in a quizzical merchant's home. Is it eroticism you are after? Then study what occurs to the neurotic wife of the merchant when she watches the hypnotist. Or are you for Rabelaisian humor? Then get those servant girls when they drink the fake love-potions and start going after the lads.
>
> As for the sheer melodrama, you'll look far to find a creepier scene than the one in which the skeptical surgeon is hounded by the "body" on which he has just performed an autopsy! The practical uses of suggestion are beautifully indicated here.
>
> As in all his pictures, Mr. Bergman (who does everything) has achieved remarkable magic with his camera and with his cast. Max von Sydow as the magician is a haunting figure who floats between the realms of an agonized mystic and a vulgar charlatan. And he recalls the late Lon Chaney in his sad unmasking scene and in the one he plays with the surgeon, brilliantly performed by Gunnar Bjornstrand.
>
> Ingrid Thulin as the wife of the magician, Erland Josephson as the merchant-dilletante, Ake Fridell as the medicine-show barker and Bibi Andersson as one of the servant girls stand out in a cast that is superior in absolutely every role.
>
> Brilliant use of the sound-track — lengthy silences broken by weird guitar phrases, thumps and strikings of clocks — is a notable feature. It is just too bad one has to read so many English subtitles to follow the Swedish dialogue.

[3] From "The Magician," by Bosley Crowther, *The New York Times*, August 28, 1959.

The second excerpt is from a review of *The Seventh Seal* by Andrew Sarris.[4] Writing for *Film Culture,* Sarris is addressing the serious student of film. As such, his work is more scholarly in tone and character than a review written for a mass audience.

It is not until Jof describes the Dance of Death that we realize that his vision is inspired by a creative imagination rather than a Divine Revelation. The people he identifies in the Dance of Death—Death, the knight, the squire, the actor, the blacksmith and his wife, and the renegade priest—are not entirely the same people Death confronts in the castle. Jof has never seen the knight's wife, and her absence from his vision is quite logical. The omission of the silent girl is more puzzling. At least two interesting theories suggest themselves. The silent girl's final expression of acceptance slowly dissolves into the watchful expression of Mia. The two women look very much alike, and whatever this means—Jof developing a mental block in imagining death for someone resembling Mia, Jof unconsciously admiring the silent girl, Jof even absent-mindedly overlooking the existence of this girl—a clear link has been established between these two archetypes of woman.

The second theory is almost frighteningly intellectual. Since Jof calls off the names of the Dancers, it is possible that the unnamed silent girl cannot operate in Jof's artistic imagination. Except for the witch, all the other recurring characters are assigned proper names, but the silent girl, like the witch, remains an abstract being beyond Jof's ability to recall in his creations. This theory raises the question of Bergman's immersion in the technical philosophies of logical and linguistic analysis, a question which can be answered ultimately only by Bergman himself. Yet, it is quite clear from his interviews and his past films that he has been influenced by the irrational ideas of illusion and existence expressed in the works of Camus, Sartre, Anouilh, Strindberg and Pirandello.

If Jof and Mia represent the continuity of man, they do so because of certain transcendent illusions—love, art, contentment and the future of their child. These futile distractions from imminent death make life endurable if not justifiable. Yet, the knight and the squire are also aspects of man, the knight as the questing mystic, the squire as the earthbound philosopher. It is possible to identify Bergman in some measure with all three characters since *The Seventh Seal* is a unique amalgam of beauty, mysticism and rational logic. What is most remarkable about Bergman's achievement is that he projects the most pessimistic view of human existence with an extraordinary vitality. Conceding that life is hell and death is nothingness, he still imparts to the screen a sense of joy in the very futility of man's illusions.

There are obvious differences between the types of film criticism represented by Crowther and Sarris. Crowther's review, written for a widely disparate audience, serves to give advance information and informed opinions about a film in order to help the reader determine whether he should see the film. Sarris' review, on the other hand, is directed toward the serious student of the art of film; as such, the article presupposes that the reader pos-

---

[4] From "The Seventh Seal" by Andrew Sarris, *Film Culture* (No. 19), 59–60. Reprinted by permission.

sesses the time and interest required for absorbing a detailed critical study. Whereas the Crowther review is most useful before seeing the film, the Sarris critique is most interesting after seeing the film.

Style

An essential element of film criticism—as, indeed, of any type of writing—is *style*. Style refers to the way a critic writes. Art of language, wit, incisiveness, clarity of expression—all these elements contribute to a critic's style of writing. One of the first writers to develop a distinct style in film criticism was the poet-novelist-playwright James Agee. The following excerpt is from Agee's review of the 1947 French film *Farrebique*.[5]

> *Farrebique* was made on a farm in southern France by Georges Rouquier, who was born and raised in the neighborhood, left home and became a linotyper, and ultimately got into movie-making because he couldn't keep away from it. Rouquier had made only one short film before this, a documentary about the making of wine vats. Both the subject of the new film and the particular kind of movie treatment happen to be obsessions of mine; so I cannot hope that many other people will be as deeply excited and satisfied by this film as I am. On the other hand, it is clear to me that because of the same obsessions I would be more merciless toward any mismanagements and betrayals, of the subject or in the treatment, than most people would.
>
> Rouquier's idea is simply to make a record of the work and living of a single farm family, and of the farm itself, and of the surrounding countryside, through one year. I cannot imagine a better subject, or one that is as a rule more degenerately perceived and presented. In a sense, all that can be said of Rouquier's treatment of it is that it is right. That means, among other things, the following:
>
> He realizes that, scrupulously handled, the camera can do what nothing else in the world can do: can record unaltered reality; and can be made also to perceive, record, and communicate, in full unaltered power, the peculiar kinds of poetic vitality which blaze in every real thing and which are in great degree, inevitably and properly, lost to every other kind of artist except the camera artist. He is utterly faithful to this realization; and it is clear in nearly every shot that he is infinitely more than a mere documentor, that his poetic intelligence is profound, pure, and vigorous; and it is clear many times over that he has the makings, and now and then the achievement, of a major poet. There is not an invented person or thing in the picture, and the reenactments, and invented incidents, are perfect examples of the discipline of imagination necessary under these difficult circumstances. One could watch the people alone, indefinitely long, for the inference of his handling of them, to realize that moral clearness and probity are indispensable to work of this kind, and to realize with fuller contempt than ever before how consistently in our time so-called simple people, fictional and nonfictional, are consciously

[5] From *Agee on Film* by James Agee, pp. 296–98. Copyright © 1958 by The James Agee Trust. Reprinted by permission of the publisher, Grosset & Dunlap, Inc.

and unconsciously insulted and betrayed by artists and by audiences: it seems as if the man is hardly alive, any more, who is fit to look another man in the eye. But this man is; and this is the finest and strongest record of actual people that I have seen.

Rouquier's sense of the discretion and power of plot and incident, such as they are, is just as sure and as rare. Even more remarkable is his ability with all the small casual scraps of existence which are neither plot nor incident nor even descriptive, nor revealing of mood or character, but are merely themselves, and of the essence of being. He never imposes poetry or rhetoric or special significance upon these scraps, and they are never left half-dead and helpless, as mere shots-for-shots'-sake: they are incredibly hard stuff to organize, but he has so ordered them that they are fully and euphoniously articulate in their own perfect language. He knows as well as any artist I can think of the power and the beauty there can be in absolute plainness: his record, for instance, of the differing faces of three men and two women as they stand in their home for night prayer; or the mere sequence of bedding down the cows. Much of the picture, and much of the finest of it, has this complete plainness; but raised against this ground bass Rouquier's sense of device and metaphor is equally bold and pure. He develops a wonderful communication of the rooted past, the flowering present, and the ungerminated future in about three minutes during which the Grandfather tells the children the history of the farm and family, while the camera examines snapshots and mementos which are like relics from a primitive grave. He does a beautiful thing in showing the dreams of the old man, his son, his son's wife, wishes as touching and naive as those of a child: then hovers the dreamless face of the Grandmother. His use of analogy and metaphor is Homeric in simplicity and force: the terrifying blooming of a sped flower, as an image of childbirth; the sound of an ax and of a falling tree as the camera watches a man's pulse die. He uses stop-motion as I have always wanted to use it: very plainly, to show the motions of darkness and light and shadow; and with complete freedom and daring, in his orgiastic sequence on spring, to show the jubilant rending and pouring upward and blossoming of the world. This sequence is a prescient and as primordially exciting as the *Pervigilium Veneris*. He also dares to add to it — almost whispered, as it should be — a poem of his own; and so well as I could hear, it is an extremely good poem. I'm not sure the picture wouldn't be still better without it; yet it adds a quality and full dimension of its own, and in principle I am for it. In one sense this film is a kind of Bible which expounds not only the grave kinds of discipline necessary to such work but also the kinds, degrees, and tremendous reaches of liberty and adventure which obedience to these kinds of discipline makes possible.

Agee begins the review with his own value judgments. He then gives the reader detailed examples of Rouquier's art that greatly enrich the viewing experience. An important element of Agee's style is his continuous interjection of the first-person pronoun, making the review seem like a dialogue between himself and the reader. Agee also has the ability to make the reader "see" the scene he is describing, to bring the scene to life through colorful, descriptive phrases.

The following excerpt, from a review written by Agee for *The Nation* on Sergei Eisenstein's *Ivan the Terrible,* is a good example of his accomplished and unique prose style.[6]

> There is a kind of frozen, catatonic deadness about the particular intensity and rigidity of style developed for this film—as if the intelligence, great as it is, could liberate only a very little of itself in the actual images of the film. The kind of liberation I mean occurs just twice in this picture, in the opening, coronation scene, a deacon's hair-raising intonation of a royal benediction (and his wonderful face as he sings), and the moment at which Eisenstein cuts from the ritualistic pouring of gold coins over the new Czar to the faces of young women, watching the sleeting gold and the monarch's tumescent face through it and blossoming into smiles of sexual delight. In their suddenness, beauty, and wildness, and in their ability to enrich the film with whole new trains of ideas and reactions, these two moments are of a different order from any others in *Ivan.* They would have been memorable in any of Eisenstein's early films; but there, ideas as good swarmed and coruscated upon his new-found, new-crowned poetry as abundantly as the anointing storm of gold itself.

Content

The second essential element of film criticism is *content.* In film criticism, as in all other writing, content is a matter of *what* is said, not how it is said. Opinions and value judgments are valid as conclusions, but the body of the critical work rises or falls on the quality of the ideas that are offered.

A film is difficult to analyze. Unlike a book, which can be read and reread, or a painting, which can be viewed for hours, a film speeds by and usually requires many viewings for full appreciation. Thus the critic often finds it difficult to isolate and understand those ideas and techniques that contribute to a film's success or failure. The quality of a work of film criticism often reflects the quality of the film being reviewed. Many critical articles say too little in too many words, and the critic who is able to present original and provocative ideas about a film is all too rare.

The following two excerpts—both dealing with Bergman's *Cries and Whispers*—can be studied as contrasts in film criticism. The first, by Vincent Canby,[7] provides some plot details and some superficial discussion of method, but there is little real analysis of the film, of its content and meanings. Even if one makes allowance for the limitations of space in a daily newspaper review, this kind of film criticism is flawed by its lack of serious content. The second piece, by Michael Wood,[8] represents a more successful attempt to analyze and understand a complex motion picture. The few paragraphs selected demonstrate Wood's ability to present, in a few words, provocative ideas and penetrating intellectual judgments. Whether or not the reader

[6] From *Agee on Film* by James Agee, pp. 249–50. Copyright © 1958 by The James Agee Trust. Reprinted by permission of the publisher, Grosset & Dunlap, Inc.

[7] From "Bergman's New 'Cries and Whispers,'" by Vincent Canby, *The New York Times,* December 22, 1972. © 1972 by The New York Times Company. Reprinted by permission.

[8] From "Seeing Bergman" by Michael Wood, *The New York Review of Books,* XX, 3. (March 8, 1973), pp. 3, 4.

agrees with Wood, this critical article certainly provides a stimulus to further thought and discussion. Because the content is solid and interesting, the criticism serves a valid function.

Set in a tranquil autumn park is a handsome eighteenth-century Swedish manor house, every room of which is decorated in a shade of red. Walls, rugs, draperies, even the blankets in the bedrooms. Depending on the light, the red may look as dark as dried blood or as brilliantly scarlet as a new azalea. The time is the turn of the century, at the end of a long night. Agnes (Harriet Andersson) awakens, moves her head fretfully from side to side on the pillow, then gets out of bed and goes to her desk. In her diary she writes: "It is early Monday morning and I am in pain."

Thus begins Ingmar Bergman's magnificent, moving and very mysterious new film, "Cries and Whispers," with a focus so sharp that it seems to have the clarity of something seen through the medium of fever. Every sense has been heightened to a supernatural degree. Fears, wishes and suspicions never spoken occasionally rustle through the house like wind. We can even hear the newly dead talk, distantly and somewhat reproachfully, mindless of the rapidity with which physical decay sets in.

Agnes, in her late 30's, unmarried and with nothing much to show for her life except some rather ordinary watercolors of flowers, is dying of cancer, slowly and with great pain.

Attending her are her older sister, Karin (Ingrid Thulin), a drawn, angry woman who is married to a diplomat she loathes; her younger sister, Maria (Liv Ullmann), an extraordinary beauty, also married but not inhibited from extramarital affairs that help pass the time; and Anna (Kari Sylwa), a peasant woman with a round, expressionless face, who is probably younger than Agnes but who acts like a forest mother to her.

When Agnes awakens in the night in pain, it is Anna who crawls into bed to hold her and fondle her until she drifts into sleep again.

Nothing that Bergman has done before is likely to prepare you for "Cries and Whispers" except in a comparatively superficial sense. Like all of his recent works, it's ever-aware of what I hesitate to call its filmicness. Sequences begin and end with close-up portraits of the character being considered. The color program of the film is designed to call attention to itself—the red interiors, a fondness for white costumes that is so insistent that the appearance of a gray dress to be a terrible omen, the periodic dissolves to the blank red screen.

All of these things are simply the methods by which Bergman dramatizes states of mind that have seldom been attempted, much less achieved, outside of written fiction. A lot, I'm afraid, will be made of the fact that "Cries and Whispers" moves, like "Persona," in and out of reality and fantasy without easily defining either, though it must now be apparent that everything we see in Bergman is "real" to the extent that we see it and that it is meaningful to the characters and to us.

. . . The film assaults us at these moments, inflicts a kind of punishment on us for being in the cinema, for coming in to spy on death and pain, or perhaps for treating real life, outside the cinema, as a movie, something to be stared at in comfort. Perhaps more simply Bergman is saying, with grim existential fervor, that he can speak to us only by showing pain, that meticulous portraits of pain are the only way to break out of celluloid and into life, to make us feel. I hope he's wrong; he certainly makes his case with a great deal of force, and the temptation to call the movie a dream in the mind of Bergman, or to insist on its careful, sumptuous photography, must in large part be a temptation to scale down the vivid, ugly reality of the film.

What goes wrong in *Cries and Whispers,* though, is not its insistence on reality but its attempt at fable. There is a failure of control in some details too. For example, Karin, early in the film, is doing the accounts. She drops her pen across the book with a dry, weary gesture, then throws down her pince-nez with a stiff, slight, sharp flick of the wrist, and these are perfect evocations of her despair, of a poverty of feeling in her and around her. On the other hand, we see Maria asleep with her dolls, which ought to do the trick, say what Bergman means well enough. But he can't resist a long excursion with the camera down and around a doll's house, which is beautiful, but suggests that Maria's childishness is more important and interesting than it is. Conversely, Liv Ullmann, as Maria, brings grace and economy and complication to the role, whereas Ingrid Thulin, as Karin cracking up, behaves as if she were the wife of Dracula, screaming and laughing and frowning in a manner quite out of key with the distinction of the rest of her performance, or even with the odd, small, eloquent gestures she manages once or twice in the middle of her ranting.

But the main problem is the dream of Anna, the maid, in which Agnes, now dead and laid out, weeps waxy tears and summons her sisters and Anna to her room, one by one. Karin is too cold, and says she doesn't love her; Maria fakes warmness but is repelled when the corpse tries to kiss her; only Anna, the faithful servant and peasant earth mother, for whom Agnes has come to replace her child lost in infancy, can face the dead woman and stanch her tears, and cradle her on her capacious bosom. The spare, rather formal narrative structure of the film invites us to consider this episode as taking place in the gothic imagination of Anna, but it resembles the over-all message of the movie too closely for that alibi to stick. The gothic imagination here is Bergman's, and the movie is flopping into bathos. When Anna says, staring at the speaking corpse, "It's all a dream," and the corpse croaks lugubriously, "It may be a dream for you, but it's not a dream for me," we seem to have struck extraordinary new film territory: Groucho Marx playing Strindberg.

In order to make his film move, to make something happen, Bergman has had to animate his intuition, his initial, undramatic image of women rustling in redness, and he does this unequally, and at the point I have just described, disastrously. The curious thing is that none of this really impairs the film, which rides so perfectly on its mood, on the intensity and mystery which are generated by whatever these women and this house mean to Bergman, that one merely registers flaws without paying any attention to them—they sink into some part of the mind that has nothing to do with one's enjoyment of the film, or even with how the film seems on reflection.

The Wood article, then, probes, dissects, and analyzes. Opinions are supported with specific references to sequences in the film, and the author's interpretation of these sequences gives the piece its integrity of content. The Canby excerpt, although easy to read and understand, is just too superficial and lacking in real content to add much to the reader's knowledge.

CONTEMPORARY FILM CRITICS

Each of the major contemporary film critics has a highly personalized style that can be readily identified. In addition, each critic is a particular combination of strengths and weaknesses. In their diversity of style, background, and orientation, the major film critics offer the serious student of film a broad spectrum of opinion and point of view. A study of their work can stimulate the potential filmmaker, enlarge the perception of the student of film, and, most important, provide a historical perspective for the filmgoer.

In style and content, in erudition and scholarship, film has not yet produced a critic equal to Edmund Wilson, Harold Schonberg, or Robert Brustein in their respective fields. The reviews presented below represent the beginnings of the art of film criticism. They have been selected to demonstrate the quality and character of the work of major contemporary film critics.

Penelope Gilliatt

Among modern film critics, Penelope Gilliatt possesses one of the finest capacities for understanding "what the film is about." Her interpretations of complex plot lines and symbolic material are always interesting. For example, her review of *Petulia* in *The New Yorker* catches the full depth and range of Richard Lester's views on human relationships in modern society and provides many fine insights into the connection between Lester's technique and his subject matter. Although her general tone is relatively serious and professional, Miss Gilliatt possesses an excellent wit. She has a wide range of experience in the other arts and an impressive grasp of history and current events. The following excerpt from her review of Godard's *Les Carabiniers* reveals the important elements of Miss Gilliatt's style.[9]

[A] War is stupid, says everyone, fighting and buying armament stocks the while. No, says Jean-Luc Godard's blandly insulting "Les Carabiniers," it is soldiers who are stupid. War itself is very clever. It gets the ill-placed to do the top brass's dirty work, it sanctions acts of arson and genocide that lone criminals might jib at, and it sells the recruitable on the idea that their lives are duller in peacetime. Without great idiocy among the men who fight, says the film—which has only just got a New York run, though Godard made it in 1963—war could scarcely work so brilliantly. This startling, craggy picture is haggard with intellect, but the brains and concern are disclaimed. "Les Carabiniers" wears an off-focus callousness that is peculiar to Godard. He proposes rock-faced paradoxes upon which familiar sympathy can obtain no purchase. They are illustrated with all the inhumanity he can muster, and he dares you to presume pity in him at the peril of your own cool. But some freezing alertness to people's suffering in the vise of modern arbitrariness seems to be there all the same, and his drive to deny that he feels affection is part of that same racking contemporary trap.

* * *

[B]   Cleopatra, Venus, Michelangelo, Ulysses. "Les Carabiniers" is about insensate people carrying legendary inscriptions of which they know no more than the postcard knows of the Parthenon. It is about minds that see history as garbage; about the way the world looks when insight and the sense of consequence have been lobotomized; about being a tool. Brecht often wrote of the same things. He was obsessed and saddened by our readiness to buy life as it comes and to believe the labels. The bemused clods in "Les Carabiniers" have been sold a fake, handed out the existence of curs, but they trust the tag and obediently act out the parts of fortunate men, just as the characters in "Mother Courage" truly suppose themselves to be doing well out of the war that exploits them. The intellectual substance of the picture is compressed into the device of attaching noble official pronouncements to scenes of harrowing military muddle that they don't match at all. Soothing slogans are intoned over images of wretchedness like benedictions uttered over a Catholic peasant woman at the end of her tether. Godard is really making a humane point of linguistics. Hang on like grim death, he says, to the difference between words and meanings. Language denies the visible truth all the time in this picture. There is a shout of *"La guerre est finie"* but the explosions continue as usual. While a voice sonorously announces triumph, civilians in a town square scatter under a low bombing raid. The womenfolk at home trot out to the mailbox for lunatically stoic letters saying that the bloodshed proceeds magnificently and that their men kiss them. On the third Christmas Day of the war, beside a stingy tree in a corner of their shack, Cleopatra and Venus experiment happily with festive ways of doing their hair.

* * *

[C]   "Les Carabiniers" is a chilling fable about habit. It is also about the dizzying impulse to push the atrocious always a little farther. There are lines dealing with the same instinct in Godard's films about private life—moments when lovers wantonly say "I do not love you," to test how much pain they can cause; and in "Pierrot le Fou," when Pierrot says to a badly-off garage boy, "You'd like a car like that? Well, you'll never have one." The men in "Les Carabiniers" are inevitably less interesting than these characters, because their responses seem devised, and not their own. They are the victims, never the agents, of the obscuring of their consciousness. The film is more of a thesis film than any other that Godard has made; it is deliberately even less particularized than usual, and sometimes even more contrary. I realize that the maddeningness is a device, but occasionally it can be—well, maddening. Perhaps it is a trick he uses to shield himself. (His ex-wife, Anna Karina, once touchingly said that his reason for wearing dark glasses all the time is not that his eyes are weak but that his universe is too strong.) The shrug that one catches in his work, the self-protective guise of cool, can sometimes look very like an updating of the hallowed and facile old French game of playing the unsurprisable cynic, but it can also strike you, when his films are most expressive, as the self-defense of a uniquely troubled, rancorous, and tender intellect. Godard regularly uses affront as a style for statement, maybe to stop our gum-chewing or maybe to give himself something to hide behind. In "Les Carabiniers," his weapon is stupidity—wooden-headedness in the soldiers, and even a surface of simplemindedness to the thesis of the picture. But after you have thought about the film for a while you haven't much doubt that what drives it is not willful flippancy but distress. In his own way, Godard belongs historically to the line of great intellectual cartoonists—the witnesses who goad by deforming the familiar and by pretending callousness, the provokers who deliberately seek to be drastic because they see themselves as the reporters of last chances.

In paragraph A, Miss Gilliatt describes what she thinks the film is about. Her use of adjectives ("startling, craggy picture," "haggard with intellect," "rock-faced paradoxes") is highly original and communicative. Miss Gilliatt uses her erudition in other arts to supplement her work and never just to show off. Her analogy to Brecht (paragraph B) helps to reveal and clarify a major point in Godard's work. The reader may even be stimulated to read *Mother Courage* before going to see *Les Carabiniers*.

Paragraph C contains Miss Gilliatt's own critical judgments. Her conclusion evolves logically from the careful architecture of the article and seems convincing and inescapable. If we have already seen the film, we can measure our own views against the judgment of this critic. If we have not seen the film, we may be stimulated to do so and can view the film with greater perception.

Miss Gilliatt is not afraid to clarify her judgments in detail. She points out specific elements of the film she considers effective. After we have read the article, we not only understand Miss Gilliatt's view of the film but have learned something about the film itself. This should be a hallmark of good criticism, and it is continually present in Miss Gilliatt's work.

John Russell Taylor

John Russell Taylor, film critic for the London *Times*, has written some of the most provocative and insightful criticism about film. The following excerpt is from an article on Fellini, which appears in Taylor's book *Cinema Eye, Cinema Ear*.[10] Of course, such a general article about a filmmaker, written, so to speak, at leisure, cannot be compared with a daily or weekly review of a specific film. However, this type of critical analysis comprises an important part of film criticism and provides rewarding material for study.

[10] From *Cinema Eye, Cinema Ear* by John Russell Taylor, pp. 31–37. Copyright © 1964 by John Russell Taylor. Reprinted by permission of Hill and Wang, Inc., and A. D. Peters & Company.

[A]   [*Il Bidone*] starts, visually and emotionally, in the bare upland world of *La Strada;* even Nino Rota's music takes up again the theme associated with the snow scenes in *La Strada.* The bidoni, disguised as priests, are practising an elaborate confidence trick on some peasants by searching for treasure on their land, near a solitary tree just such as that which brooded over the wedding feast in *La Strada.* After various other tricks played on the credulous and pitiable poor, they go back to the town and there we are at once plunged into the world of *I Vitelloni,* with a festival in progress, a wild party to which they are all invited, the entangling of the principal figures in and then their progressive detachment from this background, and inevitably the moment of truth in the small hours. Picasso might be saved; he would be if he were capable of salvation, but probably he is not, any more than Fausto; he is a spiritual lightweight. But Augusto, touched also by something akin to remorse, only hides it from himself by plunging further into shame. After an extraordinary drunken night scene in which his attitude and Picasso's are contrasted he goes off first to a meeting with his daughter which suggests an attempt at redeeming himself, but leads only to his arrest and imprisonment, and then to his final trick, where he pushes his priestly imposture to sacrilegious extremes with a crippled girl and then double-crosses his associates into the bargain, and so finally to his agony and death.

[B]   The whole final sequence, with its ultimate degradation, its bitter accent on physical pain and its ambiguous conclusion, is one the most remarkable in all Fellini, and deserves closer attention on several counts. To begin with, there are an extraordinary number of overtly symbolic correspondences where they have the most unequivocal effect: in the dialogue. Practically everything in the conversation between Augusto (disguised as a bishop) and the paralysed girl has a direct bearing on what subsequently happens to him; he becomes paralysed as she has been; when she says that suffering has shown her the way to God the implications of her words for the interior action of the last sequence are unmistakable. Then, too, the sequence offers an extreme example of Fellini's use of a real location quite realistically on one level (how many gangsters in American films have not met picturesque ends in rubbish dumps, railway sidings and other wastelands without any real significance being attached to the circumstance?), but with an unashamedly symbolic overall effect. Flung by his infuriated associates down a steep slope of stones at the roadside, Augusto finds that he is paralysed and probably dying, alone and far from help, in a dry hellish waste of infertile rock (water is conspicuous by its absence in *Il Bidone;* there is no seashore scene at all, and when at one point it rains the moisture is made to fall like a benediction on those below). Here he is at last, and this time quite inescapably, brought face to face with himself: with the falseness of his standards and his total uselessness to everyone in the world, even himself.

[C]   And so, at this deep point of self-judgement and self-condemnation, he starts what can only be described as a calvary, an agonizing ascent towards, literally and functionally speaking, the road, but much more prominently towards recovered humanity, redemption, and salvation. As he edges painfully up the slope the village bells are heard in the distance, then, later, when he is too worn out even

218

to call for help, a group of peasants pass, with a little girl singing. And finally, alone to the last, he dies, and the camera, which has clung obsessively to him and his torment of stones up to now, suddenly draws back from him with a short, discreet gesture of abandonment. Has suffering shown him the way to God? We are at liberty to believe so if we wish, and the majority opinion seems to be that he has. One wonders if Fellini himself would feel competent to give a decisive answer, but whatever the verbal reply he would offer to an intellectually formulated question, there is no doubt of the efficacy of the answer the sequence gives in film terms to the questions formulated in film terms by what has gone before. In location, in the direction and duration of Augusto's ascent (again we share the character's time, on this occasion almost unbearably long drawn out), in the grey, stone-obsessed quality of the photography, Fellini offers the perfect resolution of the film's earlier conflicts between light and dark, the worlds of La Strada and I Vitelloni. The final sequence completes the film's structure with unmistakable authority, and here director's authority: the sequence could hardly have been conceived, let alone successfully realized, by any writer who was not a director to his fingertips, dealing all the time, from the start, essentially in film rather than the words on paper which may eventually go towards making it.

[D]   If after this climax some even of Fellini's most enthusiastic admirers felt and expressed disappointment with his next film, Le Notti di Cabiria, that may be attributed to various causes, some of which on examination seem to be reasonable, some less so. The most immediate, I think, were Fellini's return, after the clear, single dramatic developments at the centre of La Strada and Il Bidone, to a loose, episodic form of organization reminiscent of I Vitelloni, only if anything less purposeful, since the argument of the film is essentially circular rather than progressive; and the fact that he used Giulietta Masina in a way which suggested to the wary that he was deliberately trying to repeat the success of La Strada with another lovable Gelsomina figure. . . .

. . . All Fellini's other films chart in some way a moral progression, upwards or downwards, and the characters in them are brought by events to a situation where truths have to be faced and decisions made. In other words, they are all dynamic, and only Le Notti di Cabiria is essentially static. That statement may provoke disagreement, and certainly at first glance the film does appear to progress by a series of such encounters with the truth for Cabiria. But, in fact, what we are shown is a series of trials, each one, if only by virtue of being one more, that little bit worse than the one before, and the point of the film is that through them all Cabiria remains the same, indestructible. She does not really develop; indeed, she is in many ways hardly a character at all, but a yardstick by which the turpitude and degradation of the world around her can be measured. And as such she is, inescapably, a sentimental device; even her apparently shocking profession—she is a prostitute and therefore might normally be expected to symbolize the very opposite —fails in its desentimentalizing effect simply because the tart with a heart, to which breed she unmistakably belongs, is itself one of the oldest clichés of sentimental fiction. So right at the film's conception, there is something wrong; perhaps, as Renzo Renzi suggests, it is that while setting up a model of perfect Christian charity and humility Fellini cannot himself believe in it as a human possibility, however passionately he is for it as a principle.

[E]   But, as ever in Fellini's work, such academic objections are swept aside (or very nearly) by the force and life of the film itself: each episode is so fully, vividly imagined and embodied in visual imagery that we do not as it goes along notice the lack of that inner development which elsewhere gives impetus and direction to Fellini's abounding invention. The first and last sequences are attacks on Cabiria, the first by a lover she has trusted who pushes her in the river and runs off with her money; the second infinitely more brutal and premeditated, a sort of nightmare intensification of the first, in which a mild, quiet-looking man leads her on to believe he loves and will marry her, lets her sell everything she owns, and then takes it all from her and leaves her apparently desperate at last, crying out that she doesn't want to live any more. But the final shots show her surrounded by happy young people who serenade her, and it is clear that from this last trial also she has emerged unscathed, with enough hope and strength to start again.

*   *   *

[F]   Whatever may be the dramatic weaknesses of Le Notti di Cabiria as a whole, there is no denying the remarkable brilliance with which these sequences are handled. The direction, in fact, is more obtrusively artful in effects than ever before—which might also be interpreted as a sign of doubt in the director's mind about the workability of the basic material. Fellini has never previously been so ready to indulge in decorative extravagance as in the various scenes in which the prostitutes squabble in the night streets, or indulged in such spectacular editing as in parts of the Divine Amore sequence. Some of the prostitutes, too—la Bomba Atomica in her cave, full of threats of a big come-back; Matilde in her leopard-skin bolero, screaming insults—are more uninhibitedly grotesque than ever before in his work. Even the style of photography favoured fluctuates considerably from scene to scene: bold chiaroscuro in the night-club scene and the street-scenes; dead grey in the sequence involving the man with the sack; blanching neo-realist daylight for the scenes near Cabiria's house; expressionistically strange and unnatural illumination for the theatre scene (reasonably) and the final disillusionment which springs indirectly from it.

Throughout the article, Taylor intersperses comments and questions that enrich his retelling of the plot and that force the reader to think. In paragraphs A and B, Taylor comes to grips with Il Bidone, a subtle and complex film, and provides an insight into techniques that are important in later Fellini films. Taylor is particularly good in presenting material that can be applied to all the films of a particular director, giving the reader a better understanding of how that filmmaker works. Paragraphs B and C contain many phrases that provide a key to all Fellini's films: "overtly symbolic correspondences," "use of a real location quite realistically on one level . . . but with an unashamedly symbolic overall effect," "grey stone-obsessed quality of the photography."

Paragraphs D and E deal with *Le Notti di Cabiria*. Taylor's assessment of this film as "essentially static" is provocative. He supports his contention by isolating the major weakness throughout Fellini's work (end of paragraph D).

In paragraph F, Taylor demonstrates a facility for convincingly applying his own value judgments to what is seen on screen. The final sentence is an excellent example of useful critical comment on one area of film (the style of photography), and it provides the reader with a touchstone by which to evaluate any Fellini film.

Taylor's style is lively and never becomes didactic. He continually adds personal comments to his recounting of the plot, giving us a feeling of his attitude toward the film. He asks questions that go directly to the heart of the film: "How many gangsters in American films have not met picturesque ends in rubbish dumps, railway sidings and other wastelands without any real significance being attached to the circumstance?" "Has suffering shown him [Augusto] the way to God?" Taylor also makes frequent references to other Fellini films, displaying a thorough familiarity with the subject. His ideas are original and well considered, and they make his reviews enjoyable and stimulating.

Taylor rarely admires a film or filmmaker unreservedly; he devotes his attention to isolating those factors that are central to a particular artist or work. He generally deals with selected details, microscopically examining all the factors that make up a scene or sequence. From this intensive look at the segments of a film, he draws his conclusions on the work as a whole. He is extremely negative on the work of Bergman, but very appreciative of and informative on Bresson, Truffaut, and Fellini.

Dwight Macdonald

Dwight Macdonald comes to the field of film criticism with a background of diverse activities in journalism. Although he lacks a scholarly grounding in film, the intellectual and artistic richness of his views adds vitality to his work. The following review of George Stevens' *The Greatest Story Ever Told*, reprinted in its entirety, is a humorous and iconoclastic attempt to upset the establishment.[11] Macdonald's aim is to entertain the reader as well as to stimulate improvements in the art. Despite the fact that Dwight Macdonald is no longer writing film criticism on a regular basis, the skill with which he uses humor and sarcasm as critical tools in the following article justifies his inclusion in this text and merits careful study by the reader.

---

[11] "The Greatest Story Ever Badly Told" by Dwight Macdonald, *Esquire* (July 1965), 52–56. Reprinted by permission of *Esquire* Magazine. Copyright © 1965 by Esquire, Inc.

[A]   It seems to be impossible for this Christian civilization to make a
decent movie about the life of its founder. From DeMille's sexy-
sacred epics — too bad those temple prostitutes were pagan — up to
the film under present consideration, George Stevens' *The Greatest
Story Ever Told,* they have all been, as art or as religion, indecent.
Yet the rules for success, deducing them inversely from the failures,
are simple enough:

(1) Use the original script.

(2) Avoid well-known performers, especially in small parts.

(3) Try to realize that the past was once a present, as everyday
and confused and banal as the present present, and that Jesus and the
people of his time didn't know they were picturesque any more than
the builders of Chartres knew they were making Gothic architecture
(though the builders of our collegiate Gothic did).

(4) Keep it small. In spirit: no dramatics, sparing use of emphatic
closeups and photography, no underlining of a story that still moves
us precisely because it is not underlined; Jesus was a throw-it-away
prophet, direct and unrhetorical even in a speech like the Sermon
on the Mount. Also keep it small literally: no wide screen, no stereophonic sound, no swelling-sobbing mood music (maybe no music
at all), no gigantic sets or vast landscapes or thousands of extras
milling around with staves, palm branches and other picturesque
impedimenta.

(5) The story of Jesus should be told with reverence for the text in
the New Testament (taking into account historical corrections by
recent scholarship), but with irreverence for the sensibilities of contemporary religious group — Buddhist, Moslem, Taoist, and even
Catholic or Jewish.

[B]   Of the three most recent stabs — *le mot juste,* I think — at the
Christ story, Nicholas Ray's *King of Kings* is lowbrow kitsch, Pier
Pasolini's *The Gospel According to St. Matthew* is highbrow kitsch,
and the present work is the full middlebrow, or Hallmark Hall of
Fame treatment. I must add, in fairness to Mr. Pasolini, that his was
the best try — see December column: it followed rules (1) and (2)
completely, observed (3) intermittently, and systematically violated
(4), which unfortunately is the most important. I can't understand
why it hasn't been imported over here; it is more interesting than
almost all the films we've had a look at this thin season. I must
also add, in fairness to Mr. Stevens, that his movie was premiered
"Under the Patronage of the President of the United States and Mrs.
Johnson"; and, in fairness to myself, that even Bosley Crowther,
normally a pushover for Biblical spectaculars, didn't like it.

[C]   For reasons which as usual escape me, George Stevens has long
enjoyed a reputation in Hollywood as a dedicated artist. Dedicated
he may be, but his films look to me overblown and pretentious,
even *A Place in the Sun,* even *Shane.* Maybe it's because he takes
so long — five years on *The Greatest Story,* including a year of cutting
which doesn't show up positively on the screen. Or perhaps it's
because he takes himself very seriously — in Hollywood it's often
all that is necessary. How can they tell out there, after all? Maybe
the guy *is* an artist. Dismissing previous Biblical films as "superficial," Mr. Stevens announced his treatment was going to be different. No clichés, he told a New York *Times* reporter, and furthermore:

"The basic theme of the story is one which unfortunately, has not always been associated with it in the past. It relates to the universality of men and how they must learn to live together. I think it is a theme of great earnestness and utmost simplicity. And I think all the usual trappings connected with Biblical productions . . . are in alarming disagreement with this simple theme. We tried, without diverging from the traditional, to think out the story anew and present it as living literature." The safety clause about not "diverging from the traditional" seems to contradict the rest, but let's be realistic: it's a $20,000,000 property, so two cheers for George Stevens. He talks a good movie.

What I saw on that wide screen was something else again. Had I not just this moment thought up my five simple rules, I might have suspected Mr. Stevens had somehow got a peek and, reasoning that whatever I like the box office wouldn't, simply inverted them.

[D]   (1) The screenplay, by Mr. Stevens and James Lee Barrett, is "based on The Books of the Old and New Testaments, Other Ancient Writings, The Book *The Greatest Story Ever Told* by Fulton Oursler, and Other Writings by Henry Denker." Decent of them to list the New Testament and nice, if puzzling, to include the Old so nobody gets left out. The Other Ancient Writings are intriguing, as are the Other Writings, presumably non-Ancient, by Mr. Denker, an unknown writer to me. I have heard of the late Mr. Oursler but have not felt it necessary to read him. He is described in the 1962 edition of *The Reader's Encyclopedia of American Literature* as "a versatile writer . . . detective stories . . . plays and motion-picture scenarios, including *The Spider* (1927) . . . in 1944 became a senior editor of *Reader's Digest*. . . . His most famous books were those on the Bible and Christianity, particularly *The Greatest Story Ever Told* (1951). Oursler had a great gift for popularization." His religious career was eclectic: "In his early years Oursler was a Baptist, for a while he was an agnostic, in his later years a devout Catholic." Just the man for a Biblical movie. There was one more litterateur involved. "Produced in Creative Association with Carl Sandburg," the titles proclaim—a job as vague as it was elevated. Mr. Sandburg seems to have been a kind of cinematic Holy Ghost. The script that emerged from this olio of writers and Other Writings teeters between the vapid and the punchy, every line destroying whatever illusion of history or religion the acting, photography and direction have accidentally spared. "The party responsible is Jesus of Nazareth." "Don't lie there, Matthew, you'll catch a sickness," says Jesus, meaning a cold, but "sickness" is more Biblical. "Your majesty, if I may be so bold. . . ." "I have never liked you, Baptist," says José Ferrer (Herod Antipas) to Charlton Heston (John the Baptist) in his most sneering tone, which is plenty. Later they have a spirited exchange: "I've heard things about you, Baptist." "And I've heard many things about *you*, Herod [pause], all bad!" "How shall I be saved?" Herod asks, trying to change the conversation—you can tell by Ferrer's expression he doesn't really mean it, just cynical and effete; his father, Herod the Great, alias Claude Rains, is even more cynical, in that world-weary style on which Mr. Rains took out a patent in 1927. But Baptist-Heston, who is neither cynical nor effete, replies with simple dignity: "By standing in the next line when you meet him—this side of Hell!" That's the stuff for the troops! But I still prefer the original dialogue by Matthew, Mark, Luke and/or John.

[E]   (2) Max Von Sydow—who must have found George Stevens an interesting contrast to his usual director, Bergman—is a gentlemanly Christ, restrained, earnest and handsome in a Nordic way. I wonder why, incidentally, all movie Christs, from H. B. Warner on (with the exception of Pasolini's, who I'm told, is a Spanish Jew, though he looked just Spanish to me), have been non-Jewish; likewise most of the disciples, except of course Judas. I also wonder why those Jewish-chauvinist groups and magazines that gave me a hard time when, in my review of *Ben-Hur*, I complained the Crucifixion was blamed entirely on the Romans, have never made a fuss about this point. Why no protests against Mr. Stevens' casting the ostentatiously Irish Dorothy McGuire as Mary? I suppose it's a tricky business: the Semiticists don't want Jews to be villains in the Christ story, but they aren't keen either to claim the heroes for their side since, despite the recent scholarly researches—with which I largely agree—proving that the Romans were more and the orthodox Jewish authorities were less responsible for sending Jesus to the Cross than the New Testament alleges, still he did preach a new religion that was—and is—in important respects opposed to Judaism. Getting back to casting, Von Sydow is not bad as Jesus; for all his lack of Semitic expressiveness, he's at least dignified and he's not so familiar as to make one think, "There's Max!" whenever he appears. But when Ed Wynn, wearing contact lenses, comes on as the blind Aram, a quaveringly ecstatic convert, I was wrenched back to the Texaco Fire Chief and, before that, to The Perfect Fool who lectured us in the Twenties as the zany professor who had invented a machine for eating corn on the cob which rang a bell, like a typewriter, when he nibbled to the end of a row. I have noted the difficulty of suspending disbelief when Ferrer, Rains and Heston go through their familiar routines, also the difficulty of keeping Dorothy McGuire in focus as Mary, but I might add that Simon of Cyrene was all too obviously Sidney Poitier, ditto Van Heflin and Sal Mineo and John Wayne and Angela Lansbury in other "cameo" parts. The illusion-destroying effect was all the greater because they came on so suddenly and briefly. I never got used to them as, respectively, Bar Amand, Uriah, The Centurion, and Claudia; like some nutty relative bursting in dressed up as Napoleon. There was also that "Woman of No Name" who pushes through the crowd as Jesus is healing the sick and, after he has grappled with her, cries out in purest Bronx, "Oi'm cured! Oi'm cured!" and turns around to run toward the camera with arms waving in triumph—and damned if it isn't Shelley Winters. A shock like that can suspend belief for quite a while.

(3) Mr. Stevens says he tried to avoid "the clichés and the usual trappings connected with Biblical productions" and to "think the story out anew and present it as living literature." His effort was unsuccessful, one might say spectacularly so. He rushed to embrace every Biblical movie cliché and trapping in sight. Picturesque effects are unremitting, beginning with the star that guides the three wise men to the manger. It is a very large star, gleaming in the shape of a Hallmark cross in the dark-blue Panavision sky, and the

wise men would have had to be extremely nearsighted to miss it. The manger is rather pictorial too, not to mention the lovely Miss McGuire ensconced there looking down with misty eyes on her miraculous babe. The wise men, like the other characters, have a tendency to get themselves photographed against the sky. I haven't seen so many skyline shots since Dassin's *He Who Must Die*, another Christ movie; it's in modern dress, but otherwise it's done in the same spirit as *The Greatest Story Ever Told*. One of Mr. Stevens' favorite effects is a skyline shot of a line of camels, very picturesque animals, going one way while a line of disciples trudges the other way.

(4) The scale is bigger in every way than any Biblical film I've seen, which is a large statement. Not just Panavision but Ultra Panavision 70. Not just sound but stereophonic sound that comes at you from all quarters. There are lots of squalling babies, to show that Life Goes On, and once the cry came so clearly from under my seat that I looked down to see if some careless mother. . . . There are also lots of screaming gulls wheeling and gliding most pictorially to show that the lower orders also reproduce themselves—the M.P.A. Code should blacklist seagulls as local color, except in art films. The music roars and throbs and nudges continually, more Wagnerian than Christian. For the finale of Part One, Handel's *Hallelujah Chorus* was belted out with such deafening *brio* that, what with Lazarus rising from the dead and the extras running around like grand-opera peasants telling each other, needlessly since we and they had seen it happen, "Lazarus has risen! He's *alive!*" and Ed Wynn recovering his sight (I *think*, but there was so much confusion) and tottering up to Herod's palace to shout triumphantly up to the guards on the high Babylonian ramparts that Lazarus has risen . . . is *alive*, etc.—I then decided I had spent a reasonable amount of time, two hours, on *The Greatest Story* and that after this the Crucifixion could only be an anticlimax. So I left.

The landscape Mr. Stevens had chosen was a factor in my decision. With his customary thoroughness, he had, according to the *Times*, spent "months of research in the Holy Land." But he was disappointed: it looked worn, beat up, mingy, *small*. Not a worthy setting for the greatest story ever told. So he returned to the U.S.A. and shot the film in Utah, Nevada and California, where vistas are quite large. "Some of the landscapes around Jerusalem," he explained, "were exciting, but many had been worn down through the years by erosion and man, invaders and wars, to places of less spectacular aspect." Therefore, as one of his handouts puts it, our own West is a "far more authentic" locale for filming the life of Christ "than is the modern Holy Land." (The Forest Lawn cemetery in Los Angeles suggests in its literature that its replicas of Michel-Angelo's sculptures, carved by hand out of the same Carrara marble he used and by Italians just like him, are really closer to his conception than those chipped, stained, dilapidated "originals" in Florence.) So what we have is a Biblical Western. Jesus and his disciples crawl like ants over the most stupendous kind of rocky terrain. The Sermon on the Mount is escalated to The Sermon on the Mountain, with Jesus on the pinnacle of a high mesa with scenery stretching for miles around him and the disciples in a circle a proper distance below and the people down in the lowest place. He begins

225

the Lord's Prayer in a meadow, then the bored camera moves off and we get some more mountain scenery and finally they camp by a broad river at the bottom of what looks like the Grand Canyon (it's somewhere in Utah, actually) and, dramatically silhouetted against the sunet, with great black cliffs beetling over him and the wide river roiling turbulently as it catches the evening light, Jesus delivers the Lord's Prayer complete. The setting is impressive enough, and indeed perhaps a little too impressive. Custer's last stand or the battle of the Alamo might compete successfully with such natural grandeur. The Lord's Prayer gets lost in the scenery.

(5) All Biblical movies are theologically circumspect, for obvious reasons, but this one overdoes it. The Romans are the bad goys again—though Pilate looks Jewish for some reason—and the Jews couldn't be more friendly to the founder of Christianity. Jesus-Sydow is walking with his disciples, and one says, "Look, some Pharisees!" (Like "Hey, Indians!", though how did he know? Movie Indians wear feathers in their hair and look fierce, but these Pharisees weren't distinguishable visually from the disciples.) And there they are, those oft-denounced Pharisees; "Woe unto you . . . ." And they have come to warn him about certain plots against him. Nor is the Catholic audience slighted. When Jesus asks the disciples just who they think he is, exactly, Judas hems and haws ("Er, um, you're a great leader, a teacher"); the others are more enthusiastic but also vague; finally Peter gives the right answer: "You are the Son of God, the Messiah." Jesus is pleased: "Peter, you are the rock on which my church will be founded." As a lapsed Presbyterian, I object to this building up of Peter. He didn't show up so well at Gethsemane. Jesus said unto him, "Verily I say unto thee, that this day, even in this night, before the cock crow twice, thou shalt deny me thrice." And he did. Some rock. These tactful touchings up to appease religious pressure groups are to be expected in Biblical movies. But Mr. Stevens has gone farther. "Do you consider wealth a crime?" the rich Lazarus asks. "Not at all," smoothly replies Max Von Norman Vincent Peale, "but it may become a burden." One of the many things I admire about Jesus is his prejudice against the rich. Give away your goods and follow me; easier for a camel to pass through the eye of a needle than for a rich man to enter heaven, etc. Mr. Stevens might have left this minority group unappeased, I think. Did he write this exchange, I wonder, or Mr. Barrett, or Mr. Oursler, or Mr. Denker, perhaps?

[F]   "The film moves to excite the imagination of the audience by rendering before it the beauty and the extraordinary nature of Him who represents many things, and one thing," states the vellum-paper program in that gnomic style of which Mr. Stevens is a master. "To recall, or is it to challenge, one's own image of Christ—an image derived from a word, a panel of stained glass, a Gothic-lettered Christmas card, a burst of organ music, an inner exaltation, an experience." You can get an image of Christ, it seems, from practically anything, including a Hallmark greeting card, except the writings of Matthew, Mark, Luke and John.

A distinctive mark of the style of Dwight Macdonald is, of course, his sardonic wit. In the above article, he uses this wit to destroy a film he does not like. However, beneath the obvious ridicule is serious and thoughtful commentary.

In paragraph A, Macdonald presents constructive suggestions for improving the quality of some of the more ambitious films dealing with the Christ story. Paragraph B contains a brief but highly useful discussion of such films. Macdonald's evaluation of Stevens (paragraph C) is interesting and provocative. This is an important function of the critic: to accept no historical idols but to spur a constant reevaluation of all films and filmmakers.

In paragraph D, Macdonald points out not only what he thinks is wrong but *why* it is wrong, and he makes his case with a vengeance. In paragraph E, Macdonald comments on the casting practices of Hollywood and provides a vivid description of the elements of Stevens' film that he feels are thoroughly absurd. In paragraph F, he draws all his comments together in a *coup de grâce* that leaves no one unclear about the nature of his views.

Macdonald's thoughtful indictment of American filmmaking, sugar-coated with genuine wit, is easy and pleasurable reading throughout. The article reveals his ability to grasp the essence of a film in idea and execution and to evaluate the film without parochial nostalgia.

Norman Mailer

Although Norman Mailer is best known for his efforts in other areas of literature, his film criticism is certainly worth study. Because of his excellence as a writer and because he brings to film an original and incisive mind, his film criticism opens up new ways of evaluating films. It is not uncommon for distinguished artists in one field to double as important critics in many areas of the arts (for example, C. P. Snow and André Malraux). Mailer is not only an important novelist but has worked in film both as filmmaker and script writer. The following sections were selected from a long critical piece on the much-discussed *Last Tango In Paris*.[12]

[A] What powerful biographical details we learn, however, on the instant they part. Paul's wife is a suicide. Just the night before, she has killed herself with a razor in a bathtub; the bathroom is before us, red as an abattoir. A sobbing chambermaid cleans it while she speaks in fear to Paul. It is not even certain whether the wife is a suicide or he has killed her — that is almost not the point. It is the bloody death suspended above his life like a bleeding amputated existence — it is with that crimson torso between his eyes that he will make love on the following days.

Jeanne, in her turn, is about to be married to a young TV director. She is the star in a videofilm he is making about French youth. She pouts, torments her fiancé, delights in herself, delights in the special idiocy of men. She can cuckold her young director to the roots of his eyes. She also delights in the violation she will make

[12] From "A Transit to Narcissus" by Norman Mailer, *The New York Review of Books*, xx, 8, (May 17, 1973).

of her own bourgeois roots. In this TV film she makes within the movie she presents her biography to her fiancé's camera: she is the daughter of a dead Army officer who was sufficiently racist to teach his dog to detect Arabs by smell. So she is well brought up—there are glimpses of a suburban villa on a small walled estate—it is nothing less than the concentrated family honor of the French army she will surrender when Brando proceeds a little later to bugger her.

These separate backgrounds divide the film as neatly between biography and fornication as those trick highball glasses which present a drawing of a man or a woman wearing clothes on the outside of the tumbler and nude on the inside. Each time Brando and Schneider leave the room we learn more of their lives beyond the room; each time they come together, we are ready to go further. In addition, as if to enrich his theme for students of film, Bertolucci offers touches from the history of French cinema. The life preserver in *Atalante* appears by way of homage to Vigo, and Jean-Pierre Léaud of *The 400 Blows* is the TV director, the boy now fully grown. Something of the brooding echo of *Le Jour Se Lève* and Arletty is also with us, that somber memory of Jean Gabin wandering along the wet docks in the dawn, waiting for the police to pick him up after he has murdered his beloved. It is as if we are to think not only of this film but of other sexual tragedies French cinema has brought us, until the sight of each gray and silent Paris street is ready to evoke the lost sound of the *Bal musette* and the sad near-silent wash of the Seine. Nowhere as in Paris can doomed lovers succeed in passing sorrow, drop by drop, through the blood of the audience's heart.

* * *

[B]   Suddenly Brando is before her again on the street. Has he been waiting for her to appear? He looks rejuvenated. "It's over," she tells him. "It's over," he replies. "Then it begins again." He is in love with her. He reveals his biography, his dead wife, his unromantic details. "I've got a prostate like an Idaho potato but I'm still a good stick man . . . I suppose if I hadn't met you I'd probably settle for a hard chair and a hemorrhoid." They move on to a hall, some near mythical species of tango palace where a dance contest is taking place. They get drunk and go on the floor. Brando goes in for a squalid parody of the tango. When they're removed by the judges, he flashes his bare ass. He is still mooning on *The Godfather*.

Now they sit down again and abruptly the love affair is terminated. Like that! She is bored with him. Something has happened. We do not know what. Is she a bourgeoise repelled by his flophouse? Or did his defacement of the tango injure some final nerve of upper French deportment? Too small a motive. Must we decide that sex without a mask is no longer love, or conclude upon reflection that no mask is more congenial to passion than to be without a name in the bed of a strange lover?

There are ten reasons why her love could end, but we know none of them. She merely wants to be rid of him. Deliver me from a fifty-year-old, may even be her only cry.

She tries to flee. He follows. He follows her on the Métro and all the way to her home. He climbs the spiraling stairs as she mounts in the slow elevator, he rams into her mother's apartment with her, breathless, chewing gum, leering. Now he is all cock. He is the memory of every good fuck he has given her. "This is the title shot, baby. We're going all the way."

She takes out her father's army pistol and shoots him. He murmurs, "Our children, our children, our children will remember . . ." and staggers out to the balcony, looks at the Paris morning, takes out his chewing gum, fixes it carefully to the underside of the iron railing in a move which is pure broth of Brando—culture is a goat turd on the bust of Goethe—and dies. The angel with the tragic face slips off the screen. And proud Maria Schneider is suddenly and most unbelievably reduced to a twat copping a plea. "I don't know who he is," she mutters in her mind to the oncoming "flics," "he followed me in the street, he tried to rape me, he is insane. I do not know his name. I do not know who he is. He wanted to rape me."

* * *

[C]   Still he lost an opportunity for his immense talent. If he has been our first actor for decades, it is because he has given us, from the season he arrived in *Streetcar*, a greater sense of improvisation out of the lines of a script than any other professional actor. Sometimes he seemed the only player alive who knew how to suggest that he was about to say something more valuable than what he did say. It gave him force. The lines other people had written for him came out of his mouth like the final compromise life had offered for five better thoughts. He seemed to have a charged subtext. It was as if, whenever requested in other films to say script lines so bad as, "I make you die, you make me die, we're two murderers, each other's," the subtext—the emotion of the words he was using behind the words—became, "I want the pig to vomit in your face." That was what gave an unruly, all but uncontrolled, and smoldering air of menace to all he did.

Now, in *Tango*, he had nothing beneath the script, for his previous subtext was the script. So he appeared to us as a man orating, not improvising. But then a long speech can hardly be an improvisation if its line of action is able to go nowhere but back into the prearranged structures of the plot. It is like the aside of a politician before he returns to that prepared text of which the press already has got copies. So our interest moved away from the possibilities of the film and was spent on the man himself, his mobility and his loutishness. But his nature was finally a less interesting question than it should have been, and weeks would go by before one could forgive Bertolucci for the aesthetic cacophony of the end.

Still, one could forgive. For, finally, Bertolucci has given us a failure worth a hundred films like *The Godfather*. Regardless of all its solos, failed majesties, and off-the-mark horrors, even as a highly imperfect adventure, it is still the best adventure in film to be seen in this pullulating year. And it will open an abyss for Bertolucci. The rest of his life must now be an improvisation. Doubtless he is bold enough to live with that.

In paragraph A Mailer not only communicates some of the plot line of the film but, writing with his own uncommon force and power, begins to establish his views concerning the film's shortcomings. He also demonstrates and uses his knowledge of film history to make a telling point. It should be noted that Mailer writes as if he is embroiled in a violent debate, which gives his criticism an unusual vitality.

In paragraph B Mailer, using the technique of retelling scenes and sequences, attacks their validity and uses his *own* retelling to criticize them. Again, his own writing here is so vivid and strong that he literally forces the reader to engage him. If one disagrees, one is forced to answer the critic at least in one's own mind. It is not possible to read this article and remain indifferent to the film or the critic.

Mailer's final paragraph is a judgment well supported by the rest of the article and, equally important, it is an interesting and well-reasoned dissent from the majority of critics who reviewed *Last Tango in Paris*. Since a valid role of the critic is to provide independence of thought and ideas, this too is a valued contribution from Mailer.

Wilfrid Sheed

Wilfrid Sheed comes to film criticism after years of successful writing in other fields. He has written theatrical and literary criticism, political commentary, and several novels (*Pennsylvania Gothic, Office Politics,* and *People Will Always Be Kind*). He was, for a time, Dwight Macdonald's successor as film critic for *Esquire*.

Sheed has the rare ability to dissect a film into its component parts. In his discussion of the quality of each element, he literally reconstructs the film. Sheed's prose style is highly effective; he bombards the reader with phrases and descriptive adjectives. The following article on *In Cold Blood* is a good example of his style and approach.[13]

> What they've done is taken Truman Capote's whatchamacallit and made a nonfiction movie (or something) out of it. Which means, if Truman has a run-of-the-play contract, that Perry Smith and Dick Hickock, the Kansas killers, may soon find themselves financing yet another glittering bash for The Beautiful People. It would probably please their particular temperaments to know that crime does pay someone. Their own cut was, of course, forty dollars and a rope.
>
> The movie is admirably plain and I almost said uncluttered—a sick Freudian slip if ever I showed one. Outside of that slickest of clichés, the splicing of sounds (door slam turns into roaring motor, woman's scream turns into police siren, etc.), the director, Richard Brooks, has been at some pains to erase his own fingerprints and to make his film artless, almost featureless.
>
> The result is simple truth, something so rare and strange in the movies as to be aesthetically thrilling. Anyone planning a movie about homicidal

[13] From "Films" by Wilfrid Sheed, *Esquire* (March 1968), 120–22. Copyright © 1968 by Esquire, Inc. Reprinted by permission of Robert Lantz-Candida Donadio Literary Agency, Inc.

punks will henceforth have to use *In Cold Blood* as his standard. The speech patterns are right — Capote's weird, gnomelike sensibility recorded the very thought waves of his subjects and left Brooks a treasure trove. The physical movements are right. Even the motions of violence, which are as rigidly stereotyped on film as the dotted-line movements of love, are freshly choreographed here. And they are not falsified by panting close-ups or look-ma-I'm-acting pauses. Hickock and Smith are not movie people at all, except in the sense that we are all movie people. They belong to the world of build-your-strength ads and add-inches-to-your-bosom ads, the world of lower-middle-class fantasy and withdrawal.

Unfortunately the movie stabs itself lightly in the back in the last reel by tacking on a vague Civics I message about capital punishment. This serves to remind us that we are at the movies after all. *In Cold Blood* is not really about capital punishment — equating the state's execution of Smith and Hickock with their execution of the Clutters is two-bit irony: the two crimes are quite separate and distinct, except for the cold blood.

The movie finally hasn't the outsize guts it takes to admit that it isn't about anything at all, in the usual sense: it is a straight rendering, à la Flaubert. You do not take sides, any more than you take sides in *Madame Bovary*. You may have been wondering about meaningless violence: well this is how it works. And nothing for *you* to get righteous about.

Hickock and Smith are superficially just like everyone else, there is very little for our indignation to grab onto, except that the sense of un-reality all of us bring to something — Vietnam, famine in India, whatever our pet turn-off may be — they can bring to anything. Murder is as morally neutral as whipping a prostitute is to one man or biting his nails is to another. There is no appeal against this fathomless indifference. If someone like that wants to kill you, Little Nell and Clarence Darrow couldn't talk him out of it. You might as well argue with the Pentagon.

Mr. Brooks conveys this so well in scene after scene that it is ab-normally churlish to quarrel with his conventionally "thoughtful" ending — which, thanks to the art has gone before it, is completely tinny and ineffective anyway. To find two actors who look like the originals (Scott Wilson and Robert Blake) and then to find that they can actually act is the kind of luck that such virtue deserves. Perry Smith's fantasies are not always too convincing: the one where he plays his guitar to empty tables is trite and movie-ish. But outside of that, there is hardly a false note in more than two hours. The banality of evil has found itself an epic.

Though Sheed has definite personal attitudes toward the film and its charac-ters ("a vague Civics I message about capital punishment," "homicidal punks"), he considers the film itself to be "morally neutral." The position he takes as critic is highly provocative. Most critics and viewers consider *In Cold Blood* to be a tract against the society that created the two killers. Sheed, however, offers an entirely original reading of the film. This is a prime role of the critic: to offer original ideas and to support them logically in an analysis of the work. The best critics are original thinkers. Only time will judge the accuracy of their statements.

Sheed excerpts, with admirable brevity, key elements that support his case for a morally neutral film. In his phraseology, he blends both fact and value judgment. For example:

Their own cut was, of course, forty dollars and a rope.

. . . the director, Richard Brooks, has been at some pains to erase his own fingerprints and to make his film artless, almost featureless.

. . . Capote's weird, gnomelike sensibility recorded the very thought waves of his subjects and left Brooks a treasure trove.

They belong to the world of build-your-strength ads and add-inches-to-your-bosom ads, the world of lower-middle-class fantasy and withdrawal.

Murder is as morally neutral as whipping a prostitute is to one man or biting his nails is to another.

The end result is a critical work that gives the reader the raw material for thought and argument.

Stanley Kauffmann

Stanley Kauffmann is one of the most active of contemporary critics. He writes for *The New Republic,* makes regular appearances on television, and has served with *The New York Times* as drama critic. His background in film is excellent, and he has the ability to understand and communicate the meaning of the most complex works of cinema. The following excerpt, which deals with a filmmaker (Antonioni) rather than a film, is a good example of Kauffmann's approach to film criticism.[14]

Antonioni . . . is achieving what many contemporary artists in his and other fields are seeking, and not often with his success: renewal of his art rather than repetition. . . . [He is] finding a way to speak to us about ourselves today without crankily throwing away all that went before and without being bound by it. He is reshaping the idea of the content of film drama, discarding ancient and less ancient concepts, redirecting traditional audience expectations toward immersion in character rather than conflict of character. He is reshaping time itself in his films, taking it out of its customary synoptic form, wringing intensity out of its distention, daring to ask us to "live through" experiences with less distillation, deriving his drama from the very texture of such experiences and their juxtaposition, rather than from formal clash and climax and resolution. Fundamentally, he gives us characters whose drama consists in facing life minute after minute rather than in moving through organized plots with articulated obstacles; who have no well-marked cosmos to use as a tennis player uses a court; who live and die without the implication of a divine eye that sees their virtues (whether men do or not) and cherishes them.

John Grierson once said that when a director dies he becomes a photographer; but Antonioni gets emotional utility—in a film about *people*—out of surfaces and compositions. He uses photography for enrichment, not for salon gasps: for example, the scene in *La Notte* where Lidia goes for a ride in the rain with a man and the downpour seems to put the car in danger of dissolution.

[14] From "La Notte" (February 26, 1962), in *A World on Film* by Stanley Kauffmann, pp. 305–07. Copyright © 1962 by Stanley Kauffmann. Originally appeared in *The New Republic,* and reprinted by permission of Harper & Row, Publishers.

The sequence in *La Notte* that best represents Antonioni's style is the one in which Lidia slips away from the publisher's party and wanders through the streets. Conditioned as we are, we *expect* something; we think she is off to meet a lover, or to kill herself, or to get involved in an accident. But nothing happens; and everything happens. She strolls past a bus conductor eating a sandwich and is fascinated by his existence and his appetite in the same universe with her; she passes two men laughing uproariously at a joke and she smiles, too, although she has not heard it, anxious to join them, to be one of the human race; she encounters a crying child and kneels briefly and unsuccessfully to comfort it; she tears a flake of rust off a corroding wall; she sees two young men punching each other ferociously, watches, horrified, then screams for them to stop. (The victor thinks she must be attracted to him and starts to pursue her, and so Antonioni touches another old tribal nerve.) Then in the suburbs she watches some boys shooting off rockets. She finds she is in a neighborhood where she and Giovanni used to come years before. She telephones him and he drives out to pick her up.

By drama-school definition, it is not a cumulative dramatic sequence. It is a miniature recapitulation, deftly done, of the possibilities of life: a child and an old woman, a man eating and a man punching, sunlight on a fountain and a greasy, lewd stallkeeper. Antonioni holds it all together with something like the surface tension of liquids and, by not commenting, comments. It is essentially as drastic a revolution as abstract-expressionist painting or Beckett's litany-like dialogue, but Antonioni has not estranged us in order to speak to us about loneliness; he has not sacrificed the link of recognition to make new images; he has not had to use absurdity to convey the absurd.

Of every directional technique he is an easy master. I specify only two. His use of sound: the low-pitched conversation in the hospital is interrupted by the passage of a helicopter like a pause in music so that the hushed key will not become tedious. His symbolism (which is unobtrusive): the mushroom cloud of smoke that envelops the boy who fires the rocket, and the fact that Giovanni meets Lidia after her walk in front of a long-abandoned church.

For me, Antonioni has made in *La Notte* and in *L'Avventura* the most subtly truthful theatrical works about the relation of the sexes since Joyce's *Exiles*. But he has done more. In *La Notte* he has used a vitiated marriage as a metaphor of the crisis of faith in our age, the faith within which profoundest love and pettiest whim have always been contained. He has used his camera as a hound of non-heaven ranging through the streets of Milan to find the beauty in necessity, the assurance in knowing that one can live without assurances. This film leaves us less deceived; thus, with the truth in us less encumbered.

In this short excerpt, Kauffmann tells us a great deal about Antonioni's style. He uses highly evocative phrases: "immersion in character rather than conflict of character," "customary synoptic form, wringing intensity out of its distention," "miniature recapitulation," "as drastic a revolution as abstract-expressionist painting or Beckett's litany-like dialogue," "hound of non-heaven." His adjectives are carefully chosen and always tell us something important about the subject: "greasy, lewd stallkeeper," "subtly truthful theatrical works," "profoundest love and pettiest whim."

Although all film critics try to use examples from the film to illustrate their points, few are as effective as Kauffmann in selecting examples that convince the reader. He has a good eye for specific detail, and his analogy to Joyce's *Exiles* leads the reader to a deeper understanding of the filmmaker.

Kauffmann brings to his work taste, knowledge, and acerbic wit. He is at his best with films that deal with complex philosophical ideas, but he shows some reluctance to accept basic innovations in the art. In the limited space of a short critique, he is able to convey much information about the film, and at the same time he expresses himself vividly and with precision.

Andrew Sarris

Andrew Sarris is one of the most knowledgeable of contemporary film critics. He moves freely about the world of modern cinema and is unfailingly eloquent and interesting. The following excerpt is from an article on *The Seventh Seal* written by Sarris *before* the film was generally accepted as a masterpiece.[15]

> "And when he had opened the seventh seal, there was silence in heaven about the space of half an hour."
> "Revelation"

> "A free mind, like a creative imagination, rejoices at the harmonies it can find or make between man and nature; and where it finds none, it solves the conflict so far as it may and then notes and endures it with a shudder."
> GEORGE SANTAYANA, "Art and Happiness"

[A] Although Ingmar Bergman's *The Seventh Seal* is set in medieval Sweden, nothing could be more modern than its author's conception of death as the crucial reality of man's existence. Appearing at a time when the anguished self-consciousness of Kierkegaard and Nietzsche has come back into favor as a statement of the human condition. *The Seventh Seal* is perhaps the first genuinely existential film. The plight of the individual in an indifferent universe would have seemed a fatuous subject for an artist a generation ago when human objectives barely extended to the next bread line, and when, it now seems ages ago, Edmund Wilson could reasonably denounce Thornton Wilder's metaphysical concerns in *The Bridge of San Luis Rey* as socially irresponsible. Liberal reform, Marxist determinism and the Social Gospel of Christianity were variously hailed as the formulas of a blissful world, but something went wrong with these collective panaceas partly because thinking men discovered that endless problem-solving reduced life to its one insoluble problem, death, and partly because population explosions, the hydrogen bomb and the Cold War scuttled the idea of Progress as a cause for rejoicing. Quite obviously, the time has come to talk of other things beside the glories of social reconstruction.

[B]   Ingmar Bergman, the son of a clergyman, is aware of the decline

[15] From "The Seventh Seal" by Andrew Sarris, *Film Culture* (No. 19), 51–61. Reprinted by permission.

of religious faith in the modern world, but unlike Dreyer, he refuses to reconstruct mystic consolations from the dead past. If modern man must live without the faith which makes death meaningful, he can at least endure life with the aid of certain necessary illusions. This is what Bergman seems to be saying in *The Seventh Seal,* a remarkably intricate film with many layers of meaning.

[C]   The Biblical context of the Seventh Seal is never fully retold on the screen, but enough excerpts are provided to keynote the theme of the Last Judgment. A hawk suspended in flight opens the film with a striking image of foreboding against a rising chorale of exultant faith. After ten years on a Crusade to the Holy Land, a knight and his squire return disillusioned to Sweden. Riding north to the knight's castle further and further away from Christianity's birthplace where God has died in their hearts, the knight and the squire are cast allegorically into the void of modern disbelief.

*   *   *

[D]   As the knight and the squire continue their homeward journey, towering overhead shots of the two riders alternate with pulsating images of the sun. This cosmic technique would be pretentious for a lesser theme, but here in the beginning, Bergman is suggesting the dimensions of the universe in which his drama will unfold. Once the philosophical size of the film is established, Bergman's camera probes more intimately into his characters.

[E]   The fact that the squire does not share the knight's first encounter with Death is consistent with Bergman's conception of the knight's solitude in his quest for God. Since the squire is a confirmed atheist, the knight cannot seek consolation in that quarter. Indeed, the squire's bawdy songs and low comedy grimaces stamp him as the knight's Sancho Panza until a startling incident transforms him into a co-protagonist. Dismounting to ask a hooded stranger the way to the next town, the squire lifts the hood and beholds the death skull of a plague victim. The squire's reaction is that of a forceful intelligence, and he displays an unexpected flair for irony when he tells the un-suspecting knight that the stranger said nothing but was quite elo-quent. Bergman achieves his shock effect here with the aid of a dog frisking about its dead master before the squire lifts the man's hood. This is more than a trick, however, and Bergman later develops the flickering idea involved here.

[F]   Bergman adds to his chess pieces as the knight and the squire ride past a carnival wagon in which an actor, a juggler, the juggler's wife and their infant son are asleep. Emerging from the wagon into a sunlit world less intensely illuminated than the world of the knight and the squire, the juggler is awed by a vision of the Virgin Mary walking the Christ Child. He calls his wife to describe this latest miracle of his imaginative existence, and as always she is kind but skeptical. (Bergman has a priceless talent for establishing states of being in quick scenes.) The juggler and his wife are suggestively named Jof and Mia at slight variance from an explicit identification with Christ's parents. They are never quite that, but when Joseph observes wistfully that his son, Michael, will perform the one im-possible juggling trick, the screen vibrates with Bergman's first intimations of immortality.

[G]   Bergman returns to his central theme as the actor steps out of the wagon to announce that he will play Death in the religious pageant at Elsinore. Donning a death mask, he asks (vanity of vanities!) if the women will still admire him in that disguise. As the pompous director of the troupe, he orders Joseph to portray the Soul of Man, a part Joseph dislikes for theatrical reasons. When the actor returns to the wagon, hanging the death skull on a pole outside, the camera lingers on this symbol long enough for the sound track to record the pleasant laughter of Jof and Mia before cutting back to the couple whose merriment operates both as a conscious reaction to the departing actor and as the director's expression of their irreverent attitude towards death. In all this symbolic by-play, Jof and Mia convey a wondrous innocence, and the scene ends on a note of emotional recollection as Mia's avowal of her love for her husband is underscored by the same musical motif which accompanied Jof's vision of the Madonna.

* * *

[H]   The various threads of the plot are woven together into the fabric of a town which represents for Bergman many of the evils of society. Art reappears in a musical pantomime of cuckoldry presented by Jof, Mia and the preening actor. The medieval approximation which Bergman attempts in this performance is carried over into the actor's flamboyant affair with a flirtatious blacksmith's wife. With dainty steps and cock-robin flourishes, the seduction in the nearby forest derives its tempo from a bawdy nonsense song rendered in the town by Jof and Mia, their faces gaily painted, their manner joyously abandoned. Their performance is meaningfully interrupted by the wailing of flagellants bearing Christ on the Cross. Bergman cuts with brilliant deliberation back and forth between the painful detail of the incense-shrouded procession and tracking shots of the soldiers and townspeople kneeling reverently in turn as the Cross goes past. The same soldiers who threw fruit at the actors (art) now kneel to their Saviour (fear).

[I]   The brutalization of a fear-crazed society reaches its climax in an inn where the patrons suspend their discourses on the End of the World to laugh sadistically at Jof's grotesque dance on a table while the renegade priest brandishes a torch at the juggler's feet. (The ordeal of a performer deprived of his mask and the sanctuary of his stage is more fully explored in Bergman's *The Naked Night*.) Joseph escapes only because of the intervention of the squire, who slashes the priest's face. In a film drenched with death, this is the only instance in which blood is drawn.

* * *

[J]   Although the knight has given the witch a drug to ease her pain, her last moments on the stake are filled with wild despair as she realizes that the Devil is not going to claim her from the emptiness which lies beyond the flames. The squire confronts the knight for the first time with evidence (?) of the void, but the knight refuses to abandon hope. One would lose all sympathy for Bergman's characters if they treated the witch's ordeal as merely a test of God's existence. Fortunately, Bergman never loses his human perspective on death even when the renegade priest is stricken by the Plague. The silent girl he once menaced rushes towards him until the squire restrains her, virtually pleading that any help would be futile. Dying never becomes a casual process for Bergman. The actor, the witch, the renegade priest all achieve a form of moral purgation in the inescapable self-pity they arouse in their audiences, both real and fictitious.

[K]   When Death confronts the knight for the final moves on the chessboard, the once stark tonal contrasts between the two antagonists have merged into relativistic grayness. Gone is the sun and the sea and the sky. Death has enveloped the forest and no longer makes striking entrances with his black cloak. Jof "sees" Death at the chessboard and takes flight with Mia and Michael. Fearing Death's intervention, the knight knocks over the pieces to allow Jof and his family to escape. Inscrutable to the end, Death does not indicate he has been taken in by this diversion, or whether he is tolerant or indifferent, or whether, after all, he *is* actually controlled by a Higher Power. Once Death has achieved checkmate and has claimed the knight and his friends at the next meeting, he still denies he possesses any secrets of the afterlife, and in a dissolving close-up, his face is slowly and memorably transformed into a hollow mask.

* * *

[L]   This elliptical declaration of awareness, perhaps miraculously extracted from the text of Revelation, is less meaningful than the glowing expression in her eyes as she awaits the end of her earthly servitude. The silent girl, more than any of the other characters, has been defeated by life, and in her defeat, has embraced the prospect of death. When we first see her, she is about to be raped and murdered. She passively accepts her role as the squire's housekeeper, and is always seen either bearing some burden or accepting the squire's protection. One almost suspects Bergman of a class statement in his conception of this memorable, yet elusive, character.

* * *

[M]   For all its intellectual complexity, *The Seventh Seal* is remarkably entertaining. In the high level of acting we have come to expect in Bergman films, Gunnar Bjornstrand as the squire, and Bengt Ekerot as Death, provide truly remarkable performances. Bjornstrand, previously seen here in *The Naked Night* and *Smiles of a Summer Night*, displays classic range in the subtlety and force of his widely dissimilar characterizations. Bengt Ekerot's playing of Death is so uncanny that it is difficult to imagine this unfamiliar actor in any other role. Max von Sydow has the most difficult part as the mystical knight who must communicate from the depths of his soul, but in his dramatic scenes, he fully captures the tortured nobility of his character. Nils Poppe, Sweden's leading comedian, is very moving as Jof through the counterpoint of his comic personality and his cosmic problems. Bibi Andersson as Mia heads a gallery of unaffectedly beautiful women which includes anonymous faces in Bergman's crowd scenes.

[N]   Bergman's camera technique is fully equal to his theme. Except for a glaring process shot in the opening scene, his medieval images are clear and solid in the best tradition of realistic cinematography.

237

Bergman is at his best in intimate scenes where his unobtrusively moving camera builds up tensions before his editing exploits them. One is always aware of the meaningful texture of faces as they react to the uncertainties they confront. Bergman indulges in the sun dissolves endemic to Swedish cinema, and the reverse cloak opening of a frame which Hitchcock invented, but which Bergman gives a special flourish in many of his films. In this instance, Death's black cloak must have been irresistible.

[O]   Bergman's overall editing maintains a steady flow of images to create visual progressions for each successive plot development. The plastic symbol of the death skull reappears in each shot at a different expressive angle, and Death himself never repeats the choreography of his comings and goings. Bergman's economy of expression actually makes it difficult to absorb all the meanings in each scene. Instead of fully developing his ideas in long, obligatory confrontations of characters, Bergman distributes fragments of what he is saying into every incident. Yet, a great deal that is implied is left unsaid, and it is possible that *The Seventh Seal* will be a source of controversy for years to come, and that like all classics of the mind, its interpretations will vary with the minds and times of its critics.

Sarris' style is a fine example of critical architecture coupled with highly literate writing. Sarris uses two quotations to open his article. The first is the source of the film's title, always important in the interpretation of the film; the second is a statement from a great philosopher, also a key to understanding the work. Through the use of quotations, Sarris immediately arrests the reader's attention and provides some clues to what will follow.

In paragraphs A and B, Sarris discusses his interpretation of the theme of the film and explains the film's social and philosophical setting. His literary allusions (Kierkegaard, Nietzsche, Wilder) and his comparison with Dreyer are much to the point, for they isolate the influences, the antecedents, of Bergman's work.

In paragraphs C and D, more than simply recounting plot, Sarris carefully describes every incident related to the film's theme. This is the essence of effective criticism: to provide a clarification and illumination of the artist's intent and to offer the reader a basis for discussion.

In paragraphs E through L, which continue the retelling of plot, Sarris uses specific examples to explain Bergman's symbols. Since visual symbolism is the core of Bergman's technique, Sarris performs a very useful function in seeking to interpret the artist's intent. In paragraph E and F, he presents several provocative statements that help the reader to understand some of the subtle ideas in this film: the idea that the shock value of the "dog and the dead man" incident is more than just a theatrical trick, the identification of Bergman's use of sunlight, the parenthetical comment on Bergman's talent for "establish-ing states of being in quick scenes," and the statement that Jof and Mia are "never quite" Christ's parents.

Sarris continually describes in detail the most important incidents in the film and in doing so clarifies its meaning:

Donning a death mask, he asks (vanity of vanities!) if the women will still admire him in that disguise.

Bergman cuts with brilliant deliberation back and forth between the painful detail of the incense-shrouded procession. . . . The same soldiers who threw fruit at the actors (art) now kneel to their Saviour (fear).

(The ordeal of a performer deprived of his mask and the sanctuary of his stage is more fully explored in Bergman's *The Naked Night.*) Joseph escapes only because of the intervention of the squire, who slashes the priest's face. In a film drenched with death, this is the only instance in which blood is drawn.

The squire confronts the knight for the first time with evidence (?) of the void, but the knight refuses to abandon hope.

Fortunately, Bergman never loses his human perspective on death even when the renegade priest is stricken by the Plague.

Dying never becomes a casual process for Bergman. The actor, the witch, the renegade priest all achieve a form of moral purgation in the inescapable self-pity they arouse in their audiences, both real and fictitious.

This elliptical declaration of awareness, perhaps miraculously extracted from the text of Revelation, is less meaningful than the glowing expression in her eyes as she awaits the end of her earthly servitude.

Throughout the article, Sarris deals in detail with Bergman's symbolic images and action:

(1) The riders on the beach as suggestive of the dimensions of the universe (paragraph D).

(2) The relationship between the Squire and the Knight as communicating the Knight's solitude in his quest for God (paragraph E).

(3) Jof and Mia as revealing Bergman's first intimations of immortality (paragraph F).

(4) The contrast between the innocence of Jof and Mia and the death symbols of the troupe's play (paragraph G).

(5) The interruption of the play by the flagellants, with the juxtaposition of art and fear (paragraph I).

(6) Bergman's "human perspective" on death in the face of "the void" (paragraph J).

(7) The "silent girl," the most difficult character to explain (paragraph L).

The heart of Sarris' technique is to communicate not only the plot (anyone can do this) but the *structure* of the plot, and at the same time to interpret its meaning.

In paragraphs M and N, Sarris communicates his value judgments in thoughtful and communicative language: "classic range in the subtlety and force of his widely dissimilar characterizations," "so uncanny that it is difficult to imagine this unfamiliar actor in any other role," "fully captures the tortured nobility of his character," "meaningful texture of faces." Sarris' comments on the editing (paragraph O) are significant because the editing techniques in the film are deceptively simple.

Sarris' work is always eloquent and original. He is perhaps a shade too didactic and fails to leaven his prose with humor, but the intense precision of his critical writing does justice to the films he studies and has had a profound influence on filmmaker and filmgoer alike.

Pauline Kael

Pauline Kael writes for *The New Yorker* and other publications and is the author of four highly successful collections of film criticism: *I Lost It at the Movies; Kiss Kiss, Bang Bang; Going Steady;* and *Deeper into Movies.* Miss Kael is one of the most influential of contemporary critics. She combines a chatty anti-film-as-art style that masks an incisive mind, an excellent wit, and a true love of film. Miss Kael tends to regard rather grimly the trend toward serious discussions of film as art, sensing perhaps the real and dangerous tendency to overintellectualize about film, to "read too much into" the filmmaker's work.

Miss Kael has written some of the finest works of contemporary film criticism. Her review of *Bonnie and Clyde* is reprinted below in its entirety as a model of excellent film criticism.[16]

> How do you make a good movie in this country without being jumped on? *Bonnie and Clyde* is the most excitingly American American movie since *The Manchurian Candidate.* The audience is alive to it. Our experience as we watch it has some connection with the way we reacted to movies in childhood: with how we came to love them and to feel they were ours — not an art that we learned over the years to appreciate but simply and immediately ours. When an American movie is contemporary in feeling, like this one, it makes a different kind of contact with an American audience from the kind that is made by European films, however contemporary. Yet any movie that is contemporary in feeling is likely to go further than other movies — go too far for some tastes — and *Bonnie and Clyde* divides audiences; as *The Manchurian Candidate* did, and it is being jumped on almost as hard. Though we may dismiss the attacks with "What good movie doesn't give some offense?," the fact that it is generally *only* good movies that provoke attacks by many people suggests that the innocuousness of most of our movies is accepted with such complacence that when an American movie reaches people, when it makes them react, some of them think there must be something the matter with it — perhaps a law should be passed against it. *Bonnie and Clyde* brings into the almost frighteningly public world of movies things that people have been feeling

[16] From *Kiss Kiss, Bang Bang* by Pauline Kael, pp. 47–63. Copyright © 1967 by The New Yorker Magazine, Inc.; first published in *The New Yorker.* Reprinted by permission of Little, Brown and Company.

and saying and writing about. And once something is said or done on the screens of the world, once it has entered mass art, it can never again belong to a minority, never again be the private possession of an educated, or "knowing," group. But even for that group there is an excitement in hearing its own private thoughts expressed out loud and in seeing something of its own sensibility become part of our common culture.

Our best movies have always made entertainment out of the anti-heroism of American life; they bring to the surface what, in its newest forms and fashions, is always just below the surface. The romanticism in American movies lies in the cynical tough guy's independence; the sentimentality lies, traditionally, in the falsified finish when the anti-hero turns hero. In 1967, this kind of sentimentality wouldn't work with the audience, and *Bonnie and Clyde* substitutes sexual fulfillment for a change of heart. (This doesn't quite work, either; audiences sophisticated enough to enjoy a movie like this one are too sophisticated for the dramatic uplift of the triumph over impotence.)

Structurally, *Bonnie and Clyde* is a story of love on the run, like the old Clark Gable–Claudette Colbert *It Happened One Night* but turned inside out; the walls of Jericho are psychological this time, but they fall anyway. If the story of Bonnie Parker and Clyde Barrow seemed almost from the start, and even to them while they were living it, to be the material of legend, it's because robbers who are loyal to each other — like the James brothers — are a grade up from garden-variety robbers, and if they're male and female partners in crime and young and attractive they're a rare breed. The Barrow gang had both family loyalty and sex appeal working for their legend. David Newman and Robert Benton, who wrote the script for *Bonnie and Clyde,* were able to use the knowledge that, like many of our other famous outlaws and gangsters, the real Bonnie and Clyde seemed to others to be acting out forbidden roles and to relish their roles. In contrast with secret criminals — the furtive embezzlers and other crooks who lead seemingly honest lives — the known outlaws capture the public imagination, because they take chances, and because, often, they enjoy dramatizing their lives. They know that newspaper readers want all the details they can get about the criminals who do the terrible things they themselves don't dare to do, and also want the satisfaction of reading about the punishment after feasting on the crimes. Outlaws play to this public; they show off their big guns and fancy clothes and their defiance of the law. Bonnie and Clyde established the images for their own legend in the photographs they posed for: the gunman and the gun moll. The naïve, touching doggerel ballad that Bonnie Parker wrote and had published in newspapers is about the roles they play for other people contrasted with the coming end for them. It concludes:

> Someday they'll go down together;
> They'll bury them side by side;
> To few it'll be grief —
> To the law a relief —
> But it's death for Bonnie and Clyde.

That they did capture the public imagination is evidenced by the many movies based on their lives. In the late forties, there were *They Live by Night,* with Farley Granger and Cathy O'Donnell, and *Gun Crazy,* with John Dall and Peggy Cummins. (Alfred Hitchcock, in the same period, cast these two Clyde Barrows, Dall and Granger, as Loeb and Leopold, in *Rope.*) And there was a cheap — in every sense — 1958 exploitation film, *The Bonnie Parker Story*, starring Borothy Provine. But the most important earlier version was Fritz Lang's *You Only Live Once*, starring Sylvia Sydney as "Joan" and Henry Fonda as "Eddie," which was made in 1937; this version, which was one of the best American films of the thirties, as *Bonnie and Clyde* is of the sixties, expressed certain feelings of its time, as this film expresses certain feelings of ours. (*They Live by Night*, produced by John Houseman under the aegis of Dore Schary, and directed by Nicholas Ray, was a very serious and socially significant tragic melodrama, but its attitudes were already dated thirties attitudes: the lovers were very young and pure and frightened and underprivileged; the hardened criminals were sordid; the settings were committedly grim. It made no impact on the postwar audience, though it was a great success in England, where our moldy socially significant movies could pass for courageous.)

Just how contemporary in feeling *Bonnie and Clyde* is may be indicated by contrasting it with *You Only Live Once*, which, though almost totally false to the historical facts, was *told* straight. It is a peculiarity of our times — perhaps it's one of the few specifically modern characteristics — that we don't take our stories straight any more. This isn't necessarily bad. *Bonnie and Clyde* is the first film demonstration that the put-on can be used for the purposes of art. *The Manchurian Candidate* almost succeeded in that, but what was implicitly wild and far-out in the material was nevertheless presented on screen as a straight thriller. *Bonnie and Clyde* keeps the audience in a kind of eager, nervous imbalance — holds our attention by throwing our disbelief back in our faces. To be put on is to be put on the spot, put on the stage, made the stooge in a comedy act. People in the audience at *Bonnie and Clyde* are laughing, demonstrating that they're not stooges — that they appreciate the joke — when they catch the first bullet right in the face. The movie keeps them off balance to the end. During the first part of the picture, a woman in my row was gleefully assuring her companions, "It's a comedy, it's a comedy." After a while, she didn't say anything. Instead of the movie spoof, which tells the audience that it doesn't need to feel or care, that it's all just in fun, that "we were only kidding," *Bonnie and Clyde* disrupts us with "And you thought we were only kidding."

This is the way the story was told in 1937. Eddie (Clyde) is a three-time loser who wants to work for a living, but nobody will give him a chance. Once you get on the wrong side of the law, "they" won't let you get back. Eddie knows it's hopeless — once a loser, always a loser. But his girl, Joan (Bonnie) — the only person who believes in him — thinks that an innocent man has nothing to fear. She marries him, and learns better. Arrested again and sentenced to death for a crime he didn't commit, Eddie asks her to smuggle a gun to him in prison, and she protests, "If I get you a gun, you'll kill somebody." He stares at her sullenly and asks, "What do you think they're going to do to me?" He becomes a murderer while escaping from prison; "society" has made him what it thought he was all along. *You Only Live Once* was an indictment of "society," of the forces of order that will not give Eddie the outcast a chance. "We have a right to live," Joan says as they set out across the country. During the time they are on the run, they become notorious outlaws; they are blamed for a series of crimes they didn't commit. (They do commit holdups, but only to get gas or groceries or medicine.) While the press pictures them as desperadoes robbing and killing and living high on the proceeds of crime, she is having a baby in a shack in a hobo jungle, and Eddie brings her a bouquet of wild flowers. Caught in a police trap, they die in each other's arms; they have been denied the right to live.

Because *You Only Live Once* was so well done, and because the audience in the thirties shared this view of the indifference and cruelty of "society," there were no protests against the sympathetic way the outlaws were pictured—and, indeed, there was no reason for any. In 1958, in *I Want to Live!* (a very popular, though not very good movie), Barbara Graham, a drug-addict prostitute who had been executed for her share in the bludgeoning to death of an elderly woman, was presented as gallant, wronged, morally superior to everybody else in the movie, in order to strengthen the argument against capital punishment, and the director, Robert Wise, and his associates weren't accused of glorifying criminals, because the "criminals," as in *You Only Live Once*, weren't criminals but innocent victims. Why the protests, why are so many people upset (and not just the people who enjoy indignation), about *Bonnie and Clyde*, in which the criminals *are* criminals—Clyde an ignorant, sly near psychopath who thinks his crimes are accomplishments, and Bonnie a bored, restless waitress-slut who robs for excitement? And why so many accusations of historical inaccuracy, particularly against a work that is far more accurate historically than most and in which historical accuracy hardly matters anyway? There is always an issue of historical accuracy involved in any dramatic or literary work set in the past; indeed, it's fun to read about Richard III vs. Shakespeare's Richard III. The issue is always with us, and will always be with us as long as artists find stimulus in historical figures and want to present their versions of them. But why didn't movie critics attack, for example, *A Man for All Seasons*—which involves material of much more historical importance—for being historically inaccurate? Why attack *Bonnie and Clyde* more than the other movies based on the same pair, or more than the movie treatments of Jesse James or Billy the Kid or Dillinger or Capone or any of our other fictionalized outlaws? I would suggest that when a movie so clearly conceived as a new version of a legend is attacked as historically inaccurate, it's because it shakes people a little. I know this is based on some pretty sneaky psychological suppositions, but I don't see how else to account for the use only against a *good* movie of arguments that could be used against almost all movies. When I asked a nineteen-year-old boy who was raging against the movie as "a cliché-ridden fraud" if he got so worked up about other movies, he informed me that that was an argument *ad hominem*. And it is indeed. To ask why people react so angrily to the best movies and have so little negative reaction to poor ones is to imply that they are so unused to the experience of art in movies that they fight it.

Audiences at *Bonnie and Clyde* are not given a simple, secure basis for identification; they are made to feel but are not told *how* to feel. *Bonnie and Clyde* is not a serious melodrama involving us in the plight of the innocent but a movie that assumes—as William Wellman did in 1931 when he made *The Public Enemy*, with James Cagney as a smart, cocky, mean little crook—that we don't need to pretend we're interested only in the falsely accused, as if real criminals had no connection with us. There wouldn't be the popular excitement there is about outlaws if we didn't all suspect that—in some cases, at least—gangsters must take pleasure in the profits and glory of a life of crime. Outlaws wouldn't become legendary figures if we didn't suspect that there's more to crime than the social workers' case studies may show. And though what we've always been told will happen to them—that they'll come to a bad end—does seem to happen, some part of us want to believe in the tiny possibility that they can get away with it. Is that really so terrible? Yet when it comes to movies people get nervous about acknowledging that there must be some fun in crime (though the gleam in Cagney's eye told its own story). *Bonnie and Clyde* shows the fun but uses it, too, making comedy out of the banality and conventionality of that fun. What looks ludicrous in this movie isn't *merely* ludicrous, and after we have laughed at ignorance and helplessness and emptiness and stupidity and idiotic deviltry, the laughs keep sticking in our throats, because what's funny isn't only funny.

In 1937, the movie-makers knew that the audience wanted to believe in the innocence of Joan and Eddie, because these two were lovers, and innocent lovers hunted down like animals made a tragic love story. In 1967, the movie-makers know that the audience wants to believe — maybe even prefers to believe — that Bonnie and Clyde were guilty of crimes, all right, but that they were innocent in general; that is, naïve and ignorant *compared with us*. The distancing of the sixties version shows the gangsters in an already legendary period, and part of what makes a legend for Americans is viewing anything that happened in the past as much simpler than what we are involved in now. We tend to find the past funny and the recent past campy-funny. The getaway cars of the early thirties are made to seem hilarious. (Imagine anyone getting away from a bank holdup in a tin lizzie like that!) In *You Only Live Once,* the outlaws existed in the same present as the audience, and there was (and still is, I'm sure) nothing funny about them; in *Bonnie and Clyde* that audience is in the movie, transformed into the poor people, the Depression people, of legend — with faces and poses out of Dorothea Lange and Walker Evans and *Let Us Now Praise Famous Men.* In 1937, the audience felt sympathy for the fugitives because they weren't allowed to lead normal lives; in 1967, the "normality" of the Barrow gang and their individual aspirations toward respectability are the craziest things about them — not just because they're killers but because thirties "normality" is in itself funny to us. The writers and the director of *Bonnie and Clyde* play upon our attitudes toward the American past by making the hats and guns and holdups look as dated as two-reel comedy; emphasizing the absurdity with banjo music, they make the period seem even farther away than it is. The Depression reminiscences are not used for purposes of social consciousness; hard times are not the reason for the Barrows' crimes, just the excuse. "We" didn't make Clyde a killer; the movie deliberately avoids easy sympathy by picking up Clyde when he is already a cheap crook. But Clyde is not the urban sharpster of *The Public Enemy;* he is the hick as bank robber — a countrified gangster, a hillbilly killer who doesn't mean any harm. People so simple that they are alienated from the results of their actions — like the primitives who don't connect babies with copulation — provide a kind of archetypal comedy for us. It may seem like a minor point that Bonnie and Clyde are presented as not mean and sadistic, as having killed only when cornered; but in terms of legend, and particularly movie legend, it's a major one. The "classic" gangster films showed gang members betraying each other and viciously murdering the renegade who left to join another gang; the gang-leader hero no sooner got to the top than he was betrayed by someone he had trusted or someone he had double-crossed. In contrast, the Barrow gang represent family-style crime. And Newman and Benton have been acute in emphasizing this — not making them victims of society (they are never that, despite Penn's cloudy efforts along these lines) but making them absurdly "just-folks" ordinary.

When Bonnie tells Clyde to pull off the road—"I want to talk to you"—
they are in a getaway car, leaving the scene of a robbery, with the police
right behind them, but they are absorbed in family bickering: the traditional all-American use of the family automobile. In a sense, it is the
absence of sadism—it is the violence without sadism—that throws the
audience off balance at *Bonnie and Clyde*. The brutality that comes out
of this innocence is far more shocking than the calculated brutalities of
mean killers.

Playfully posing with their guns, the real Bonnie and Clyde mocked
the "Bloody Barrows" of the Hearst press. One photograph shows slim,
pretty Bonnie, smiling and impeccably dressed, pointing a huge gun at
Clyde's chest as he, a dimpled dude with a cigar, smiles back. The famous
picture of Bonnie in the same clothes but looking ugly squinting into the
sun, with a foot on the car, a gun on her hip, and a cigar in her mouth,
is obviously a joke—her caricature of herself as a gun moll. Probably,
since they never meant to kill, they thought the "Bloody Barrows" were a
joke—a creation of the lying newpapers.

There's something new working for the Bonnie-and-Clyde legend
now: our nostalgia for the thirties—the unpredictable, contrary affection
of the prosperous for poverty, or at least for the artifacts, the tokens, of
poverty, for Pop culture seen in the dreariest rural settings, where it truly
seems to belong. Did people in the cities listen to the Eddie Cantor show?
No doubt they did, but the sound of his voice, like the sound of Ed Sullivan
now, evokes a primordial, pre-urban existence—the childhood of the race.
Our comic-melancholic affection for thirties Pop has become sixties Pop,
and those who made *Bonnie and Clyde* are smart enough to use it that way.
Being knowing is not an artist's highest gift, but it can make a hell of a
lot of difference in a movie. In the American experience, the miseries of
the Depression are funny in the way that the Army is funny to draftees—a
shared catastrophe, a leveling, forming part of our common background.
Those too young to remember the Depression have heard about it from
their parents. (When I was at college, we used to top each other's stories
about how our families had survived: the fathers who had committed
suicide so that their wives and children could live off the insurance; the
mothers trying to make a game out of the meals of potatoes cooked on
an open fire.) Though the American derision of the past has many offensive
aspects, it has some good ones, too, because it's a way of making fun not
only of our forebears but of ourselves and our pretensions. The toughness
about what we've come out of and what we've been through—the honesty
to see ourselves as the Yahoo children of yokels—is a good part of American popular art. There is a kind of American poetry in a stickup gang seen
chasing across the bedraggled back drop of the Depression (as true in
its way as Nabokov's vision of Humbert Humbert and Lolita in the cross-
country world of motels)—as if crime were the only activity in a country
stupefied by poverty. But Arthur Penn doesn't quite have the toughness
of mind to know it; it's not what he means by poetry. His squatters'-jungle
scene is too "eloquent," like a poster making an appeal, and the Parker-
family-reunion sequence is poetic in the gauzy mode. He makes the sequence a fancy lyric interlude, like a number in a musical (*Funny Face*, to
be exact); it's too "imaginative"—a literal dust bowl, as thoroughly be-
calmed as Sleeping Beauty's garden. The movie becomes dreamy-soft
where it should be hard (and hard-edged).

If there is such a thing as an American tragedy, it must be funny.
O'Neill undoubtedly felt this when he had James Tyrone get up to turn

off the lights in *Long Day's Journey Into Night*. We are bumpkins, haunted by the bottle of ketchup on the dining table at San Simeon. We garble our foreign words and phrases and hope that at least we've used them right. Our heroes pick up the wrong fork, and the basic figure of fun in the American theatre and American movies is the man who puts on airs. Children of peddlers and hod carriers don't feel at home in tragedy; we are used to failure. But, because of the quality of American life at the present time, perhaps there can be no real comedy—nothing more than stupidity and "spoof"—without true horror in it, Bonnie and Clyde and their partners in crime are comically bad bank robbers, and the backdrop of poverty makes their holdups seem pathetically tacky, yet they rob banks and kill people; Clyde and his good-natured brother are so shallow they never think much about anything, yet they suffer and die.

If this way of holding more than one attitude toward life is already familiar to us—if we recognize the make-believe robbers whose toy guns produce real blood, and the Keystone cops who shoot them dead, from Truffaut's *Shoot the Piano Player* and Godard's gangster pictures, *Breathless* and *Band of Outsiders*—it's because the young French directors discovered the poetry of crime in American life (from our movies) and showed the Americans how to put it on the screen in a new, "existential" way. Melodramas and gangster movies and comedies were always more our speed than "prestigious," "distinguished" pictures; the French directors who grew up on American pictures found poetry in our fast action, laconic speech, plain gestures. And because they understood that you don't express your love of life by denying the comedy or the horror of it, they brought out the poetry in our tawdry subjects. Now Arthur Penn, working with a script heavily influenced—one might almost say inspired—by Truffaut's *Shoot the Piano Player*, unfortunately imitates Truffaut's artistry instead of going back to its tough American sources. The French may tenderize their American material, but we shouldn't. That turns into another way of making "prestigious," "distinguished" pictures.

Probably part of the discomfort that people feel about *Bonnie and Clyde* grows out of its compromises and its failures. I wish the script hadn't provided the upbeat of the hero's sexual success as a kind of sop to the audience. I think what makes us not believe in it is that it isn't consistent with the intelligence of the rest of the writing—that it isn't on the same level, because it's too manipulatively clever, too much of a gimmick. (The scene that shows the gnomish gang member called C.W. sleeping in the same room with Bonnie and Clyde suggests other possibilities, perhaps discarded, as does C.W.'s reference to Bonnie's liking his tattoo.) Compromises are not new to the Bonnie-and-Clyde story; *You Only Live Once* had a tacked-on coda featuring a Heavenly choir and William Gargan as a dead priest, patronizing Eddie even in the afterlife, welcoming him to Heaven with "You're free, Eddie!" The kind of people who make a movie like *You Only Live Once* are not the kind who write endings like that, and, by the same sort of internal evidence, I'd guess that Newman and Benton, whose Bonnie seems to owe so much to Catherine in *Jules and Jim*, had more interesting ideas originally about Bonnie's and Clyde's (and maybe C.W.'s) sex lives.

But people also feel uncomfortable about the violence, and here I think they're wrong. That is to say, they *should* feel uncomfortable, but this isn't an argument *against* the movie. Only a few years ago, a good director would have suggested the violence obliquely, with reaction shots (like the famous one in *The Golden Coach*, when we see a whole bullfight reflected in Anna Magnani's face), and death might have been sym-bolized by a light going out, or stylized, with blood and wounds kept to a minimum. In many ways, this method is more effective; we feel the vio-lence more because so much is left to our imaginations. But the whole point of *Bonnie and Clyde* is to rub our noses in it, to make us pay our dues for laughing. The dirty reality of death—not suggestions but blood and holes—is necessary. Though I generally respect a director's skill and intelligence in inverse ratio to the violence he shows on the screen, and though I questioned even the Annie Sullivan-Helen Keller fight scenes in Arthur Penn's *The Miracle Worker,* I think that this time Penn is right. (I think he was also right when he showed violence in his first film, *The Left Handed Gun,* in 1958.) Suddenly, in the last few years, our view of the world has gone beyond "good taste." Tasteful suggestions of violence would at this point be a more grotesque form of comedy than *Bonnie and Clyde* attempts. *Bonnie and Clyde* needs violence; violence is its mean-ing. When, during a comically botched-up getaway, a man is shot in the face, the image is obviously based on one of the most famous sequences in Eisenstein's *Potemkin,* and the startled face is used the same way it was in *Potemkin*—to convey in an instant how someone who just happens to be in the wrong place at the wrong time, the irrelevant "innocent" by-stander, can get it full in the face. And at that instant the meaning of Clyde Barrow's character changes; he's still a clown, but *we've* become the butt of the joke.

It is a kind of violence that says something to us; it is something that movies must be free to use. And it is just because artists must be free to use violence—a legal right that is beginning to come under attack—that we must also defend the legal rights of those film-makers who use violence to sell tickets, for it is not the province of the law to decide that one man is an artist and another man a no-talent. The no-talent has as much right to produce works as the artist has, and not only because he has a sur-prising way of shifting from one category to the other but also because men have an inalienable right to be untalented, and the law should not discriminate against lousy "artists." I am not saying that the violence in *Bonnie and Clyde* is legally acceptable because the film is a work of art; I think that *Bonnie and Clyde,* though flawed, is a work of art, but I think that the violence in *The Dirty Dozen,* which isn't a work of art, and whose violence offends me *personally,* should also be legally defensible, however morally questionable. Too many people—including some movie reviewers—want the law to take over the job of movie criticism; perhaps what they really want is for their own criticisms to have the force of law. Such people see *Bonnie and Clyde* as a danger to public morality; they think an audience goes to a play or a movie and takes the actions in it as examples for imitation. They look at the world and blame the movies. But if women who are angry with their husbands take it out on the kids, I don't think we can blame *Medea* for it; if, as has been said, we are a nation of mother-lovers, I don't think we can place the blame on *Oedipus Rex.* Part of the power of art lies in showing us what we are *not* capable of. We see that killers are not a different breed but are *us* without the insight or understanding or self-control that works of art strengthen. The tragedy of *Macbeth* is in the fall from nobility to horror; the comic tragedy of *Bonnie and Clyde* is that although you can't fall from the bottom you can reach the same horror. The movies may set styles in dress- or love-making, they may advertise cars or beverages, but art is not examples for imitation—that is not what a work of art does for us—though that is what guardians of morality *think* art is and what they want it to be and why they think a good movie is one that sets "healthy," "cheerful" examples of behavior, like a giant all-purpose commercial for the American way of life. But people don't "buy" what they see in a movie quite so simply; Louis B. Mayer did not turn us into a nation of Andy Hardys, and if, in a film, we see a frightened man wantonly take the life of another, it does not encourage us to do the same, any more than seeing an ivory hunter shoot an elephant makes us want to shoot one. It may, on the contrary, so sensitize us that we get a pang in the gut if we accidentally step on a moth.

Will we, as some people have suggested, be lured into imitating the violent crimes of Clyde and Bonnie because Warren Beatty and Faye Dunaway are "glamorous"? Do they, as some people have charged, confer glamour on violence? It's difficult to see how, since the characters they play are horrified by it and ultimately destroyed by it. Nobody in the movie gets pleasure from violence. Is the charge based on the notion that simply by their presence in the movie Warren Beatty and Faye Dunaway make crime attractive? If movie stars can't play criminals without our all wanting to be criminals, then maybe the only safe roles for them to play are movie stars—which, in this assumption, everybody wants to be anyway. After all, if they played factory workers, the economy might be dislocated by everybody's trying to become a factory worker. (Would having criminals played by dwarfs or fatties discourage crime? It seems rather doubtful.) The accusation that the beauty of movie stars makes the anti-social acts of their characters dangerously attractive is the kind of contrived argument we get from people who are bothered by something and are clutching at straws. Actors and actresses are *usually* more beautiful than ordinary people. And why not? Garbo's beauty notwithstanding, her Anna Christie did not turn us into whores, her Mata Hari did not turn us into spies, her Anna Karenina did not make us suicides. We did not want her to be ordinary looking. Why should we be deprived of the pleasure of beauty? Garbo could be all women in love because, being more beautiful than life, she could more beautifully express emotions. It is a supreme asset for actors and actresses to be beautiful; it gives them greater range and greater possibilities for expressiveness. The handsomer they are, the more roles they can play; Olivier can be anything, but who would want to see Ralph Richardson, great as he is, play Antony? Actors and actresses who are beautiful start with an enormous advantage, because we love to look at them. The joke in the glamour charge is that Faye Dunaway has the magazine-illustration look of countless uninterestingly pretty girls, and Warren Beatty has the kind of high-school good looks that are generally lost fast. It's the role that make *them* seem glamorous. Good roles do that for actors.

There is a story told against Beatty in a recent *Esquire*—how during the shooting of *Lilith* he "delayed a scene for three days demanding the line 'I've read *Crime and Punishment* and *The Brothers Karamazov*' be changed to 'I've read *Crime and Punishment* and *half* of *The Brothers Karamazov*.'" Considerations of professional conduct aside, what is odd is why his adversaries waited three days to give in, because, of course, he was right. That's what the character he played *should* say; the other way, the line has no point at all. But this kind of intuition isn't enough to make an actor, and in a number of roles Beatty, probably because he doesn't have the technique to make the most of his lines in the least possible time, has depended too much on intuitive non-acting—holding the screen far too long as he acted out self-preoccupied characters in a lifelike, boringly self-conscious way. He has a gift for slyness, though, as he showed in *The Roman Spring of Mrs. Stone,* and in most of his films he could hold the screen—maybe because there seemed to be something going on in his mind, some kind of calculation. There was something smart about him—something shrewdly private in those squeezed-up little non-actor's eyes—that didn't fit the clean-cut juvenile roles. Beatty was the producer of *Bonnie and Clyde,* responsible for keeping the company on schedule, and he has been quoted as saying, "There's not a scene that we have done that we couldn't do better by taking another day." This is the hell of the expensive way of making movies, but it probably helps to explain why Beatty is more intense than he has been before and why he has picked up his pace. His business sense may have improved his timing. The role of Clyde Barrow seems to have released something in him. As Clyde, Beatty is good with his eyes and mouth and his hat, but his body is still inexpressive; he doesn't have a trained actor's use of his body, and, watching him move, one is never for a minute convinced he's impotent. It is, however, a tribute to his performance that one singles this failure out. His slow timing works perfectly in the sequence in which he offers the dispossessed farmer his gun; there may not be another actor who would have dared to prolong the scene that way, and the prolongation until the final "We rob banks" gives the sequence its comic force. I have suggested elsewhere that one of the reasons that rules are impossible in the arts is that in movies (and in the other arts, too) the new "genius"—the genuine as well as the fraudulent or the dubious—is often the man who has enough audacity, or is simpleminded enough, to do what others had the good taste not to do. Actors before Brando did not mumble and scratch and show their sweat; dramatists before Tennessee Williams did not make explicit a particular substratum of American erotic fantasy; movie directors before Orson Welles did not dramatize the techniques of film-making; directors before Richard Lester did not lay out the whole movie as cleverly as the opening credits; actresses before Marilyn Monroe did not make an asset of their ineptitude by turning faltering misreadings into an appealing style. Each, in a large way, did something that people had always enjoyed and were often embarrassed or ashamed about enjoying. Their "bad taste" shaped a new accepted taste. Beatty's non-actor's "bad" timing may be this kind of "genius"; we seem to be watching him *think out* his next move.

It's difficult to know how Bonnie should have been played, because the character isn't worked out. Here the script seems weak. She is made too warmly sympathetic—and sympathetic in a style that antedates the style of the movie. Being frustrated and moody, she's not funny enough—neither ordinary, which, in the circumstances, would be comic, nor perverse, which might be rather funny, too. Her attitude toward her mother is too loving. There could be something funny about her wanting to run home to her mama, but, as it has been dòne, her heading home, running off through the fields, is unconvincing—incompletely motivated. And because the element of the ridiculous that makes the others so individual has been left out of her character she doesn't seem to belong to the period as the others do. Faye Dunaway has a sixties look anyway—not just because her eyes are made up in a sixties way and her hair is wrong but because her personal style and her acting are sixties. (This may help to make her popular; she can seem prettier to those who don't recognize prettiness except in the latest styles.) Furthermore, in some difficult-to-define way, Faye Dunaway as Bonnie doesn't keep her distance—that is to say, an actor's distance—either from the role or from the audience. She doesn't hold a characterization; she's in and out of emotions all the time, and though she often hits effective ones, the emotions seem *hers,* not the character's. She has some talent, but she comes on too strong; she makes one conscious that she's a willing worker, but she doesn't seem to know what she's doing—rather like Bonnie in her attempts to overcome Clyde's sexual difficulties.

Although many daily movie reviewers judge a movie in isolation, as if the people who made it had no previous history, more serious critics now commonly attempt to judge a movie as an expressive vehicle of the director, and a working out of his personal themes. Auden has written, "Our judgment of an established author is never simply an aesthetic judgment. In addition to any literary merit it may have, a new book by him has a historic interest for us as the act of a person in whom we have long been interested. He is not only a poet . . . he is also a character in our biography." For a while, people went to the newest Bergman and the newest Fellini that way; these movies were greeted like the latest novels of a favorite author. But Arthur Penn is not a writer-director like Bergman or Fellini, both of whom began as writers, and who (even though Fellini employs several collaborators) compose their spiritual autobiographies step by step on film. Penn is far more dependent on the talents of others, and his primary material—what he starts with—does not come out of his own experience. If the popular audience is generally uninterested in the director (unless he is heavily publicized, like DeMille or Hitchcock), the audience that is interested in the art of movies has begun, with many of the critics, to think of movies as a directors' medium to the point where they tend to ignore the contribution of the writers—and the directors may be almost obscenely content to omit mention of the writers. The history of the movies is being rewritten to disregard facts in favor of celebrating the director as the sole "creative" force. One can read Josef von Sternberg's autobiography and the text of the latest books on his movies without ever finding the name of Jules Furthman, the writer who worked on nine of his most famous movies (including *Morocco* and *Shanghai Express*). Yet the appearance of Furthman's name in the credits of such Howard Hawks films as *Only Angels Have Wings, To Have and Have Not, The Big Sleep,* and *Rio Bravo* suggests the reason for the similar qualities of good-bad-girl glamour in the roles played by Dietrich and Bacall and in other von Sternberg and Hawks heroines, and also in the Jean Harlow and Constance Bennett roles in the movies he wrote for *them.* Furthman, who has written about half of the most entertaining movies to come out of Hollywood (Ben Hecht wrote most of the other half), isn't even listed in new encyclopedias of the film. David Newman and Robert Benton may be good enough to join this category of unmentionable men who do what the directors are glorified for. The Hollywood writer is becoming a ghost-writer. The writers who succeed in the struggle to protect their identity and their material by becoming writer-directors or writer-producers soon become too rich and powerful to bother doing their own writing. And they rarely have the visual sense or the training to make good movie directors.

Anyone who goes to big American movies like *Grand Prix* and *The Sand Pebbles* recognizes that movies with scripts like those don't have a chance to be anything more than exercises in technology, and that this is what is meant by the decadence of American movies. In the past, directors used to say that they were no better than their material. (Sometimes they said it when they weren't even up to their material.) A good director can attempt to camouflage poor writing with craftsmanship and style, but ultimately no amount of director's skill can conceal a writer's failure; a poor script, even well directed, results in a stupid movie — as, unfortunately, does a good script poorly directed. Despite the new notion that the direction is everything, Penn can't redeem bad material, nor, as one may surmise from his *Mickey One*, does he necessarily know when it's bad. It is not fair to judge Penn by a film like *The Chase*, because he evidently did not have artistic control over the production, but what happens when he does have control and is working with a poor, pretentious mess of a script is painfully apparent in *Mickey One* — an art film in the worst sense of that term. Though one cannot say of *Bonnie and Clyde* to what degree it shows the work of Newman and Benton and to what degree they merely enabled Penn to "express himself," there are ways of making guesses. As we hear the lines, we can detect the intentions even when the intentions are not quite carried out. Penn is a little clumsy and rather too fancy; he's too much interested in being cinematically creative and artistic to know when to trust the script. *Bonnie and Clyde* could be better if it were simpler. Nevertheless, Penn is a remarkable director when he has something to work with. His most interesting previous work was in his first film, *The Left Handed Gun* (and a few bits of *The Miracle Worker*, a good movie version of the William Gibson play, which he had also directed on the stage and on television). *The Left Handed Gun*, with Paul Newman as an ignorant Billy the Kid in the sex-starved, male-dominated Old West, has the same kind of violent, legendary, nostalgic material as *Bonnie and Clyde*; its script, a rather startling one, was adapted by Leslie Stevens from a Gore Vidal television play. In interviews, Penn makes high, dull sounds — more like a politician than a movie director. But he has a gift for violence, and, despite all the violence in movies, a gift for it is rare. (Eisenstein had it, and Dovzhenko, and Buñuel, but not many others.) There are few memorable violent moments in American movies, but there is one in Penn's first film: Billy's shotgun blasts a man right out of one of his boots; the man falls in the street, but his boot remains upright; a little girl's giggle at the boot is interrupted by her mother's slapping her. The mother's slap — the seal of the awareness of horror — says that even children must learn that some things that look funny are not only funny. That slap, saying that only idiots would laugh at pain and death, that a child must develop sensibility, is the same slap that *Bonnie and Clyde* delivers to the woman saying "It's a comedy." In *The Left Handed Gun*, the slap is itself funny, and yet we suck in our breath; we do not dare to laugh.

Some of the best American movies show the seams of cuts and the confusions of compromises and still hold together, because there is enough energy and spirit to carry the audience over each of the weak episodes to the next good one. The solid intelligence of the writing and Penn's aura of sensitivity help *Bonnie and Clyde* triumph over many poorly directed scenes: Bonnie posing for the photograph with the Texas Ranger, or — the worst sequence — the Ranger getting information out of Blanche Barrow in the hospital. The attempt to make the Texas Ranger an old-time villain doesn't work. He's in the tradition of the mustachioed heavy who foreclosed mortgages and pursued heroines in turn-of-the-century plays, and this one-dimensional villainy belongs, glaringly, to spoof. In some cases, I think, the writing and the conception of the scenes are better (potentially, that is) than the way the scenes have been directed and acted. If Gene Hackman's Buck Barrow is a beautifully controlled performance, the best in the film, several of the other players — though they are very good — needed a tighter rein. They act too much. But it is in other ways that Penn's limitations show — in his excessive reliance on meaning-laden closeups, for one. And it's no wonder he wasn't able to bring out the character of Bonnie in scenes like the one showing her appreciation of the fingernails on the figurine, for in other scenes his own sense of beauty appears to be only a few rungs farther up that same cultural ladder.

The showpiece sequence, Bonnie's visit to her mother (which is a bit reminiscent of Humphrey Bogart's confrontation with his mother, Marjorie Main, in the movie version of *Dead End*), aims for an effect of alienation, but that effect is confused by all the other things attempted in the sequence: the poetic echoes of childhood (which also echo the child sliding down the hill in *Jules and Jim*) and a general attempt to create a frieze from our national past — a poetry of poverty. Penn isn't quite up to it, though he is at least good enough to communicate what he is trying to do, and it is an attempt that one can respect. In 1939, John Ford attempted a similar poetic evocation of the legendary American past in *Young Mr. Lincoln*; this kind of evocation, by getting at how we *feel* about the past, moves us far more than attempts at historical re-creation. When Ford's Western evocations fail, they become languorous; when they succeed, they are the West of our dreams, and his Lincoln, the man so humane and so smart that he can outwit the unjust and save the innocent, is the Lincoln of our dreams, as the Depression of *Bonnie and Clyde* is the Depression of our dreams — the nation in a kind of trance, as in a dim memory. In this sense, the effect of blur is justified, is "right." Our memories *have* become hazy; this is what the Depression has faded into. But we are too conscious of the technical means used to achieve this blur, of the *attempt* at poetry. We are aware that the filtered effects already include our responses, and it's too easy; the lines are good enough so that the stylization wouldn't have been necessary if the scene had been played right. A simple frozen frame might have been more appropriate.

The editing of this movie is, however, the best editing in an American movie in a long time, and one may assume that Penn deserves credit for it along with the editor, Dede Allen. It's particularly inventive in the robberies and in the comedy sequence of Blanche running through the police barricades with her kitchen spatula in her hand. (There is, however, one bad bit of editing: the end of the hospital scene, when Blanche's voice makes an emotional shift without a corresponding change in her facial position.) The quick panic of Bonnie and Clyde looking at each other's face for the last time is a stunning example of the art of editing.

The end of the picture, the rag-doll dance of death as the gun blasts keep the bodies of Bonnie and Clyde in motion, is brilliant. It is a horror that seems to go on for eternity, and yet it doesn't last a second beyond what it should. The audience leaving the theatre is the quietest audience imaginable.

Still, that woman near me was saying "It's a comedy" for a little too long, and although this could have been, and probably was, a demonstration of plain old-fashioned insensitivity, it suggests that those who have attuned themselves to the "total" comedy of the last few years may not know when to stop laughing. Movie audiences have been getting a steady diet of "black" comedy since 1964 and *Dr. Strangelove, Or: How I Learned to Stop Worrying and Love the Bomb*. Spoof and satire have been entertaining audiences since the two-reelers; because it is so easy to do on film things that are difficult or impossible in nature, movies are ideally suited to exaggerations of heroic prowess and to the kind of lighthearted nonsense we used to get when even the newsreels couldn't resist the kidding finish of the speeded-up athletic competition or the diver flying up from the water. The targets have usually been social and political fads and abuses, together with the heroes and the clichés of the just preceding period of film-making. *Dr. Strangelove* opened a new movie era. It ridiculed *everything* and *everybody* it showed, but concealed its own liberal pieties, thus protecting itself from ridicule. A professor who had told me that *The Manchurian Candidate* was "irresponsible," adding, "I didn't like it—I can suspend disbelief only so far," was overwhelmed by *Dr. Strangelove:* "I've never been so involved. I had to keep reminding myself it was only a movie." *Dr. Strangelove* was clearly intended as a cautionary movie; it meant to jolt us awake to the dangers of the bomb by showing us the insanity of the course we were pursuing. But artists' warnings about war and the dangers of total annihilation never tell us how we are supposed to regain control, and *Dr. Strangelove*, chortling over madness, did not indicate any possibilities for sanity. It was experienced not as satire but as a confirmation of fears. Total laughter carried the day. A new generation enjoyed seeing the world as insane; they *literally* learned to stop worrying and love the bomb. Conceptually, we had already been living with the bomb; now the mass audience of the movies—which is the youth of America—grasped the idea that the threat of extinction can be used to devaluate everything, to turn it all into a joke. And the members of this audience do love the bomb; they love feeling that the worst has happened and the irrational are the sane, because there is the bomb as the proof that the rational are insane. They love the bomb because it intensifies their feelings of hopelessness and powerlessness and innocence. It's only three years since Lewis Mumford was widely acclaimed for saying about *Dr. Strangelove* that "unless the spectator was purged by laughter he would be paralyzed by the unendurable anxiety this policy, once it were honestly appraised, would produce." Far from being purged, the spectators are paralyzed, but they're still laughing. And how odd it is now to read, "*Dr. Strangelove* would be a silly, ineffective picture if its purpose were to ridicule the characters of our military and political leaders by showing them as clownish monsters—stupid, psychotic, obsessed." From *Dr. Strangelove* it's a quick leap to *MacBird* and to a belief in exactly what it was said we weren't meant to find in *Dr. Strangelove*. It is not war that has been laughed to scorn but the possibility of sane action.

Once something enters mass culture, it travels fast. In the spoofs of the last few years, everything is gross, ridiculous, insane; to make sense would be to risk being square. A brutal new melodrama is called *Point Blank* and it is. So are most of the new movies. This is the context in which *Bonnie and Clyde,* an entertaining movie that has some feeling in it, upsets people—people who didn't get upset even by *Mondo Cane.* Maybe it's because *Bonnie and Clyde,* by making us care about the robber lovers, has put the sting back into death.

Since the subject material of *Bonnie and Clyde* is a part of America's social history, Miss Kael carefully develops the background of both the film and the real-life characters. She explores the forces that inspired the film and examines the values that underlie its theme. In doing so, she gives us more than simply a review of the film; she provides a starting point from which many other ideas and discussions can be developed.

Miss Kael uses her extensive knowledge of film history to enrich her review, providing us with a detailed background of the "Bonnie and Clyde" theme in American cinema. She also interprets the relationship between changes in the cinematic treatment of this theme and changes in society.

Miss Kael is not afraid to utilize literary references to enrich and clarify her discussion. Although some critics tend to intimidate their readers by their erudition, Miss Kael never talks down to her audience and avoids the ivory-tower, look-how-much-I-know approach. Her carefully chosen references are clear in their intent and fall within the experience of most readers. Miss Kael's critical judgments are always interesting and well supported. One usually has the feeling that her ideas are original and not borrowed from any other source.

Throughout the article, the reader feels involved in a friendly conversation with the critic. Miss Kael's personal style makes the reading of criticism an easy and pleasurable experience without diminishing the validity or impact of the ideas presented. Her critical work is deserving of careful study and serves as a model of good film criticism.

Film criticism is an important part of the future of film as art. The above examples of contemporary criticism are the beginnings of what will inevitably emerge as an important literary adjunct to the art itself. When present in a single work, the key elements of effective criticism — intelligence, perception, intellectuality, originality, validity of ideas, knowledge of many art forms, wit, style, and, above all, depth of content — make a substantial contribution to both artist and audience.

SUPPLEMENTARY READING

Agee, James. *Agee on Film.* 2 vols. New York: Grosset & Dunlap, Inc., 1958.

Bentley, Eric. *In Search of Theater.* New York: Random House, Inc., 1953.

Brustein, Robert. *Seasons of Discontent.* New York: Simon and Schuster, Inc., 1965.

——. *The Theatre of Revolt.* Boston: Little, Brown and Co., 1964.

Crist, Judith. *The Private Eye, the Cowboy and the Very Naked Girl.* New York: Holt, Rinehart & Winston, Inc., 1968.

Kael, Pauline. *I Lost It at the Movies.* Boston: Little, Brown and Co., 1965.

——. *Kiss Kiss, Bang Bang.* Boston: Little, Brown and Co., 1968.

——. *Going Steady.* Boston: Little, Brown and Co., 1970.

——. *Deeper into Movies.* Boston: Little, Brown and Co., 1973.

Kazin, Alfred. *On Native Grounds.* New York: Harcourt Brace Jovanovich, Inc., 1942.

Schickel, Richard, and John Simon (eds.). *Film 67/68.* New York: Simon and Schuster, Inc., 1968.

Schonberg, Harold. *The Great Conductors*. New York: Simon and Schuster, Inc., 1967.

Taylor, John Russell. *Cinema Eye, Cinema Ear*. New York: Hill and Wang, Inc., 1964.

Wilson, Edmund. *Axel's Castle*. New York: Charles Scribner's Sons, 1931.

——. *The Bit Between My Teeth*. New York: Farrar, Straus & Giroux, Inc., 1965.

INDEX

INDEX

259

Quinn, Anthony, 174

ILLUSTRATION ACKNOWLEDGMENTS

ILLUSTRATION ACKNOWLEDGMENTS

Chapter 3
Figure 1. Photo supplied by author   p. 85
Figure 2. Courtesy of Nagra Magnetic Recorders, Inc., New York, New York   p. 86
Figure 3. Photo supplied by author   p. 86
Figures 4A and 4B. Photos supplied by author   p. 87

Chapter 4
Figure 1A. Courtesy of Magnasync Moviola Company   p. 111
Figure 1B. Courtesy of Kem Electronic Mechanic Corporation   p. 111

Chapter 5
Figure 1. *Through a Glass Darkly*, dir. Ingmar Bergman (Janus Films)   p. 135
Figure 2. *In Cold Blood*, dir. Richard Brooks (Columbia Pictures)   p. 135
Figure 3. *State of Siege*, dir. Costa-Gavras (Cinema V)   p. 139
Figure 4. *La Guerre Est Finie*, dir. Alain Resnais (Audio Brandon)   p. 145
Figure 5. *The Seventh Seal*, dir. Ingmar Bergman (Janus Films)   p. 146
Figure 6. *Hiroshima, Mon Amour*, dir. Alain Resnais (Audio Brandon)   p. 146
Figure 7. *Red Desert*, dir. Michelangelo Antonioni (Audio Brandon)   p. 147
Figure 8. *A Clockwork Orange*, dir. Stanley Kubrick (© 1972 by Warner Brothers)   p. 149

Chapter 7
Figure 1. Culver Pictures   p. 169
Figures 2 through 11. Museum of Modern Art/Film Stills Archive   pp. 171, 174, 176, 179, 181, 184, 186, 189, 192, 195

Color Plates
Plates I and II. *Images,* dir. Robert Altman (© 1973 by Columbia Pictures)   following p. 52
Plate III–V. *Cries and Whispers,* dir. Ingmar Bergman (Courtesy of Jon Davison, New World Pictures)   following p. 52
Plates VI–VII. *Deliverance,* dir. John Boorman (Warner Brothers)   following p. 52

C 5
D 6
E 7
F 8
G 9
H 0
I 1
J 2
3